Taking Stock

Research on Teaching and Learning in Higher Education

Edited by
Julia Christensen Hughes
and Joy Mighty

Queen's Policy Studies Series
School of Policy Studies, Queen's University
McGill-Queen's University Press
Montreal & Kingston • London • Ithaca

SCHOOL OF
Policy Studies

Publications Unit
Robert Sutherland Hall
138 Union Street
Kingston, ON, Canada
K7L 3N6
www.queensu.ca/sps/

The preferred citation for this book is:
Christensen Hughes, J. and J. Mighty, eds. 2010. *Taking Stock: Research on Teaching and Learning in Higher Education*. Montreal and Kingston: Queen's Policy Studies Series, McGill-Queen's University Press.

Library and Archives Canada Cataloguing in Publication

　　　　Taking stock : research on teaching and learning in higher education / edited by Julia Christensen Hughes and Joy Mighty.

Includes bibliographical references.
ISBN 978-1-55339-272-9 (bound).—ISBN 978-1-55339-271-2 (pbk.)

　　　　1. College teaching. 2. Learning. 3. College students. 4. Education, Higher.
I. Christensen Hughes, Julia, 1959- II. Mighty, Joy III. Queen's University (Kingston, Ont.). School of Policy Studies

LB2322.T25 2009　　　　378.1'25　　　　C2009-905976-2

Contents

About the Authors

THOMAS CAREY is a professor of management sciences in the Faculty of Engineering at the University of Waterloo, currently on leave to lead collaborative projects to enhance teaching and learning across higher-education institutions and systems in Canada and the US. In Canada, Dr. Carey is a visiting senior scholar at the Higher Education Quality Council of Ontario, where he heads a program in Knowledge Mobilization for Exemplary Teaching and Learning across colleges and universities in the province. In the US, he is a visiting senior scholar at San Diego State University and the Chancellor's Office of the California State University. He is a principal investigator for the Faculty Collaborations for Course Transformations (FACCTS) program of collaborative course transformation teams in the California community colleges, funded by the William and Flora Hewlett Foundation. He is also program leader for the Engaging Learners in X at R (ELIXR) research and innovation program funded by the US Department of Education. Dr. Carey has an extensive record of innovative leadership in higher-education institutions and organizations, including most recently roles as chief learning officer for the MERLOT Consortium in the US and the University of Waterloo's associate vice-president for support of teaching and learning.

JULIA CHRISTENSEN HUGHES is dean of the College of Management and Economics at the University of Guelph in Ontario. She is also past-president of the Society for Teaching and Learning in Higher Education, a predominantly Canadian organization committed to enhancing the quality of teaching in learning in post-secondary institutions. Previously, Dr. Christensen Hughes served for ten years as director of Teaching Support Services at the University of Guelph. A long-time advocate for educational reform, her research interests include academic integrity, student-centred learning, curriculum assessment and development, universal instructional design, and organizational effectiveness. An award winning instructor, educational consultant, and frequent keynote speaker,

Dr. Christensen Hughes has facilitated several national events in support of the scholarship of teaching and learning and the teaching-research-learning nexus. In 2007, she was the recipient of the Edward F. Sheffield Award from the Canadian Society for Studies in Higher Education for the author judged to be most excellent in the *Canadian Journal of Higher Education*. In 2008, she was honored with the John Bell Award from the University of Guelph for outstanding contributions to education.

JAMES DOWNEY has been president of three universities: Carleton University, the University of New Brunswick, and the University of Waterloo. He also served as president of the Canadian Bureau for International Education, chair of the Association of Atlantic Universities, and chair of the Corporate Higher Education Forum. Dr. Downey was also special adviser to the premier of New Brunswick, special adviser to the Association of Universities and Colleges of Canada, and co-chair of the New Brunswick Commission on Excellence in Education. He founded and directed Canada's first center for the study of co-operative education. In 2000, he was awarded the Symons Medal for outstanding service to higher education in the Commonwealth by the Association of Commonwealth Universities, and in 2003, he received the David C. Smith award from the Council of Ontario Universities for his contributions to universities and public policy in Canada. Dr. Downey is an Officer of the Order of Canada.

NOEL ENTWISTLE is a Professor Emeritus of Education at the University of Edinburgh and has been an editor of the *British Journal of Educational Psychology* and of the international journal, *Higher Education*. He has honorary degrees from the Universities of Gothenburg and Turku, and holds an Oeuvre Award from the European Association for Research on Learning and Instruction. His main research interests have been in the identification and measurement of approaches to studying in higher education, as well as influences on these, and in exploring the nature of academic understanding. Between 2001 and 2005, Dr. Entwistle was co-director of a four-year Economic and Social Research Council research project on "Enhancing teaching-learning environments in undergraduate degree courses," within the Teaching and Learning Research Programme. His most recent publications are *Student Learning and University Teaching* (edited for British Psychological Society 2007), and *Teaching for Understanding at University* (Palgrave Macmillan 2009).

JILLIAN KINZIE is the associate director of the Indiana University Center for Postsecondary Research and the NSSE Institute for Effective Educational Practice. Dr. Kinzie co-ordinates research and project activities to facilitate the use of student-engagement data to promote educational effectiveness. She earned a Ph.D. in higher education with a minor in women's studies at Indiana University Bloomington. She is co-author of *Student*

Success in College: Creating Conditions that Matter (Jossey-Bass 2005) and *Piecing Together the Student Success Puzzle: Research, Propositions, and Recommendations* (Jossey Bass 2007). Dr. Kinzie serves on the editorial board for the *Journal of College Student Development* and is on the Advisory Board of the National Resource Center for the First Year Experience and Students in Transition. In 2001, she was awarded a Student Choice Award for Outstanding Faculty at Indiana University, and in 2005, she received the Robert J. Menges Honored Presentation by the Professional Organizational Development (POD) Network.

CHRISTOPHER KNAPPER was the first director of the Instructional Development Centre at Queen's University and of the Teaching Resource Office at the University of Waterloo. He is a 3M teaching fellow, and was founding president of the Society for Teaching and Learning in Higher Education, which in 2002 created the Knapper Lifetime Achievement Award in his honour. He has written many books and articles on teaching and learning in higher education and served for eight years as co-editor of the *International Journal for Academic Development*. He was also one of the originators of the teaching-portfolio concept. Dr. Knapper currently works as a consultant for universities in Canada and internationally, and recently completed a study for Oxford University on the leadership of teaching in research-intensive universities in North America, Europe, and Australia.

SARI LINDLOM-YLÄNNE is a professor of higher education and director of the Helsinki University Centre for Research and Development in Higher Education, Finland. Dr. Lindblom-Ylänne is currently serving as president of EARLI (European Association for Research on Learning and Instruction, 2009–2011). She is a licensed psychologist and received her Ph.D. in educational psychology in 1999. Dr. Lindblom-Ylänne is actively involved in many international research projects with a focus on teaching and learning at university. Her specific interests include approaches to teaching and learning; the scholarship of university teaching; personal epistemology; assessment practices and quality enhancement in higher education; and on different learning environments, such as problem-based learning.

JAN H.F. MEYER is a professor of education and director of the Centre for Learning, Teaching, and Research in Higher Education at Durham University in the UK. He is also an adjunct professor at the University of South Australia and a Professor Emeritus of the University of Cape Town. Dr. Meyer has a sustained track record of research on student learning in higher education, particularly in terms of modelling individual differences in the transition from school to university study. The focus of his current work is on developing metalearning capacity in students. In 2002, Dr. Meyer proposed the notion of threshold concepts and in a series of subsequent publications with Ray Land, and drawing on the work of David Perkins, a theoretical framework of threshold concepts and troublesome knowledge was developed and is now being applied across a range of disciplinary contexts in higher education.

JOY MIGHTY is director of the Centre for Teaching and Learning and a professor in the School of Business at Queen's University. She is also president of the Society for Teaching and Learning in Higher Education and represents Canada on the Council of the International Consortium for Educational Development. Dr. Mighty has an eclectic academic background in English, Education, and Organizational Behaviour, and a wealth of experience as an administrator, teacher, educational developer, researcher, and consultant. Her special interests are organizational development and change, as well as equity and diversity issues as they relate to both management and education. An award-winning teacher, Dr. Mighty is also a recipient of the Association of Atlantic Universities Distinguished Service Award and winner of the 2004 Emerald Literati Award of Excellence for best article published in the *Journal of Management Development*. A frequent keynote speaker at regional, national, and international conferences, she has published in various conference proceedings, journals, and books, and has provided consulting services to private, public, and not-for-profit organizations in Canada, the Caribbean, England, and the US.

MICHAEL PROSSER is a professor and executive director of the Centre for the Advancement of University Teaching, The University of Hong Kong. Dr. Prosser's teaching, research, and academic-development interests are in the field of student learning in higher education, focussing primarily on the relationship between students' experiences of learning and teachers' experiences of teaching and research. He has published widely, including a well-cited book analysing much of his research until 1999 with Dr. Keith Trigwell. Dr. Prosser has been elected a life member of the Higher Education Research and Development Society of Australasia for distinguished contributions to teaching and research in higher education, is co-president of the International Society for the Scholarship of Teaching and Learning, is listed in the top 1 percent of cited authors in the Social Sciences in the ISI Citation Index, and has been elected by the Australian Research Council's College of Experts as an "Expert of International Standing."

ALENOUSH SAROYAN is a full professor and chair of the Department of Educational and Counselling Psychology at McGill University in Montreal. Her research expertise and interest is in the area of the quality of teaching and learning, with a specific focus on the pedagogical development of academics, academic leadership, quality assurance, and the reform of post-secondary systems. Dr. Saroyan teaches graduate courses in the Learning Sciences program in the department and serves regularly as a consultant to various international organizations including the World Bank, the European Commission, the Organisation for Economic Co-operation and Development, and UNESCO on matters related to higher education. She disseminates findings of her research and development work in peer-reviewed journals, books, and scholarly conferences. As an invited speaker, she has participated in numerous international minister-ial conferences on quality and relevance of higher education, challenges and opportunities for the 21st century, and strategic choices for tertiary education reform in the Middle East, China, Thailand, India, and Nepal.

ALASTAIR J.S. SUMMERLEE is the seventh president of the University of Guelph. His career as a scholar, professor, researcher, and administra-tor spans nearly 30 years. Dr. Summerlee is passionate about teaching and learning: he has continued teaching while holding administrative positions and was awarded a prestigious 3M Teaching Fellowship for outstanding leadership in teaching, education, and academic-program development. Dr. Summerlee serves on the board of directors of World University Service of Canada, one of the country's leading international development agencies aiming to foster human development through education and training. His research in biomedical sciences is acclaimed internationally; he has attracted significant financial support, published extensively, and been invited to speak around the world. He holds a B.Sc., B.V.Sc., Ph.D., and Doctor of Laws (Honoris causa) from the University of Bristol, and is a member of the Royal College of Veterinary Surgeons.

KEITH TRIGWELL is the director of the Institute for Teaching and Learning and a professor of higher education at the University of Sydney. He was previously the director of the Oxford Centre for Excellence in Preparing for Academic Practice, a fellow of Kellogg College, and a reader in higher education at the University of Oxford. He has a Ph.D. in chemistry, university teaching experience in chemistry and education, and has published more than 100 journal articles, conference papers and books, including *Understanding Learning and Teaching: The Experience in Higher Education*, which is a summary of ten years of learning/teaching research with Michael Prosser. His research work in Oxford and Sydney focuses on investigations into qualitative differences in university teaching and in the students' learning experience, on teaching-research relations, the scholarship of teaching, and emotions in teaching. He is a past president of the International Society for the Scholarship of Teaching and Learning, and in 2005 was appointed a co-ordinating editor of the international journal *Higher Education*.

MARYELLEN WEIMER is a Professor Emeritus of Teaching and Learning at Penn State where she has taught communication courses and first-year seminars, amongst others. In 2005, she won Penn State's Milton

S. Eisenhower award for distinguished teaching. She has acted as the associate director of the National Center on Postsecondary Teaching, Learning and Assessment and also spent ten years directing Penn State's Instructional Development Program. Dr. Weimer is a well-known writer, speaker, and proponent of effective-teaching practices. She has numerous publications, including articles in refereed journals, book chapters, and books reviews. She has also edited or authored eight books on various aspects of teaching and has served on the editorial boards of several journals. Dr. Weimer regularly keynotes national meetings and regional conferences and has consulted with over 450 colleges and universities on instructional issues.

CARL WIEMAN became director of the Carl Wieman Science Education Initiative and a professor of Physics at the University of British Columbia in 2007. He maintains a part-time appointment at the University of Colorado where he is a Distinguished Professor of Physics, Presidential Teaching Scholar and director of the Science Education Initiative. Dr. Wieman has carried out extensive research in experimental atomic physics. He was awarded the Nobel Prize in Physics in 2001 for the first creation of the Bose-Einstein condensate. Dr. Wieman also carries out physics and chemistry-education research, and developed a popular website (phet.colorado.edu) that provides interactive educational simulations. He was named the US University Professor of the Year in 2004 by the Carnegie Foundation, and in 2006, was awarded the Oersted Medal for contributions to physics education. He is a member of the National Academy of Sciences and is the founding chair of the NAS Board on Science Education.

W. ALAN WRIGHT holds degrees from Mount Allison University, McGill University, and the Université de Montréal. Before assuming his current duties as vice-provost, teaching and learning, at the University of Windsor, he worked for several years as a dean and director of undergraduate studies in the Université du Québec multi-constituent system, as well as for Dalhousie University, where he was the founding director of the office of instructional development and technology. Dr. Wright is active as a teacher, researcher, and author, and is the former series editor of the *Green Guides*, a collection of pedagogical manuals published by the Society for Teaching and Learning in Higher Education. Over the past decade, Dr. Wright has participated in a $2.5 million Major Collaborative Research Investigation sponsored by the Social Sciences and Humanities Research Council of Canada, as well as several projects funded by other research agencies.

FOREWORD

In a speech he gave in 1969, Professor J. Percy Smith told this story: Two rabbis are standing at the fringe of the crowd listening to the Sermon on the Mount. As it ends, one turns to the other and says, "A wonderful teacher. But what has he published?"

The title of Professor Smith's speech was "Teach, or Get Lost," and the theme was a rejection of the academic imperative implicit in the slogan, "Publish or Perish." Professor Smith was arguing that "Teach, or Get Lost" was a better mantra, one more consistent with the mission and tradition of the academy.

My invocation of Percy Smith, however, has another purpose: to remind us that the search for a just balance between teaching and research has been going on for a long time—indeed for the whole of my academic career, and then some. For much of that time I have been critical of the relative neglect of teaching in our universities. And I still am. Of late, however, I have begun to experience mild spasms of hope.

One reason is that Ontario's colleges and universities have of late been investing more time and resources in the theory and practice of teaching and learning. For their part, colleges—always engaged with curriculum design, effective teaching, and learning outcomes—have been giving weight to pedagogical theory and research. Likewise, an increasing number of universities have begun to make significant investments in teaching programs and centres to help professors and graduate students improve their teaching and communication skills, acquaint them with a bit of the scholarship of teaching and learning, and enable them to adapt their courses to changing interests and technologies.

These developments are all the more encouraging because they are happening in what seems like a critical mass of colleges and universities, and some of the initiatives being taken are highly innovative. Our own involvement in research to support the quality of teaching and learning stems from the action four years ago of the Ontario government—Premier McGuinty, in particular—to create a council, the one I have the privilege of directing, to conduct independent research and give policy advice on all aspects of higher education. While the mandate of the Higher Education Quality Council of Ontario (HEQCO) is broad, it seems inevitable that its primary focus will be on the educational experience of students at universities and colleges. In this regard the council is in part a response to the growing interest in the quality of the student experience, and its research will, we believe, lead to better policy advice on how to enhance that experience and improve outcomes.

To help us take stock of what we know about teaching and learning and what, through further research, we need to know, we sponsored the symposium whose proceedings are published in this volume. We are grateful to Julia Christensen Hughes, Joy Mighty, and staff at the University of Guelph for leadership and support in the design and execution of this event. We are equally grateful to all who accepted to participate in what proved to be a stimulating conference.

In his report, *Ontario: A Leader in Learning*, the Honourable Bob Rae rejected the urging of some for the creation of a teaching and learning centre in the province of Ontario. He did so on the sound basis that experimentation and engagement with teaching and learning will only prove effective if universities and colleges are individually engaged with educational theory and practice.

And theory is important. As Derek Bok suggests in *Our Underachieving Colleges* (2006), for too long, universities have been dismissive of educational research on the grounds that it is not rigorous enough to meet the exacting standards of the academy. Setting aside the fact that the same might be said of a good deal of the scholarship for which people are generously rewarded, we can admit that it is indeed true that perfectly matched control groups or double-blind experiments are hard to conduct in this field, and disagreements will arise about how to measure proficiency in such competencies as critical thinking and writing. To allow such challenges to discredit institutional research, however, would be to let the perfect become the "enemy of the good" (Bok 2006, 320). Bok argues that "the proper test for universities to apply is not whether their assessments meet the most rigorous scholarly standards but whether they can provide more reliable information than the hunches, random experiences, and personal opinions that currently guide most faculty decisions about educational issues" (320).

To strengthen its culture for teaching and learning, an institution should have its own ways and means of fostering on-campus research and experimentation. There is a growing body of scholarship in the fields of science and social science to help us do this, as the essays in this book so richly illustrate. Participants in the symposium will be pleased to learn that their deliberations have already led to practical results. To cite just one example, HEQCO has initiated a program called Knowledge Mobilization for Exemplary Teaching and Learning, in which teams of faculty and instructional developers from across Ontario are working together in pilot projects to apply knowledge about teaching and learning in their subject areas. These teams are building on the research base discussed in these proceedings: exploring, synthesizing, adapting, evaluating, extending, and disseminating.

Percy Smith would take heart.

James Downey

REFERENCE

Bok, D. 2006. *Our Underachieving Colleges: A Candid Look at How Much Students Learn and Why They Should Be Learning More.* Princeton, NJ: Princeton University Press.

SECTION I

TAKING STOCK: SETTING THE STAGE

Much is known about effective pedagogical practice in higher education, yet many faculty members continue to use methods that are at odds with this evidence. It is time to identify the forces behind these practices of convenience and work collectively to transform our students' learning experiences.

1

PRACTICES OF CONVENIENCE: TEACHING AND LEARNING IN HIGHER EDUCATION

Julia Christensen Hughes and Joy Mighty

INTRODUCTION

This book is intended for those with an interest in improving the quality of teaching and learning in higher education—faculty, educational developers, administrators, policy makers—people who ideally already have some familiarity with the research on teaching and learning and want to strengthen it; those who are committed to taking an evidence-based approach to this critical work. The contents are based upon a research symposium that was held in the spring of 2008 in Guelph, Ontario. The symposium was sponsored and organized by the Higher Education Quality Council of Ontario (HEQCO),[1] with the support of Frank Iacobucci Q.C., chair; James Downey, president; and Ken Norrie, vice-president research. It was conceptualized and facilitated by us—Julia Christensen Hughes and Joy Mighty, past and current presidents of the Society for Teaching and Learning in Higher Education (STLHE),[2] respectively—and hosted by the University of Guelph.

The impetus for this event was the recognition that researchers have discovered much about teaching and learning in higher education, but that dissemination and uptake of this information have been limited. As such, the impact of educational research on faculty-teaching practice and the student-learning experience has been negligible.

Inspired by Al Gore's documentary, *An Inconvenient Truth*, and the associated "climate project" through which individuals, communities, and even nations have been motivated to reduce their environmental impact as a result of becoming better informed, we wondered what might happen if the same was done for teaching and learning in higher education. We even wondered about using a similar project title (with apologies to Al Gore), namely, "An (In)convenient Practice: Teaching and Learning in Higher Education." Such a title, we thought, might help communicate that—despite the pockets of pedagogical innovation that exist on most campuses, and the best intentions of many hardworking faculty, educational developers, and administrators—much of our current approach to teaching in higher education might best be described as practices of *convenience*, to the extent that traditional pedagogical approaches[3] continue to predominate. Such practices are convenient insofar as large numbers of students can be efficiently processed through the system. As far as learning effectiveness is concerned, however, such practices are decidedly *inconvenient*, as they fall far short of what is needed in terms of fostering "self-directed" learning[4] (Brookfield 1986), "transformative learning"[5] (Kitchenham 2008; Mezirow 1981, 1991, 2000) or "learning that lasts"[6] (Mentkowski and Associates 2000).

It is without question our bias that effective teaching and learning go beyond the traditional lecture and rote learning. Rather, they are transformative in nature; providing students with opportunities to become self-directed as well as to examine critically their assumptions and views of themselves, their subjects, their contexts, and the world in general, helping them to develop new habits of perceiving, thinking, and acting (Mezirow 1981).

In embarking on this project, we also recognized that one of the challenges we would face in "taking stock" would be to make the language of this research accessible. Like all disciplines, the education literature is replete with its own concepts, terminology, and acronyms. While these are arguably useful to those in the field, they can serve as barriers to those who are not. Throughout this opening chapter, definitions and further references are therefore provided in the form of endnotes.

The objectives of the symposium were to identify and synthesize what is already known about teaching practice and student approaches to learning in higher education, what we still need to know, and the implications of what is known for improving the quality of education. Through this book, we now endeavour to make this information available to the academic community at large. Given the enormity of the educational literature, we are not claiming to have provided an exhaustive treatment by any means. Indeed, we are aware that many other factors (including philosophy, policy, curriculum, and the use of educational technology, to name a few) contribute to the complexity of the higher-education field. We chose to focus on those subject areas considered seminal by our distinguished contributors, who include empirical educational researchers, heads of teaching and learning centres, and university administrators well respected in the educational development community. A common theme among their contributions is the impact of approaches to teaching on students' approaches to learning and, in particular, on students' choice of either a *deep* or *surface* approach (Marton 1976; Marton and Säljö 1976). Our ultimate goal is to have more faculty members adopt teaching approaches that are likely to foster deep approaches to learning. Our concluding chapter presents suggestions for helping to make this happen.

Organization of the Book

Section 1 of the book features a comprehensive overview of the research by Noel Entwistle, who provided the opening keynote address for the symposium. Dr. Entwistle introduces the seminal concepts of deep and surface approaches to learning (Marton 1976; Marton and Säljö 1976), citing research that convincingly demonstrates that students vary their learning approaches depending on a host of factors, many of which are influenced by the learning environment. Dr. Entwistle suggests that faculty conceptions of teaching can also vary, and that the approach taken is potentially influenced by how faculty members conceive of their disciplines. The interacting influences of student characteristics, subject content, and the learning environment on student learning are then presented in a heuristic model, which underscores the complexity of the topic. Dr. Entwistle concludes his chapter by calling for a renewed focus on learning processes within higher education. He also calls for a renewed commitment by faculty to think "critically about the nature of learning within the discipline or professional area," to adapt their approach in keeping with an increasingly diverse student body, and to model effective approaches to learning.

Following Dr. Entwistle's contribution, each of the remaining four sections focuses on a specific issue that was addressed by a panel of presenters at the symposium. Given that several of our presenters were colleagues (i.e., they had worked together for decades), and in order to ensure breadth of perspective, each panel was organized to include at least one international and one North American speaker. Within this volume each section is additionally introduced and concluded by a Canadian discussant—a participant at the symposium who is well known for his or her role in helping reform higher education in Canada and beyond. The discussants were asked to provide a critical perspective, identifying key themes in the chapters, as well as to introduce additional literature, research, or questions they felt to be relevant to the topic.

Section 2 focuses on what we know about student learning and is introduced by Alenoush Sarayon, followed by chapters by Sari Lindblom-Ylänne and Maryellen Weimer.

Sari Lindblom-Ylänne's chapter begins with a review of research that shows a positive relationship among positive student perceptions of the teaching-learning environment, the deep approach to learning, and higher-quality learning outcomes. Drawing on her own research, Dr. Lindblom-Ylänne emphasizes the importance of concepts such as *self-regulation*[9] (Vermunt 1998), i.e., the ability to monitor, adapt, and improve the effectiveness of one's own learning processes, and student *study orchestrations*[10] (Meyer 1991) or conceptualizations of learning. In particular, she discusses the concept of dissonant study orchestrations, which are related to student attempts to adapt to the teaching-learning environment.

Citing a number of meta-analyses and research studies, Maryellen Weimer's chapter suggests that traditional deductive pedagogical approaches—which remain dominant in higher education today—are contributing to a number of disappointing learning outcomes, such as little retention of material. In contrast, she suggests that there is general support for a number of active or inductive teaching methods, "such as discovery learning, inquiry-based learning, problem-based learning, case-based teaching, and just-in-time teaching." Dr. Weimer advocates for the adoption of evidence-based pedagogical practice, more accessible teaching and learning scholarship, and enhanced institutional support for the achievement of these outcomes.

According to Alenoush Sarayon, both chapters suggest that students' learning approaches have significant impacts on student retention of material as well as their ability to transfer or apply what they have learned to new situations and contexts. Further, students' learning approaches and strategies are influenced by the broader learning environment, including faculty-teaching methods. Dr. Sarayon also introduces other literature (e.g., Centra 1993; Windschitl 2002) that helps to identify system level barriers and changes that are needed to enhance student learning. Dr. Saroyan calls on educational researchers to make their work accessible, to collaborate with faculty from other fields, and to contribute to policy debates.

Section 3 is introduced by W. Alan Wright and includes chapters by Keith Trigwell, Michael Prosser, and Jillian Kinzie. This section focuses on how teaching and learning impact one another.

Keith Trigwell's chapter similarly begins with a discussion of variation in student learning (deep/surface) and underscores its association with the learning environment and the quality of learning outcomes. Drawing on his own research—and his work with Dr. Prosser—Dr. Trigwell identifies five qualitatively different approaches to teaching: teacher-focused information transmission, teacher-focused concept acquisition, teacher/student interaction concept acquisition, student-focused concept development, and student-focused concept transformation. Dr. Trigwell reports having found a strong and positive association between transmission/teacher-focused pedagogies and surface approaches to learning and between student-focused pedagogies and deep approaches to learning. He concludes by calling for further research focusing on the relationship between teaching and learning, particularly work that helps to clarify the direction of the relationship and moves beyond self-report data to include direct observation.

Michael Prosser's chapter begins with a brief but compelling summary of 30 years of teaching and learning research that further establishes that students adopt either surface or deep learning approaches, depending upon their prior learning experiences and their perceptions of the current teaching and learning environment. Furthermore, student-learning approaches are associated with the quality of learning outcomes. Dr. Prosser then presents a summary of his most recent work (Prosser et al. 2008), which compares the research and teaching approaches of faculty. He suggests that faculty approaches to research may be associated with faculty approaches to teaching. He concludes that the research norms of a discipline may be particularly important to understanding the pedagogical inclinations of faculty and suggests that more theoretical, conceptually based research in this area be encouraged.

Jillian Kinzie's chapter focuses on the concept of student engagement[11] and the National Survey of Student Engagement. Dr. Kinzie reports that there is a positive association between learning activities that foster student engagement and undergraduate grade point average (GPA). She also cites longitudinal research which has found an association between effective teaching practices, levels of student engagement, and desirable learning outcomes such as "moral reasoning, leadership, well-being, critical thinking, intercultural effectiveness...." Dr. Kinzie concludes her chapter with four propositions in support of student learning. These are that educators should: (a) establish high expectations for student learning, provide support, and hold students accountable, (b) provide all students with "at least two high-impact practices during their undergraduate education," (c) emphasize those practices that are consistent with student engagement, and (d) "be concerned with the total learning environment—in and outside the classroom."

In his summary chapter, W. Alan Wright questions what he terms "missing knowledge and implementation dilemmas" with respect to the issues earlier raised by Drs. Trigwell, Prosser, and Kinzie. Of note, he draws attention to research dealing with the importance of understanding student backgrounds and characteristics. He also raises issues pertaining to the professional development of teachers, the leadership of deans and academic department heads, and the importance of teaching awards. Dr. Wright suggests that the choice of teaching approach is dynamic rather than fixed and that, in the long run, significant change will be dependent on collective rather than individual action. Dr. Wright reminds us that there is still much that we do not know about teaching and learning in higher education, not the least of which is the effectiveness of educational developers in providing the bridge among theory, research, and practice.

Section 4 is introduced by Thomas Carey and includes contributions by Carl Wieman and Jan H.F. Meyer. This section focuses on "exemplary teaching practices."

Carl Wieman's chapter, which has been reproduced with permission, was originally published in the September/October 2007 issue of *Change* (Wieman 2007). Dr. Wieman's chapter suggests that traditional deductive pedagogy is problematic for at least three reasons: it leads to poor short-term retention of information, poor understanding of basic concepts, and more novice beliefs about science and learning. Dr. Wieman suggests that faculty need to focus on helping students create their own understanding of the material, guide them to be more expert-like and, through such an approach, better engage the learner. Dr. Wieman also emphasizes the importance of developing a common understanding of desired learning outcomes and authentic assessments for effectively testing what students actually learn.

Jan H.F. Meyer's chapter is framed by his review of four decades of research. In it he too emphasizes variation in student learning (deep/surface) and cites research that clearly demonstrates the causal efficacy between various learning processes and outcomes (Richardson 2006). He also questions the benefit of training faculty to be more effective teachers to the extent that it is provided in a generalized as opposed to a discipline-specific manner. Finally, Dr. Meyer introduces the idea of "threshold concepts,"[12] and advocates keeping such concepts at the centre of research on teaching and learning on the basis that once threshold concepts are learned, student learning can be significantly enhanced and their journeys as learners accelerated.

While agreeing with the ideas advocated by Drs. Meyer and Wieman, Thomas Carey, like Dr. Wright, emphasizes the role of the educational developer in identifying and promoting exemplary practices. Drawing on the evidence of several past and ongoing educational development projects across a range of contexts in post-secondary educational institutions and systems, Dr. Carey acknowledges the contributions that can be made by teachers without formal knowledge or training in pedagogy. Delineating among craft knowledge, professional knowledge, and scientific knowledge, he argues that advances in the scholarship of teaching and learning may be seriously threatened if we only accept "scholarly teaching" as valuable.

Section 5 contains contributions by Julia Christensen Hughes, Joy Mighty, Christopher Knapper, and Alastair J.S. Summerlee. This section includes a call for action, focusing on catalysts and barriers to change, as well as strategies for transforming teaching and learning in higher education.

Christopher Knapper's chapter presents the results of his recent study with Graham Gibbs and Sergio Piccinin, which focused on identifying the attributes of academic departments in which training and learning innovation are embraced. They found that drivers of effective teaching include: changes to methods, curriculum, and learning outcomes; the existence of a crisis; leadership, a clear and compelling vision, shared goals, and broad consultation / communication; celebration and reward; adequate resources (time and money); evidence / research; and vigilance. In order to leverage these drivers effectively, Dr. Knapper advocates broad-based structural change, including changes in hiring practices, reward structures, quality assurance and accreditation mechanisms, increased support of teaching and learning scholarship, and changes to how we prepare new faculty.

The chapter by Alastair J.S. Summerlee and Julia Christensen Hughes strengthens the calls for change made elsewhere in this volume, by identifying the pressures for change now confronting universities worldwide and suggesting that if we fail to respond effectively to these pressures, we may ultimately face obsolescence. In arguing that we need a renaissance in higher education in which we once again embrace the role of the university as a conduit for social reform, they call for increased attention to the concepts of student self-efficacy and motivation, the reformation of teaching and learning processes, and a fundamental rethinking of how institutional resources are allocated. Using examples from the University of Guelph, they also provide concrete examples of how one institution is trying to bring such change about.

The concluding chapter of this section—and the book—by Julia Christensen Hughes and Joy Mighty synthesizes the preceding chapters, drawing attention to the key findings and presenting a historical overview of calls for change. What is clear from this review is that, while ensuring faculty and administrators are better informed of the research on teaching and learning is important, such a step is likely to be insufficient in bringing about broad-scale change. The reform of teaching and learning in higher education is a complex, systemic issue, and as such a complex, systemic response is required. Such a response would ideally include:

- Effective pedagogical leadership at all levels;
- Departmental cultures in which teaching and learning are valued, and in which an ethos of pedagogical creativity and experimentation is encouraged;
- Professional-development opportunities that are offered in collaboration with educational developers and local teaching centres and

that encourage faculty to engage with discipline-specific pedagogical literature, to identify threshold concepts, and to participate in research projects with respect to their own pedagogical practice;
- Support for the scholarship of teaching and learning, including the provision of grants and the establishment of teaching chairs;
- Faculty recruitment, selection, promotion, and tenure processes where teaching and learning competence and scholarship are adequately assessed and valued;
- Pedagogically sound physical and virtual learning spaces;
- A focus on curriculum assessment and development and the achievement of generic program-level learning outcomes.

Throughout this book the point is consistently made that research suggests there is an association between how faculty teach and how students learn, and how students learn and the learning outcomes achieved. Further, research suggests that many faculty members teach in ways that are not particularly helpful to deep student learning. Much of this research has been known for decades, yet we continue to teach in ways that are contrary to these findings.

An important first step has been "taking stock" of the evidence. We have also enhanced our understanding of why dissemination and up-take have been so limited. We need to further explore these issues and develop a collective understanding of why—given what we know—so many well-intentioned and committed faculty members continue to teach in sub-optimal ways. Then we need to develop a multi-faceted strategy for addressing the situation. Several components of such a strategy have been suggested. It is our hope that these ideas will take root and in so doing help us to create systems and cultures in which deep learning is more likely to occur for the benefit of our students and society as a whole.

NOTES

We are grateful for the support of the Higher Education Quality Council of Ontario in the completion of this project, and for the contributions of two anonymous reviewers, whose comprehensive input undoubtedly strengthened the result.

[1] "The Higher Education Quality Council of Ontario is an independent agency of the Government of Ontario dedicated to supporting the ongoing improvement of Ontario's system of postsecondary education. The Council was created through the *Higher Education Quality Council of Ontario Act, 2005.* Its mandate is to conduct research, evaluate the postsecondary education system and provide policy recommendations to the Minister of Training, Colleges and Universities with a view to enhancing the quality, access, and accountability of higher education in Ontario" (HEQCO 2008).

[2] "The Society for Teaching and Learning in Higher Education (STLHE) is a national association of academics interested in the improvement of teaching

and learning in higher education. Its members comprise faculty and teaching and learning professionals from institutions of post-secondary education across Canada and beyond" (STLHE 2009).

[3] The term "pedagogy" commonly refers to one's teaching philosophy and practice, including choice of student-learning and assessment activities. "Traditional pedagogical practice" typically implies a lecture format, whereby the faculty member attempts to orally transmit content knowledge to the students, who in turn take notes on what they have heard and are assessed on their ability to recall and accurately reproduce such information. This approach may also be referred to as a transmission model of education, deductive pedagogy, teacher-focused pedagogy, or instructivism. Within higher education, and particularly for adult learners in effective learning environments, the term "andragogy" may more appropriately apply, which is defined as "an organized and sustained effort to assist adults to learn in a way that enhances their capability to function as self-directed learners" (Mezirow 1981, 21).

[4] Self-directed learning "focuses on the process by which adults take control of their own learning, in particular how they set their own learning goals, locate appropriate resources, decide on which learning methods to use and evaluate their progress" (Brookfield 1995). While Brookfield's definition pertains specifically to adult learners, helping students to become more self-directed is appropriate to higher education in general and supports the concept of helping students to become effective life long learners.

[5] Transformative learning has been defined as "a deep, structural shift in basic premises of thought, feelings, and actions" (Transformative Learning Centre 2004, as cited in Kitchenham 2008, 104). Reflecting the underlying belief that learning should be emancipatory in nature, transformative-learning theory stems largely from the work of Mezirow (1981), and is based on the work of Kuhn (1962), Freire (1970), and Habbermas (1971, 1984). Mezirow posited that transformative learning typically begins with a "disorienting dilemma" that causes the student to uncover and question previously unexamined assumptions. Accompanied by critical self-reflection, such learning can lead to changes in how the student perceives, thinks, and acts.

[6] Learning that lasts—learning that involves "change in behavior and flexibility in perspective, enduring commitments, and transformative elements that carry the individual forward through unexpected experiences, roles and life events" (Mentkowski & Associates 2000, xv). Learning that lasts is in direct contrast to learning for a moment in time, demonstrated through one's ability to recall facts or repeat what one has been told for a test or exam.

[7] Deep-learning approaches are largely intrinsically motivated (the student has a genuine interest in engaging with the subject and extracting meaning for themselves in order to understand and become expert). Critical analysis, the integration of new knowledge with prior understanding, application, the effective transfer of knowledge to new situations, and retention are the hallmarks of deep learning.

[8] Surface-learning approaches are largely extrinsically motivated (effort is expended in order to get a particular grade or credit) and are concerned with trying to reproduce information without seeking personal understanding. Memorizing facts with only superficial understanding and the uncritical acceptance of ideas are hallmarks of a surface approach to learning.

[9] Self-regulation refers to the ability to monitor, adapt, and improve the effectiveness of one's own learning processes on the basis of self-reflection and feedback in the pursuit of academic goals. It requires self-awareness with respect to one's emotions and behaviours and is arguably essential to the success of student-centered learning approaches. Self-regulation is similar to metalearning (Biggs 1985), which pertains to a student's ability to realistically assess and enhance his or her capabilities with respect to the demands of a particular learning activity.

[10] Study orchestrations are student-learning approaches captured at a conceptual and/or philosophical (as opposed to a task) level. They are a "preferred" approach to learning, which may or may not be congruent with what the learning environment encourages. Study orchestrations in practice may therefore be described as consonant or dissonant with respect to one's preferences or beliefs.

[11] Student engagement is the focus of the National Study of Student Engagement (NSSE) and is defined by Kinzie in this volume as being comprised of two factors: (a) "the amount of time and effort students put into their studies and other educationally purposeful activities," and (b) "how the institution deploys its resources and organizes the curriculum, other learning opportunities, and support services."

[12] Threshold concepts, according to Meyer in this volume, may be viewed as "portals" or "objects of learning that really matter," and are "transformative waypoints" in students' learning journeys. Threshold concepts open up "a new and previously inaccessible way of thinking about something.... As a consequence of comprehending a threshold concept, there may thus be a transformed internal view of subject matter, subject landscape, or even world view" (Meyer and Land 2006, 3; see also Land, Meyer, and Smith 2008).

REFERENCES

Biggs, J. 1985. The Role of Metalearning in Study Processes. *British Journal of Educational Psychology* 55:185-212.

Brookfield, S. 1986. *Understanding and Facilitating Adult Learning*. San Francisco: Jossey-Bass.

Brookfield, S. 1995. Adult Learning: An Overview. In *International Encyclopedia of Education,* ed. A. Tuinjman. Oxford: Pergamon Press. Accessed 14 August 2009 at www.resources.scalingtheheights.com/stephen_brookfield.htm

Centra, J.A. 1993. *Reflective Faculty Evaluation: Enhancing Teaching and Determining Faculty Effectiveness*. San Francisco: Jossey-Bass.

Freire, P. 1970. *Pedagogy of the Oppressed*. New York: Herter and Herter.

Habbermas, J. 1971. *Knowledge of Human Interests*. Boston: Beacon Press.

Habbermas, J. 1984. *The Theory of Communicative Action, Vol. 1: Reason and the Rationalization of Society,* trans. T. McCarthy. Boston: Beacon Press.

Higher Education Quality Council of Ontario (HEQCO). 2008. *Annual Report 2007-2008*. Toronto: Queen's Printer for Ontario. Accessed 29 November 2009 at http://www.heqco.ca/SiteCollectionDocuments/0708%20Annual%20Report%20English.pdf

Kitchenham, A. 2008. The Evolution of John Mezirow's Transformative Learning Theory. *Journal of Transformative Education* 6(2):104-23.

Kuhn, T. 1962. *The Structure of Scientific Revolutions*. Chicago: University of Chicago Press.

Land, R., J.H.F. Meyer, and J. Smith. 2008. *Threshold Concepts within the Disciplines*. Rotterdam: Sense Publishers.

Marton, F. 1976. What Does It Take to Learn? Some Implications of an Alternative View of Learning. In *Strategies for Research and Development in Higher Education*, ed. N.J. Entwistle, 32-43. Amsterdam: Swets & Zeitlinger.

Marton, F. and R. Säljö. 1976. On Qualitative Difference in Learning. I- Outcomes and Processes. *British Journal of Educational Psychology* 46:4-11.

Mentkowski and Associates. 2000. *Learning that Lasts: Integrating, Learning, Development, and Performance in College and Beyond*. San Francisco: Jossey-Bass.

Meyer, J.H.F. 1991. Study Orchestration: The Manifestation, Interpretation and Consequences of Contextualized Approaches to Studying. *Higher Education* 22:297-316.

Meyer, J.H.F. and R. Land, eds. 2006. *Overcoming Barriers to Student Understanding: Threshold Concepts and Troublesome Knowledge*. London and New York: Routledge.

Mezirow, J. 1981. A Criticial Theory of Adult Learning and Education. *Adult Education* 32(1):3-24.

Mezirow, J. 1991. *Transformative Dimensions of Adult Learning*. San Fransisco: Jossey-Bass.

Mezirow, J. 2000. *Learning as Transformation: Critical Perspectives on a Theory in Progress*. San Francisco: Jossey Bass.

Prosser, M., E. Martin, K. Trigwell, P. Ramsden, and H. Middleton. 2008. University Academics' Experiences of Understanding of their Subject Matters and the Relationship to their Experiences of Teaching and Learning. *Instructional Science* 36:3-16.

Richardson, J.T.E. 2006. Investigating the Relationship between Variations in Students' Perceptions of their Academic Environment and Variations in Study Behaviour in Distance Education. *British Journal of Educational Psychology* 76:867-93.

Society for Teaching and Learning in Higher Education (STLHE). 2009. Accessed 29 November 2009 at http://www.stlhe.ca/en/stlhe/

Transformative Learning Centre. 2004. The Transformative Learning Centre. Accessed 27 July 2004 on the Transformative Learning Centre website at http://tle.oise.utoronto.ca/index.htm

Vermunt, J.D. 1998. The Regulation of Constructive Learning Processes. *British Journal of Educational Psychology* 68:149-71.

Wieman, C. 2007. Why Not Try a Scientific Approach to Science Education? *Change: The Magazine of Higher Learning* 39(5):9-15.

Windschitl, M. 2002. Framing Constructivism as the Negotiation of Dilemmas: An Analysis of the Conceptual, Pedagogical, Cultural, and Political Challenges Facing Teachers. *Review of Educational Research* 72(2):131-75.

2

TAKING STOCK: AN OVERVIEW OF
KEY RESEARCH FINDINGS

Noel Entwistle

INTRODUCTION

This chapter takes stock of research into teaching and learning in higher education as a basis for considering ways of improving practice. Rather than setting about the utterly impossible task of reviewing the total picture, I have narrowed the focus. By setting out the main issues and then selecting a set of concepts that hang together sufficiently closely, I have endeavoured to offer a coherent research-based perspective on how teaching and learning environments influence the quality of student learning. A series of questions are used to provide a structure for the chapter and a heuristic model is introduced as a framework to support ways of thinking about teaching and learning. This conceptual framework is, however, just one "take" on a complex and confusing research area, and inevitably draws mainly on the research I am most familiar with.

My starting point is the role research can play in improving teaching and learning. I then move on to definitions of high-quality learning and how it can be brought about.

Taking Stock: Research on Teaching and Learning in Higher Education, ed. J. Christensen Hughes and J. Mighty. Montreal and Kingston: McGill-Queen's University Press, Queen's Policy Studies Series. © 2010 The School of Policy Studies, Queen's University at Kingston. All rights reserved.

What Do We Expect Research to be Able to Offer in Guiding Teaching Practice?

All too often in education, pundits, and some researchers for that matter, seem to believe that they have found *the* method which all teachers should use. And policy makers have been urging educational researchers to discover "what works" among the wide range of available teaching methods used in education, relying on "research-based" or at least "research-informed" techniques. But Dahllöf (1991), among others, has been strongly critical of attempts to identify "best practice" in university teaching, arguing that:

> Too much attention is directed towards finding ... "the best method," even though 50 years of educational research has not been able to support such generalisations. Instead, we should ask which method—or which combination of methods—is best ... for which goals, for which students, and under which conditions. (148)

Thus, claims that e-learning or problem-based learning or communities of practice—or whatever else is the "best" way to encourage student learning—cannot be substantiated. The effectiveness of teaching inevitably depends on its purpose and a host of interacting influences. Making use of just one general approach could never suit all topics, all subjects, all students, and for all purposes. Nevertheless, we can expect to find certain general principles of teaching and learning to guide thinking about effective practice within these more specific situations. And research can offer a conceptual framework and detailed findings to guide the way we think about teaching and learning in specific contexts.

Where Can we Find Evidence on Teaching and Learning in Post-Secondary Education?

There are some important questions to ask when considering how much weight to place on evidence or how valuable a theory will be for pedagogy. For example:

- Is the theory derived from data or observations in an educational context?
- Is the theory presented in language that is readily intelligible to teachers?
- Can the aspects identified as affecting learning be readily changed?
- Does the theory have direct implications for teaching and learning in post-secondary education (PSE)?
- How realistic and practicable are the suggested implications?
- Will the theory spark off new ideas about teaching?

It is not sufficient for a pedagogical theory simply to explain how people learn; it has also to provide clear indications about how to improve the quality and efficiency of learning.

In the early years of research into teaching and learning in PSE, the conceptual frameworks were derived almost entirely from mainstream psychology, and so lacked the ecological validity necessary to draw convincing implications for practice. Nevertheless, a sound understanding of the fundamentals of human learning is still important, as there are clear limitations on, for example, cognitive processing, as well as particular strengths created by the flexible ways in which the brain is able to identify and combine related ideas. We need to be aware of these.

In more recent years, educational researchers have not only been carrying out studies within the everyday context of teaching and learning in PSE, but they have also been developing their own concepts and conceptual frameworks to supplement those offered by psychology and the other social sciences. One problem for education is that there has been a great deal of interest shown by psychologists and sociologists who are more concerned with developing general theories based on data collected in totally different contexts—experimental or social—and then seeking to apply them to education without fully understanding the limitations of their work, or when different groups of learners or different types of learning are involved. One could cite as examples the development of programmed learning advocated by B.F. Skinner from his experiments on the conditioning of animals (see, e.g., Skinner 1953); the change in the teacher's role suggested by Carl Rogers from his experiences in psychotherapy (see, e.g., Rogers 1969); and the more recent ideas of anthropologist Jean Lave (see, e.g., Lave 1988; Lave and Wenger 1991), based on her observations of apprentice tailors, but seen as directly relevant to student learning. Such approaches have validity in their original context, of course, but when extrapolated to teaching and learning within PSE contexts, they may well overemphasize just one aspect, prove impracticable, or be just plain wrong in an educational context.

What Research Approaches Are Most Effective?

It is also important to consider the research methodology used. The early approaches used in psychology—controlled experiments and questionnaire surveys—still figure prominently in the educational literature. Controlled experiments allow greater precision in investigating learning, but are almost impossible to carry out in the everyday contexts of teaching and learning, particularly in PSE where introducing specific experimental interventions, or allocating students randomly to differing educational treatments, is generally unacceptable. The experiments often have to be carried out with small groups of volunteer students in constrained contexts, resulting in questionable generality or applicability to the real world.

Questionnaire surveys have the advantage of large samples, although the conditions under which the data are collected often lead to relatively low response rates, with the less successful students being overrepresented in the non-response category. There are also issues about the accuracy of any measurements made and the potentially misleading findings coming from students wishing to present themselves in the best possible light.

Since the 1970s, with the pioneering work of William Perry (1970) at Harvard and Ference Marton and his research team at Gothenburg (1976), much of the research into teaching and learning has involved in-depth interviewing of students and academics, and it is from this work that some of the most influential concepts and insights have emerged. These concepts have often been operationalized through specially designed inventories, leading to increasingly complex statistical analysis of large data sets. These developments have made possible an interplay between survey and interview research, and the emergence of convergent and complementary findings from these contrasting methodological approaches has produced more convincing descriptions of teaching and learning in PSE.

In writing this chapter, I have been aware of the differing emphases in research on teaching and learning in North America, and particularly in the US, compared with those in Europe and Australasia. In the US, there has been a substantial reliance on psychological conceptualizations, for example: linking learning strategies to elaboration in the memory (Weinstein, Zimmerman, and Palmer 1988); drawing on psychological theories of motivation in relation to study strategies and learning environments (Rotter 1954; Rotter, Chance, and Phares 1972; Pintrich and Garcia 1994); using psychometric techniques to interpret students' evaluations of teaching (Marsh and Dunkin 1997); and the application of ideas from social psychology to developing a college curriculum (Mentkowski and Associates 2000). In contrast, in what has come to be described as student-learning research, much of the published material outside the US draws on concepts derived directly from educational contexts through interviews and inventory surveys (Biggs 1987; Marton, Hounsell, and Entwistle 1997; Bowden and Marton 1998; Prosser and Trigwell 1999; Biggs 2007). Although the concepts used in the US and elsewhere in the world often differ greatly, it is reassuring to find that the emerging conclusions about the relationship between teaching and learning are leading in very similar directions.

What Is Meant by "High-Quality Learning" in Higher Education?

Higher education, at least in the UK, is currently beset by terms intended to increase managerial control and increase the cost-effectiveness of the enterprise. Of course, governments have the responsibility to ensure that public money is used economically, but the measures put into place to monitor efficiency seem sometimes to run counter to what good teaching requires. There can be no doubt that we have to accept quality assurance, but the procedures that are used to implement it do raise concerns. If the value of PSE is judged mainly in terms of "throughputs" and outputs, if degrees are seen as branded commodities, and as teaching quality continues to be weighed less in career terms than research output, the notion of "high-quality learning" and the broad aims of a higher education can be pushed into the background.

In contrast, in much of the research on teaching and learning in higher education there is an underlying assumption that high-quality learning depends not just on pass or completion rates, but on the nature of the knowledge, skills, and conceptual understanding that students have acquired during their degree course. In a recent large-scale British study—the Enhancing Teaching-Learning Environments in Undergraduate Courses (ETL) project (described later on)—it became clear that what faculty sought was not so much the overtaking of specific "intended learning outcomes," as the development of more general ways of thinking and practising in the discipline or professional area (Anderson and Hounsell 2007). They had a much broader view of what students were expected to achieve than could be expressed through disaggregating knowledge and understanding into unconnected bite-sized elements.

> These [ways of thinking and practising] were not confined to knowledge and understanding but also included subject-specific skills, an evolving familiarity with the values and conventions of scholarly communication within a discipline and an understanding of how new knowledge was generated in the field. (Hounsell and Hounsell 2007, 98)

Many of these ideas are also central to the US-based "Preparation of the Professions Program" initiated by Lee Schulman and carried out by the Carnegie Foundation. Within this program, research questions included: "How does the formal and informal curriculum support the professional development of knowledge, skills, and professionalism? How do students / residents learn to think, perform, and act like a physician?" (Carnegie Foundation for the Advancement of Teaching 2009).

While there is benefit to some degree of mastery of instrumental knowledge, the danger of an over-reliance on tightly specified outcomes under the auspices of quality assurance is that it affects the quality of learning that then takes place. Drawing on the ideas of Habermas (1986), O'Brien (2008a) concludes that:

> Subject matter that is construed, constructed and presented in instrumentalist, technical terms will facilitate ... [equivalent] outcomes, effective for the mastery of key skills and competencies. In contrast, learning that requires

the development of higher forms of knowledge and knowing, entailing transformation of perspective and worldview, relies on more sophisticated views of subject matter and of learning. (151)

Other writers have pointed out that universities and colleges currently need to prepare students for a rapidly changing world in which they experience super-complexity (Barnett 2007)—situations in which no single agreed solution to problems can be reached. Increasingly, knowledge acquired in PSE can be no more than a springboard for coping with change and complexity in everyday life and the workplace, so students need to leave higher education with what Mentkowski and her colleagues (2000) call *learning that lasts*, which involves:

> an integration of learning, development, and performance [during and after college]. It connotes change in behaviour and flexibility in perspective, enduring commitments, and transformative elements that carry the individual forward through unexpected experiences, roles, and life events.... (xv)

> … to encompass the integration of learning with the development of the whole person. (11)

Higher education should thus be concentrating on helping students develop skills, attitudes, knowledge, and understanding that will be of maximum value beyond academe; not just an induction into the world of work in a specific profession, but also an effective preparation for life in the 21st century. We need to remind government and management alike of the dangers of creating policies and quality-assurance procedures that may unintentionally lose the essence of learning in higher education while promoting a production model of efficient teaching. Somehow, the two aims in improving higher education need to become complementary, rather than oppositional.

With some understanding of the roots and context of teaching and learning research in higher education established, I now turn my attention to the research findings themselves.

What is Known about Human Learning?

From behaviourist psychology we know that actions that are practised, and those that are systematically rewarded, are likely to be repeated in the future. While those conclusions now seem obvious, varied repetition in contrasting circumstances and reward through prompt feedback about relative success remain crucially important, particularly in skill learning. Many of these concepts are reflected in principles of instructional design, such as those advocated by Gagné (see, e.g., Gagné, Briggs, and Wager 1992).

With respect to knowledge and understanding, however, we turn to cognitive psychology which stresses the critically important role of attention, and both short-term and long-term memory in learning. Without attention, little can be remembered, and the strength, the extent, and the direction of that attention all affect learning. *Short-term memory* is not only limited in time, fading quickly, but also in size, allowing relatively few (7 ± 2) bits of information to be held there simultaneously, although we do develop ways of grouping related information to cope with more. This limitation can cause severe problems in student learning when too much material is presented within a short period of time, making it impossible for students to process it effectively, or to discover the relationships among the features being presented (Van Merriënboer, Kirschner, and Kester 2003).

Long-term memory can be separated into the semantic aspect, where conceptually based material is stored, and the episodic, where events (episodes) are remembered. There are important cross-links between the two, however, hence the efficacy of mnemonics and illustrations or anecdotes. And neurological research is making clear the importance of aroused interest in putting neurons on "stand-by" and of the complex linkages and neuronal pathways that are experienced as memory and understanding (Zull 2002; Hall 2005). Repeated use of connections leads to myelinisation, insulating the links within a neural network and so making them more efficient. The experience of understanding, or a newly established skill, produces chemicals in the brain that produce a feeling of well-being, and so reinforce those activities.

The well-known biologist, Edward Wilson (1998), sums up these processes as follows:

> By spreading activation, the conscious mind summons information from the store of long-term memory ... and holds it for a brief period in short-term memory. During this time it processes the information ... while scenarios arising from the information compete for dominance. As the scenarios of consciousness fly by, driven by stimuli and drawing upon memories of prior scenarios, they are weighted and modified by emotion ... which animates and focuses mental activity.... What we call meaning is the linkage among neural networks created by spreading activation that enlarges imagery and engages emotion. (119, 121-123, 126)

Concept development depends on the formation of these linkages, but incorrect or ineffective neural networks, once firmly established, are difficult to undo afterwards. While research has found delayed feedback beneficial in certain circumstances (see, e.g., Butler, Karpicke, and Roediger 2007), Greenfield (2008) suggests that immediate personalized feedback, through discussions about the processes of forming concepts and developing understanding, can help to encourage the kinds of meaningful learning for which teachers are aiming. However, implications derived from brain processes alone ignore the social nature of learning and contexts within PSE.

What is Known about Students' Ways of Learning and Studying?

A substantial body of research has accumulated over the last 30 years that has established how students go about learning and studying in higher education, with substantial agreement about the main differences, even though differing terminology is used. The concepts that emerge come at different levels of generality, with the broadest level describing goals and personal epistemology.

The research on students' goals contrasts the focus on the extrinsic rewards of qualifications alone with an *intrinsic orientation* towards the subject or the profession, seeking to understand the academic content and to become an expert in that area (Beaty, Gibbs, and Morgan 1997). And, not surprisingly, the intrinsic orientation leads to higher-quality learning.

Conceptions of Knowledge and Learning

An interview study by Perry (1970) was seminal in demonstrating that students developed *conceptions of knowledge* along common pathways during the college experience; beginning by seeing knowledge as either right or wrong and moving, first, towards a recognition of how evidence is used to reach conclusions, then beyond that, to accept that knowledge is still developing and open to challenge, and so ultimately uncertain and socially constructed (relativism). He also showed that acceptance of the implications of relativism came slowly and often with a difficulty not fully appreciated by faculty. Subsequent research has largely supported Perry's developmental scheme, but has suggested gender differences in the extent to which the learning is seen through personal or impersonal referents (Belenky et al. 1986), and also led to debates about whether his scheme should be seen as a general trend or as differentiated across different facets of knowledge and across subject areas (Shommer-Aikins 2002).

Changes in conceptions of knowledge are paralleled by equivalent development in students' *conceptions of learning*. Säljö (1979) found that students with little academic background saw learning in terms of memorizing and reproducing knowledge, whereas those who had experienced higher education had more sophisticated conceptions involving seeking personal meaning, suggesting the trend illustrated in Figure 1. The diagram draws attention to a common feature of developmental schemes, namely, that the more limited conceptions become integrated within the more sophisticated ones; with the higher conceptions, students show a greater awareness of their own cognitive processes (*metacognition*) and can monitor their own activities in carrying out academic tasks (*metalearning*).

FIGURE 1
The Development of Conceptions of Knowledge and Learning

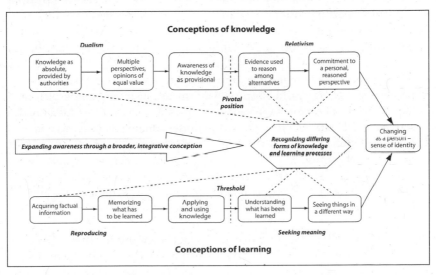

Source: Entwistle (2007, 129).

Figure 1 also highlights the parallel development of the conceptions of knowledge and learning and shows the existence, in both, of a crucial threshold at which an important qualitative change in conception takes place, affecting the ways in which students subsequently tackle their academic work (Entwistle 2007). The similarity in these independent descriptions of conceptions suggests that the processes are intimately related within the experiences of students, even though they remain largely subconscious during the process of everyday studying.

Approaches to Learning and Studying

As we look at how students actually go about their academic work, the main distinction that has emerged can be traced back to the ideas of Ausubel and his colleagues (1978) who distinguished between *meaningful* and *rote learning*: extracting personal meaning from what is being learned, or simply seeking to force it into memory. They also noted that learning in educational contexts varies along another dimension, from reception learning to discovery learning, with much of the learning in schools or higher education involving reception learning from lectures or textbooks, rather than the active, independent discovery of ideas. Whether the learning was meaningful or rote depended partly on the teaching and partly on the student.

In the literature, various labels have been attached to this distinction, but the terms introduced by Marton and his colleagues at Gothenburg

(Marton 1976; Marton and Säljö 1997)—*deep* and *surface approaches to learning*—have the advantage of emerging directly from students' descriptions of their own learning, after they had read an academic text on which they expected to be questioned. The difference in the approaches is rooted in the students' intentions, as became clear in analyzing the interviews.

> All our readings and re-readings, our iterations and reiterations, our comparisons and groupings, finally turned into an astonishingly simple picture. We had been looking for the answer to the question of why the students had arrived at qualitatively different ways of understanding the text as a whole. What we found was that the students who did not get "the point," failed to do so simply because they were not looking for it. The main difference we found in the process of learning concerned whether the students *focused on the text itself or on what the text was about* [original emphasis]—the author's intention, the main point, the conclusion to be drawn. (Marton and Säljö 1997, 43)

Students who had the intention to extract meaning for themselves engaged with the subject matter actively and generally reached a thorough understanding of the author's meaning, while those who used a surface approach were more concerned with trying to remember the answers to the questions they were expecting to be asked and so couldn't explain the author's meaning. Since the original naturalistic experiment, the distinction between deep and surface approaches has been widely confirmed across most subject areas (Richardson 2000; Long 2003), but the specific learning processes used to reach a deep understanding depend on the ways of thinking and practicing that are fundamental to each specific area of study (Entwistle 2009).

The research group at Gothenburg saw approaches to learning as relational, being affected by the teaching and learning environment experienced. As a result, individual students are found to vary their approach from course to course and even from topic to topic, and yet often with an underlying consistency created by well-honed study habits, creating a relative stability at least within a specific course that enables general approaches to be estimated through self-report inventories (Entwistle and McCune 2004). The decision to adopt a deep approach in a specific instance, however, will depend on being interested in the subject matter and having the necessary prior knowledge to be able to make sense of the study material. But actually reaching a deep understanding also depends on the amount and quality of the effort put into learning, now described as *organised* effort (TLRP 2007), although earlier seen as a strategic approach (Entwistle and McCune 2004).

Students adopting a deep approach may also differ in their preferences for particular learning strategies or *learning styles*. Some students—*holists*—prefer to tackle a topic by seeing it first as a whole, which can then be used to guide their developing understanding; others—*serialists*—are more comfortable with building up their understanding step-by-step through concentration on the details (Pask 1988). Students' reactions to different forms of presentation, whether in lectures or writing, to some extent reflect their preferred styles of learning (Witkin et al. 1977). A full understanding of academic topics, however, generally depends on an alternation between the two processes, as students examine the implications of evidence in detail and also the patterns of interconnections which relate ideas and concepts.

Survey research using inventories has shown that a deep approach seems to incorporate this interplay, with three sub-scales being directly involved: "relating ideas," "use of evidence," and "interest in ideas." The deep approach is also linked to an "intrinsic orientation to the subject" as reason for entering higher education, and a conception of learning as involving "learning as transforming," as opposed to reproducing (Entwistle 1998, 19; Entwistle and Peterson 2004). Vermunt (1998) also showed that students adopting a deep approach were likely to take greater responsibility for their own learning (self-regulation), while Entwistle, McCune, and Hounsell (2003) found the deep approach was associated not only with monitoring studying but also with organized effort (see the analysis in Appendix 1).

While the correlational links between differing aspects of students' self-reports of their experiences of studying are clear, the developmental progression of students towards a deep approach during a degree course is neither as consistent nor as strong as might be hoped. It appears to be much easier to change student conceptions of knowledge than it is to move students away from a surface approach to learning (Lonka and Lindblom-Ylänne 1996; Rodriguez and Cano 2007).

Psychological research studies have identified other student characteristics that affect the outcomes of learning. Some of these exist prior to entering college, such as prior qualifications and previous knowledge; these have to be taken into account when planning and carrying out teaching, but cannot be changed. Other student characteristics have been firmly established prior to entry, such as general ability and fundamental personality traits, and are not normally seen as amenable to much change after late adolescence (Deary 2000). But another group of characteristics— including specific abilities, self-confidence, interest, motivation, and learning strategies—are all affected by experiences at university (Pascarella and Terenzini 1991, 2005; Pintrich, Brown, and Weinstein 1994; Rotter 1954). More recently, it has been recognized that groups of variables work in consort to bring about learning, in particular, triads made up of cognitive, motivational, and affective components. Perkins and Ritchhart (2004) have described a *thinking disposition*, which is made up of a triad of ability, inclination, and alertness to situations that call for thinking. Following this line of argument, we can now suggest a *disposition to understand for yourself* in academic study, involving a symbiotic relationship between learning strategies and the confidence to use them effectively, a willingness to put concentrated effort into reaching a personal understanding of academic topics, and also an alertness to possibilities for learning provided within a learning environment and to opportunities for using understanding thereafter (Entwistle and McCune 2009). Such a disposition involves a continuing inclination to engage with learning so as to reach a personal understanding, and yet it can be stimulated, systematically encouraged, and supported through the teaching and learning experiences provided (Janssen 1996).

The Nature of Academic Learning and Understanding

The importance of developing conceptual understanding in higher education led to a series of studies in the 1990s on the nature of academic understanding in Edinburgh. A distinction was made between *target understanding* set up by the teacher and *personal understanding* achieved by the student (Entwistle and Smith 2002); and the development of this personal understanding was seen in students' descriptions of their experiences as they prepared for final examinations. What was striking was the way understanding was described in terms of seeing a topic as a related whole, in which "all the pieces fitted together" (Entwistle and Entwistle 1997). Indeed, by the end of their intensive revision, some students experienced a tightly integrated form of understanding that they reported seeing as an entity in their mind's eye—*a knowledge object*—which they then used to guide their exam answers (Entwistle and Entwistle 2003). Ongoing research in London is exploring the use of concept maps to identify the gradual development of understanding, seen in terms of the number and salience of the interconnections shown between concepts within a web (Hay 2007).

Elsewhere, the continuing research of Marton and his collaborators led, first, to a series of studies looking at variations in how students had understood specific concepts (Marton and Booth 1997) and, more recently, to a *variation theory* of learning within educational contexts (Marton 2007). Conceptual learning depends on students being able to discern the *critical features* of a concept or topic, and the relationships between those features, simultaneously.

> We should ... be clear about the difference between "discerning" and "being told." Medical students, for instance, might be advised by their professor to try to notice the different features of their patients, such as the colour of the lips, the moisture of the skin, the ease of breathing, and so on. This is "being told." But in order to follow this advice the students must experience those features, and the only way to experience them is to experience how they can vary.... By experiencing variation, people ... become "sensitized" to those aspects. This means that they are likely to see future events in terms

of those aspects ... [so learning depends] on experiencing variation. (Marton and Tsui 2004, 10-11)

Recent work has been exploring how variation theory can be used within higher education to teach problematic areas of a subject. Cope and Prosser (2005) identified the concept of an *information system* as problematic for students and interviewed students to identify the different ways in which they understood it. The researchers found several distinctive conceptions (for phenomenographic categories of description, see Marton and Booth 1997); some saw an information system simply as something which retrieved information, while others viewed it as just a computer system linking individuals within an organisation. The target understanding for the teachers was a much more complex conception: involving the processes of gathering, disseminating, and communicating the various kinds of information required to support several different organisational functions. Students adopting a surface approach tended to focus on the limited conceptions; only with a deep approach were students likely to appreciate the more sophisticated interpretation.

A deep approach starts, as always, with an intention to work out the meaning for oneself and, in this instance, depended on alertness to the importantly different ways of describing an information system. For a full understanding to become possible, though, the teaching-learning environment had to provide opportunities for students to recognize the significance of these different perspectives through carefully varied tasks and explicit discussion of the critical features of the concept. In this way, students began to see the variations that existed in the descriptions of information systems and, through that experience, to reach the required conceptual understanding.

> To improve the quality of students' outcomes, the educationally critical aspects ... need to become explicit, thematised parts of the undergraduate curricula, textbooks, teaching strategies, and learning activities. Importantly, students need to be aware, from the beginning of their studies, of the nature of the target level of understanding of the concept of an information system and how that understanding can be achieved.... Learning tasks need to be designed ... [to] make students aware of *the experience of learning about an information system* [original emphasis]. (Cope and Prosser 2005, 366)

How do Teaching and Learning Environments Influence Student Learning?

This brings us to what we, as university or college teachers, can do to assist students to learn more effectively and more congenially. The first thing to note is that it is not so much the teaching-learning environment we provide that affects the learning approaches of individual learners, as their perceptions of it. Teaching-learning environments, nevertheless, do markedly affect overall student learning approaches, but the effects work in both directions (Richardson 2007). Students already adopting deep approaches tend to view teaching designed to promote conceptual understanding favourably, while those having surface approaches react negatively to the same environments (Entwistle and Tait 1990). And students giving high ratings to teaching effectiveness and the support provided for learning also report deep approaches to organized effort in studying (Entwistle, Nisbet, and Bromage 2005).

While individual differences in perceptions of teaching are important to keep in mind, the overall reactions of students to differing teaching-learning environments allow us to determine which aspects of those teaching arrangements are most likely to induce deep approaches, and so encourage conceptual understanding. Analyses of course-evaluation forms from students have provided a clear idea about what aspects of teaching students find most helpful, with several studies being reported in Perry and Smart (1997). From these and other studies it seems clear that, in lectures, at least seven aspects are seen to be important—clarity, level, pace, structure, explanation, enthusiasm, and empathy. The first four describe the essentials for effective lecturing, while the remaining "3 Es" seem to be the aspects most likely to encourage deep approaches in the students (Entwistle 2000).

These studies focus exclusively on what happens in face-to-face teaching, but the most important conclusion from the research findings on the effects of teaching on learning is that all elements within a whole teaching-learning environment act together in affecting the quality of learning. The encouragement of deep approaches depends on designing teaching, assignments, and assessment that act synergistically to support student learning and understanding; and synergy is crucial because even one important aspect "out of sync" with the aims, or interfering with the effects, of other components can impede learning.

> Since the interaction between the learner and the learning environment depends on perceptions ... the challenge in any educational programme is to prevent misperception and mismatch.... Inappropriate approaches to learning are simply induced by teaching: just one piece of the "jigsaw" that is out of place ... may interfere with the relation between the learner and the content.... Encouraging students to adopt deep approaches and to employ them holistically is ... difficult because [all] the pieces need to fit together. (Eizenberg 1988, 196-97)

Going even further, we begin to see the teaching-learning environment as an *interacting system,* an idea developed independently by Entwistle (1987; 2009) and Biggs (1993), drawing on soft-systems and general-system theories respectively. The conclusions were almost identical; we can understand the outcomes of learning only by seeing students interacting with the whole teaching-learning environment provided by university teachers and institutions. External and institutional influences are largely unnoticed by students; they experience what has been called the "inner teaching-learning environment," the domain over which faculty have most control and that also has the greatest impact on the quality learning.

Figure 2 illustrates an inner teaching-learning environment described in the ETL project study (Entwistle, Nisbet, and Bromage 2005), using electronic engineering as an example. The diagram also indicates how each part of that environment contributes, in rather different ways, to the overall target understanding for a course. Later, after looking at subject area differences, we shall consider the ways in which this environment interacts with the characteristics of students to help explain the outcomes of learning.

FIGURE 2
A Teaching-Learning Environment Experienced in Electronic Engineering

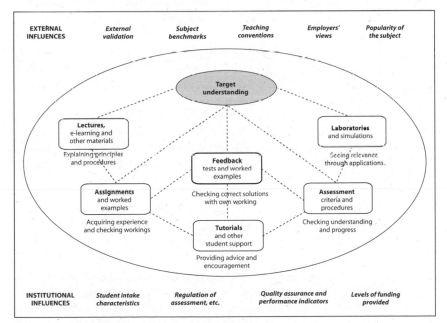

Source: Author's compilation.

How Does Subject Matter Influence What Constitutes Effective Teaching?

So far the research reviewed has sought to provide generalised conclusions about teaching and learning in higher education, but one of the main differences between schooling and PSE is the divergence between subjects and the ways in which they are taught. For educational researchers, it is particularly difficult to investigate teaching and learning within specific subject areas, as the subject matter has to be understood at least as well as the undergraduates understand. While there are vast numbers of studies carried out by academics about teaching within their own disciplines, they are mostly anecdotal reports of innovations in practice, often with little knowledge of the existing literature on teaching and learning, or sufficient expertise in educational research methods. It is relatively rare to find studies that are well-designed, conceptually sound, and also look in depth at the subject matter being taught. The picture is, however, becoming clearer, and the crucial implications of teaching and learning for the very different nature of academic disciplines and professional areas are now evident.

Differing Epistemologies. Donald (1994) reported an influential series of studies across subject areas, interviewing teaching staff and students in five contrasting disciplines. At a broad level of analysis there were noticeable similarities, such as the need to validate knowledge either against observations in the physical world or against a consensus of scholarly interpretations, a search for coherence or internal consistency among evidence and arguments, and critical or analytic thinking in reaching interpretations of evidence (Donald 1995). But there were also important differences both in the nature of the knowledge and in the match between the adopted approaches to teaching and the students' perceptions of the support they were receiving. In physics, the abstract nature of the subject and the overly theoretical explanations provided by their teachers created difficulties for the students, whereas the practical nature of engineering meant that the goals were easier to perceive. In psychology, students came to realize that the development of inferential skills was important. But what seemed to be generally lacking in the teaching was an explicit discussion of the ways of thinking that were characteristic of the discipline and how conclusions came to be validated.

Contrasting Beliefs about Teaching. Research into beliefs about and typical approaches to teaching has found important differences among faculty, even within a discipline. One example of such differences is captured in the Teaching Perspectives Inventory (Pratt, Collins, and Jarvis Selinger 2001), which is based upon 13 studies conducted in the 1980s and 1990s. It provides faculty with the opportunity to classify their own approach with respect to five distinct approaches to teaching, each with its own implicit learning focus. These approaches include: The Transmission Perspective: Effective Delivery of Content; The Apprenticeship Perspective: Modeling Ways of Being; The Developmental Perspective: Cultivating Ways of Thinking; The Nurturing Perspective: Facilitating Self-Efficacy; and The Social Reform Perspective: Seeking a Better Society.

Another classification of faculty approaches to teaching is found in the research by Prosser and Trigwell (1999), which focuses on the extent to which the approach is *teacher-focused, content-oriented* or *student-focused, learning-oriented*; whether teachers concentrate on presenting the subject matter in terms of how they themselves see its structure and meaning, or whether they also recognize the importance of making that knowledge readily accessible to the students at the stage they have then reached.

The student-focused approach is more likely to keep the needs of the student firmly in mind and to encourage conceptual understanding by recognizing potential difficulties and stressing interconnections within and between topics (Prosser and Trigwell 1999). As all lecturers have to take account of content, there is a sense that the student-focused approach will necessarily incorporate the content-focused approach, but there seems to be a complication. In several studies, there is a gross disparity between the sciences and the humanities in the proportion of lecturers who have adopted the more inclusive student-focused approach. In one recent study, half of the science and engineering lecturers interviewed fell clearly into the teacher-focused category, while among lecturers in the humanities and social sciences over 70 percent were in the student-focused group (adapted from Prosser et al. 2005, Table 4). Does this difference represent deficiencies in science teaching, or a contrast in how conceptual development is encouraged in science compared with the humanities?

In an earlier review of both school- and university-based research, and drawing on Shulman's (1987) idea of *pedagogical content knowledge*, it was suggested that effective teachers were drawing from three overlapping knowledge bases—about the subject, about the range of teaching methods available to them, and about how students learn their subject (Entwistle and Walker 2002). A recent study has begun to show how these three elements come together in different subject areas; how the nature of the subject area affects the way faculty think about pedagogy (O'Brien 2008a, 2008b). Knowledge in the sciences is more firmly established and more impersonal, while it remains more contested and people-centred in the social sciences. What does that imply for perceptions of pedagogy? Does the teaching of science really have to remain impersonal?

Prosser and his colleagues have recently come up with the intriguing finding that the main differences in approaches to teaching are also related to the way in which the subject itself is understood by the lecturer, either broadly integrated or in discrete packages.

> At one extreme, the subject is seen as a series of topics or issues with little or no attention being paid to the whole discipline. When the subject is seen in this way, lecturers tend to talk about "delivering" discreet "packages" of information to students.... In such a scenario, there is little opportunity for students to see how they might integrate what they learn into a larger field of knowledge; what they know is likely to remain a series of isolated facts.

At the other extreme, when the subject matter is seen by an academic as a coherent whole, students are more likely to be helped into a relationship with the field as a whole and to experience and develop a personal understanding of that whole. (Prosser, Martin, and Trigwell 2007, 56)

In their study, social science lecturers were found to think in broader and more integrated ways than science lecturers about both disciplinary knowledge and ways of teaching (Prosser et al. 2005, Table 4). It may be, then, that the ways science faculty tend to think about teaching remains both too impersonal and too atomistic to make it easy for many students to develop an integrated personal understanding, but that is also the way of thinking that science requires. Still, a more conscious awareness of the nature of knowledge in their discipline, and its implications for effective teaching, would be valuable for them, and indeed for all faculty.

If we want to change and develop the ways in which teachers approach their teaching and help their students to learn, we need to help them to think carefully about what they are teaching and how it relates to and coheres with the field as a whole. This is a particularly important issue for teachers new to teaching or teaching a topic for the first time. (Prosser et al. 2005, 153)

Identifying Threshold Concepts and Dealing with Troublesome Knowledge. Another influential idea introduced during the ETL project, but developed much further since, is that of *threshold concepts* (Meyer and Land 2003, 2006; Land, Meyer, and Smith 2008). These concepts have a crucial role to play within degree courses as they open up the subject for students by providing a gateway into a different and more powerful way of thinking about the subject; but one which often proves difficult for students to open.

A threshold concept … is likely to be … *transformative*, in that, once understood, its potential effect on student learning and behaviour is to occasion a significant shift in the perception of the subject.… [It is also] *integrative*, that is, exposes the previously hidden interrelatedness of something … [and it is] probably irreversible, in that the change of perspective occasioned by acquisition of a threshold concept is unlikely to be forgotten. (Meyer and Land 2003, 4)

Recent work within the field of economics teaching and learning (Davies and Mangan 2007) indicates that it is possible to identify a series of basic concepts in that subject area that then become integrated within overarching threshold concepts, and that webs of these higher-order concepts and theories can be used to map the knowledge domain that is to be taught, and so provoke discussions among faculty about better ways of teaching the subject.

Threshold concepts ... focus our attention on the relationship between big shifts in thinking in the subject and transformative changes that learners have to experience in their thinking. These changes are transformative in the sense that learners are not simply making connections between new learning and ideas they have already acquired. In order to truly understand the new idea—if it is a threshold concept—they must rework prior understanding (Davies and Mangan 2007, 721).

Examples of how faculty identify threshold concepts in their own disciplines, and how this process can transform their own pedagogical thinking, can be found in recent studies of threshold concepts (Land, Meyer, and Smith 2008). Essentially, discussion of threshold concepts can transform lecturers' ways of thinking about the nature of knowledge in their subject area and, in so doing, also affect their ideas about teaching and learning. In her study, O'Brien (2008a, b) used discussions between university teachers to focus on their thinking about a nominated threshold concept. O'Brien's work explored in depth the nature of "pedagogical content knowledge," showing how teachers' accounts of why particular aspects of their subject acted as threshold concepts, and how best to teach them, depended on individual understandings of the epistemology of the discipline, as well as on distinctive personal theories about the nature of knowledge and its uses.

Considering troublesome knowledge in general, Perkins (2006, 2007) has argued that university teachers need to take the existence of "trouble spots" in students' understanding more seriously. He suggests that there are different reactions from teachers when difficult areas are identified: to *blame* the students and continue to teach as before, to *focus* the teaching on the area of difficulty by teaching in the same way but working at it harder, and to try to *explain* the difficulty through a deeper understanding of what caused it and then changing the teaching accordingly. Perkins was also involved in the *Teaching for Understanding* project in schools, carried out in Harvard, where the main teaching aims were kept in students' minds through *throughlines*. These often took the form of major questions or issues, such as in history teaching—"How do we find out *"the truth"* about things that happened long ago?" and "How do we see through the bias in sources?"—which created a framework for the most general understandings sought during the course (Wiske 1998).

Teaching within the Disciplines to Encourage Conceptual Understanding

There have been important breakthroughs in teaching within specific subject areas through recognizing difficulties encountered by students and devising imaginative ways of overcoming them. One influential example comes from physics, where Mazur (1997) had been trying to understand why many first-year students were doing badly and found the lectures boring. He found that students were concentrating on learning "recipes" or problem-solving routines, which allowed them to arrive at solutions with little understanding of the underlying principles. Mazur decided that traditional forms of lecture were the main cause of surface approaches to learning. He therefore tried to make students more actively involved in their own learning during lectures, and eventually devised what he called *peer instruction*, in which lecture-based instruction was interspersed with occasional five-minute concept tests. Students were required to note down an answer and then justify their answers to nearby students to increase student activity and involvement. This technique has been adapted to work with the computer-based Personal Response System (PRS) that displays analyses of the answers given by the whole class, allowing a more general discussion of any misconceptions emerging (Mazur 2001).

A related approach, which also began in the sciences, has been encouraging faculty to make use of concept maps, not just in planning a new course or thinking about an existing one, but also by training students to use them in their own studying in ways that make the connections between the concepts hierarchical and explicit. Students are also encouraged to discuss the differences in their concept maps and revise their diagrams repeatedly until they are satisfied with their understanding (Hay 2007). This technique has recently been extended to a variety of disciplinary areas, but ongoing work suggests that, in the humanities, hierarchical structures are inappropriate and the links between concepts need to be explained, rather than just indicated in a few words (Hay in press). The success of concept maps depends on engaging the cognitive activities involved in developing personal understanding, processes whose importance is also supported through neurological research.

Innovations in other areas, such as problem-based learning (PBL) in medicine, have similar intentions in engaging students more actively with the main aims of the subject. As a recent study of medical students argues, what PBL can offer to students is a learning environment that encourages students to take responsibility for their own learning and to think critically and deeply about abstract concepts in relation to everyday medical contexts and problems (Fyrenious, Wirell, and Silén 2007). One of the students in that study felt that the experience of PBL had fostered a different kind of understanding, one which made sense of theory within practice.

> If you don't know how to apply it in practice, you only have it in theory, then you haven't understood…. If you can sort of think what happens practically, even if you don't have all the theory, so that you can apply what happens practically, then you have understood. And then you can draw parallels and be able to see relations and so on…. But if you've only learned something

really narrow in the book, and when you have to apply something that's not in the book, you find it difficult to understand because you … only know the language of the book. (Fyrenious, Wirell and Silén 2007, 156)

Personal Response System (PRS), problem-based learning (PBL), and other similar discipline-based innovations have been adopted in other subject areas, but with varying success. Where independent, integrative reviews of evaluations of such teaching have been carried out (e.g., TLRP 2004), the findings are almost always inconsistent—with good reason, as they are rarely able to compare like with like. The innovations are, quite sensibly, implemented in differing ways to fit in with local circumstances, but in the process prevent any easy comparison of outcomes. And it is not so much the use of any specific method in itself, but how it is implemented in relation to the broad aims of a particular course that is important.

Research at the school level has been looking at so-called "powerful learning environments," which have been shown to influence the quality of learning (De Corte et al. 2003). This approach encourages teachers to use authentic, open problems and learning materials presented in a variety of formats. Teaching methods are intended to arouse interest, activate prior knowledge, clarify meaning, and model appropriate thinking strategies and reflective processes. Where new ways of learning or problem-solving are being introduced, these are scaffolded by providing detailed guidelines to follow. This support is then gradually removed so as to encourage subsequent self-regulation in learning. And, above all, students are encouraged to monitor their own strategies and discuss these with other students, so as to produce a classroom culture that encourages reflection on process.

What General Principles are There for Designing Teaching-Learning Environments?

The earlier discussions made it clear why we cannot expect to find specific teaching methods that will "work" in all, or even most, areas of PSE. Rather we have to take full account of the diversity that is found, both in institutions with contrasting intakes and purposes and among students with very different backgrounds and previous experiences of education. In the process, it is possible to suggest guidelines for creating teaching-learning environments that are likely to encourage deep approaches among students, and so lead to high-quality learning outcomes. But the specifics have to be left to individual course teams and individual teachers. Judging from the work carried out in the ETL project (mentioned earlier) and in a more recent study by O'Brien (2008a, 2008b), it is clear that university teachers typically embrace broad aims for student learning that guide their thinking about teaching methods. They concentrate on how to develop the characteristic ways of thinking and practising within their subject through the teaching methods adopted. Indeed, there appears to be an inner logic of the subject and its pedagogy (TLRP 2007; Entwistle 2009) linking the nature of knowledge in the discipline to the specific set of methods most likely to work well in helping students learn.

This implies that much more weight should be given in educational development activities to encouraging academic staff to think critically about the nature of their subject area, to make explicit the ways of thinking and practising they want students to acquire, and to identify the threshold concepts which can open up the subject for students, but which often become stumbling blocks for them. Such critical consideration of the subject matter has been found to act as a threshold for faculty in clarifying their understanding of the relationship between teaching and learning, and making clearer which teaching methods are most likely to support the types of learning they want students to carry out (Land, Meyer, and Smith 2008).

While face-to-face teaching continues to play an important part in higher education, we have already argued that it is important to see how other aspects of the overall teaching-learning environment affect the quality of student learning. Figure 3 offers a heuristic map to summarize some of the more important influences on student learning that have been identified in the research.

The upper half of the model focuses on the characteristics of students, and these interact with the aspects of the teaching-learning environment shown in the lower half. The left-hand side shows the influences of students' abilities, knowledge, and learning processes, linked to perceptions of meaning and relevance, and to the subject matter and how it is taught. The right-hand side brings in the effects of motives, feelings, and organized effort, associated with perceptions of the task requirements and other aspects of the teaching-learning environment, particularly assessment and feedback. It must be stressed, however, as we think about aspects of the model in more detail, that this separation between cognitive and emotional aspects, and between teaching and the learning environment, is just an analytic device intended to clarify the nature of the influences on learning which are, in reality, closely interrelated.

Student Characteristics

All of the student characteristics shown in Figure 3 affect the outcomes of learning in one way or another, and interact with aspects of the teaching and the learning environment provided. As a result, they need to be kept in mind when planning and carrying out teaching. Some aspects like interest, motivation, and approaches to learning are directly affected by the teaching provided, while others like intelligence and prior knowledge, as already mentioned, have to be taken into account in judging what is appropriate for a particular group of students.

FIGURE 3
Heuristic Model of Interacting Influences on Student Learning

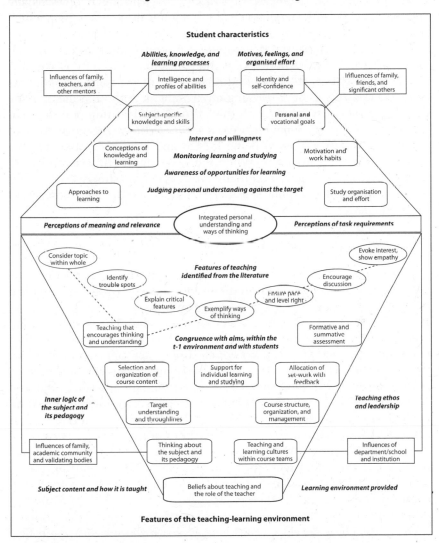

Source: Author's compilation.

Besides the specific influences on learning, the top half of the model also draws attention to certain broad characteristics that need to be kept in mind when thinking about the design of degree programmes. First, there is the crucial effect of *interest* in the subject and willingness to put the requisite effort into learning. Then, there is the need for students to *monitor* the effects of their learning and studying processes, and to be aware of opportunities provided by the various components within the teaching-learning environment for developing their understanding. And perhaps the most important aspect of monitoring learning involves *judging personal understanding* in relation to the academic targets being set, which brings us to the centre of the diagram and the most distinctive aims of university education—the development of conceptual understanding and characteristic ways of thinking and practising within the discipline.

The lower half of the model outlines some of the main components of a generalized teaching-learning environment. Although the analytic separation between teaching on the left and the learning environment on the right is artificial, nevertheless it serves to highlight the distinctive nature of the subject matter being taught and how that influences the choice of teaching methods. While the learning environment also, of course, depends on the subject matter, the influences shown on the right are somewhat less discipline specific, partly because of institutional policies about assessment procedures.

Subject Content and How it is Taught

The boxes on the left-hand side have mostly been covered in the previous discussion, but each box within the model relates to a series of critical features or defining characteristics that can be opened up, rather like an Internet link, to explain what lays behind the label. The box describing "teaching that encourages thinking and understanding" can be further elaborated by each of the ellipses, including "exemplify ways of thinking," for example. Decisions made in each of these areas should reflect an understanding of student characteristics previously described. Without doubt, one of the main problems facing faculty in planning their teaching is the diversity of previous knowledge and ability across students in their courses. Aiming at the average student does not work well, because of these wide differences. Instead strategies are needed to provide material in different ways that will suit students with different starting points and contrasting goals. One example of how that has been accomplished comes from a physicist, Paul Walker:

> Over time, I have developed a teaching approach which begins to satisfy simultaneously a tacit demand for content, for understanding of content, for relevance and applicability of that content, and yet still challenges [the students].... Within this *multipli-inclusive* approach, information is provided in logical order for those who want it.... For students who need to relate to other course content or to the world, there is a thread of conversation making such links, often unexpected ones.... [And] for students who seek to apply the knowledge, there is at least conversational reference to that, which ... is not unusual. But an explicit awareness of inclusively serving the interests and learning approaches of a diversity of students seems to be much less common. (Entwistle and Walker 2002, 27-28)

Although many features of good teaching have already been discussed, an obvious gap is the pervasive effect of information technology on teaching and learning. So far, however, there is a lack of research that brings together technological advances with the findings about teaching and learning in a coherent way. They seem at times to be marching to different drums: the one creating excitement about the latest way of presenting information or administering courses and the other focusing more on students' conceptual development and change. Although the literature described above has derived mainly from traditional approaches to teaching, nevertheless the principles emerging do seem to contain important messages for those devising e-learning environments (Ginns and Ellis 2007). There is also a growing interest in *blended learning*, with its concern to find the most appropriate ways in which e-learning and traditional teaching can work together to support deep and meaningful learning (Garrison and Kanuka 2004). And that is probably the most important trend to encourage in conventional universities and colleges, as the wholesale use of e-learning to deliver content knowledge no longer seems desirable. In publications on e-learning:

> ... a lot of the hype has vanished and ... the talk of "death of traditional educational methods" ... has been replaced by a renewed realism about the importance of blending face-to-face methods with e-learning, and that real learning is hard whatever methods are used—there are no "silver bullets".... [Also it shows that] individual innovation by academic staff does not lead automatically to real educational progress, as it is random and not strategically focused. Nor does it lead to containment in costs but rather to an escalation in them. (Haywood 2004, 26)

Learning Environment Provided

The broader context that makes up the full teaching-learning environment depicted in Figure 3 involves the influences of the institution and departments or other academic divisions, of which faculty are generally all too well aware. Attempts to introduce innovations in either teaching or assessment can be encouraged or constrained by the resources provided and the types of teaching rooms available, while institution-wide curriculum changes can sometimes be bitterly opposed within departments.

The attitudes of faculty can also be seen in the ways in which they work collaboratively to create a teaching culture within a course team or department and these clearly influence student learning. Much has been made recently about *communities of practice* (Wenger 1998), and course teams fit into that model. But the descriptions of these communities tend to stress the communality, whereas the reality often involves tensions and disagreements. Recently, Trowler (2009) has been exploring how these workgroups function within teaching-learning environments, teasing out the sociological aspects seen to govern their activities.

> In terms of theory, my thinking was much influenced by Lave and Wenger (1991). I was looking for different communities of practice ... interacting with each other. What I found surprised and puzzled me. The problem was summed up by one head of department who said "There are more factions than people in my department." Where was the "community of practice" here, then? What was being revealed largely centred around diversity and conflict, not "legitimate peripheral participation:" gentle induction into a shared set of understandings and practices. (Trowler 2009, Preface)

In his analysis, Trowler focused on issues of leadership, authority, and teaching ethos within departments and course teams, and how these affect the "take-up" of new approaches to teaching and learning, but those remain as a background to the current review. The teaching and learning policies and strategies evolved within institutions and policies clearly frame what is possible for faculty to achieve within their teaching activities, but how lecturers feel about them affects how these are implemented, and whether they will be successful. Students will generally not be aware of how these are influencing the teaching, but they are an everyday reality for the faculty.

The remaining aspects highlighted in the heuristic model (Figure 3) derive mainly from the ETL project, directed by Dai Hounsell and myself, within the Teaching and Learning Research Programme of the Economic and Social Research Council (ESRC) on *Enhancing teaching-learning environments in undergraduate courses* (TLRP 2007). The researchers worked with course teams teaching 26 undergraduate modules in four contrasting subject areas—electronic engineering, biological sciences, economics, and history—across 12 institutions. We interviewed faculty and groups of students and also collected questionnaires from students before and after the course unit had been taught. The first questionnaire covered students' approaches to learning and studying and was similar to the version shown in Appendix 2.

The second questionnaire asked about students' experiences and was a longer version of that shown in Appendix 3. Feedback on the analyses of these data was given to course teams, with subsequent discussions usually leading to a "collaborative initiative," involving some fine-tuning of the teaching to encourage greater student engagement in their learning. Equivalent data were then collected from the following year-group of students to explore their reactions to the modified teaching-learning environment provided.

Several of the concepts emerging from the project have already been mentioned: *ways of thinking and practising within the subject, threshold concepts,* and *the inner logic of the subject and its pedagogy.* We also built on the notion of *constructive alignment* (Biggs 1996)—matching teaching to constructivist aims—to examine what we called congruence, the "goodness-of-fit" between the teaching as a whole and the course teams' targets of deep understanding and development of the ways of thinking and practising. This also involved identifying any element which seemed to be interfering with such learning, and considering how the teaching seem to match the backgrounds, prior knowledge, and aspirations of the students taking a module.

The questionnaire we designed to capture students' experiences of the teaching on the target module proved to have six main dimensions (see Appendix 3 scoring procedure), all of which were closely interrelated to create a factor describing a teaching-learning environment seen by students to support their learning. This factor showed quite strong correlations with factors indicating a deep approach and organized effort, and significant correlations with both surface approach (negative) and students' self-ratings of their achievement as indicated by the grades they had received to date (see Appendix 1 for details). This final factor was defined most strongly, not by grades but by perceptions of the pace, difficulty level, and prior knowledge, and could be seen as a proxy for ability level, which it was not possible to measure directly.

The six scales describing students' experiences of teaching can be seen within the abbreviated version of the whole questionnaire shown as Appendix 3, and provided indications of where problems might lay. But the environment described by faculty, and emerging from the group interviews with students, made the nature of the relationships with learning outcomes much clearer. For example, the damaging effect of inappropriate level and pace in lectures was apparent, particularly in electronic engineering where the notion of *delayed understanding* introduced by Scheja (2006) was found to be important. A lack of understanding of the main principles underlying the subject in the early stages of a course created demoralization, which led students to transfer their efforts to more rewarding course units (Entwistle, Nisbet, and Bromage 2005).

The importance of *course management* was striking in large first-year classes and, from the student perspective, was most noticeable where the course team seemed not to be fully aware of what other members of the team were saying, and where tutors were not well prepared or seemed to be applying different standards in their marking.

The most consistent problem encountered related to the *feedback* provided on set work. The crucial importance of getting prompt comments and explanations from teaching faculty on the work submitted was mentioned repeatedly by students, and from a theoretical viewpoint is essential to complete any learning cycle. The competing pressures on faculty among teaching, research, and administration, along with substantial increases in student numbers, are making it difficult to provide appropriate feedback in a full and timely way. The adverse effects of the lack of good feedback were clear, but the allocation of resources in departments meant that relatively more faculty time was provided for final-year rather than first-year courses, and yet the need for feedback to inexperienced students, supplemented by support and guidance, is much greater during the early years than for those approaching the end of their degree.

In the literature, the effects of *assessment* on approaches to studying are repeatedly stressed, as assessment is the main "driver" of study behaviour and the form it takes strongly affects students' approaches to learning (Entwistle 2000). The assessment that students experience during the course is "formative" in the sense that it enables students to see what is required of them, but their perceptions of its purposes also affect their approaches to learning. Assessment tasks that are open-ended, encouraging engagement with the topic and requiring personal understanding, evoke a deep approach, while multiple-choice tests are notorious for pushing students into surface approaches (Scouller 1998). But it is not the multiple-choice question (MCQ) format itself that is to blame: items can demand understanding, but the vast majority of them do not (Gardiner 1994), and students come to perceive multiple-choice tests in general as implying rote learning of detail. However, in our ETL project, we found that a careful combination of MCQs and short-answer questions (SAQs) focusing on conceptual understanding proved valuable.

> MCQs made the students revise [review] the entire syllabus rather than concentrating on selected topics only. Most of the students' concerns were centred around MCQs being badly written, ambiguously worded, or aimed at "catching them out." Students who obtained high exam scores on MCQs also scored high for SAQs, and the students' approaches to studying ... were significantly related to their *overall* grades, rather than to [those from] the different types of questions. Changing the examination format seemed to have set in motion a process of constructively aligning [the assessment], which resulted in conveying to the students a very clear sense of what was expected [in preparing for the exam]. (Reimann et al. 2007)

The final box in Figure 3 pertaining to the learning environment describes *support for individual learning and studying*, which is most at risk from the "massification" of higher education. Meetings with individual students, and small-group tutorial classes, have become much less frequent, and yet discussion of students' developing understanding is crucial for high-quality learning, from both pedagogical and neurological perspectives (Greenfield 2008). As the teaching resources available for each student seem likely to continue to decline, the only alternatives seem to be an extended use of online facilities and the time-tabling of small-group sessions in which students discuss their work with each other.

CONCLUSION

After this review of research into teaching and learning in PSE, what can be said about effective teaching and learning in higher education? The research suggests that for each discipline there is an inner logic of the subject and its pedagogy. In other words, approaches to teaching and the methods used to encourage conceptual understanding necessarily reflect the nature of knowledge and ways of thinking within a particular discipline. But there is also a *way of thinking about the pedagogy* that *can* be generalized, and there are actions that can be taken to embody that approach within the teaching-learning environments provided for students. So what is that way, and what are the actions?

Following the evidence presented in this paper, the way of thinking that emerges involves seeing the purpose of higher education as going beyond the acquisition of knowledge and skills; to recognize that for the demands of current society and employment, graduates need to have acquired a personal conceptual understanding of the main ideas and ways of thinking in their area of study so as to experience "learning that lasts." Only this will provide flexibility in applying knowledge, skills, and understanding that will suffice at a time of rapid change and "super-complexity" in dealing with emerging issues and new problems.

In terms of what students have to develop during their degree courses, we should be emphasizing the importance of their being able to recognize what is needed when meeting a new challenge, and to monitor their own processes of thinking in tackling the tasks they meet, as well as being aware of the opportunities available within their current environment to help in those tasks. This depends on having appropriately sophisticated conceptions of knowledge and learning, and the necessary disposition to seek a deep level of understanding. That disposition brings with it deep approaches in studying—thinking critically about evidence and looking for links between new ideas and previous knowledge—processes which, in alternation, can lead to tight, integrated forms of understanding, and to an awareness of their understanding as a knowledge object.

Such understanding can be encouraged by developing courses that set a broad agenda from the start, highlighting the ways of thinking and practicing that are required, and introducing broad questions as "throughlines" that keep students focused on the importance of reaching an understanding for themselves. Using concept maps is also a good way of keeping the focus of personal understanding, as well as introducing topics in an open-ended way, setting authentic problems rather than giving just repetitive book-based work, and giving choice in the assignments set—together help to set the tone for a learning-environment that will evoke deep approaches. In the past, too little use was made of the students themselves as peer teachers or discussion groups focused not just on topics of problems, but also on the processes of learning and working together collaboratively. Students also have to come to see that without putting in their own "organized effort" and maintaining concentration, they will make little academic progress, notwithstanding that student culture, and the need to earn money, compete with the students' readiness to put in the necessary time and focused effort. Nevertheless, encouraging a greater awareness of students' own responsibilities in learning can help.

Of course, university teachers also have responsibilities—to put in adequate time and effort into preparing their teaching and to be aware of potential difficulties facing students. They also have to devise ways of making their presentations interesting and set up learning environments that act synergistically to encourage and support a deep engagement with the subject. In devising a course along these lines, the starting point involves thinking critically about the nature of learning within the discipline or professional area, and establishing what students need to do in order to reach a broad, transferable understanding of that subject area. If "intended learning outcomes" have to be set, then they should be made explicitly subservient to the broader aims established for the degree course as a whole. Courses then need to be carefully monitored to identify potential trouble spots and, through understanding why these difficulties occur, establish ways of overcoming them. Introducing "threshold concepts," which open up the subject in important ways, seems to trigger revealing discussions among faculty about the nature of knowledge in the discipline or professional area. Fortunately, this approach leads discussions of pedagogical issues along a path that most teachers will find congenial to follow—even exciting—in contrast to the skill-based pedagogical training that can have the opposite effect.

In preparing for face-to-face teaching, the greater diversity in student backgrounds and knowledge needs to be kept in mind with "multipli-inclusive" approaches in order to provide provocative ideas for those students already committed to learning the subject in a deep way, and enough simplicity and direct teaching for those who are less engaged. But the traditional qualities of good presentation remain: lectures should use language that is readily intelligible to the students, be pitched at the right level (or preferably at multiple levels), develop at a pace that allows students to think about the ideas introduced, point out relevance and links between ideas, and contain a structure that is easy to follow. They should also make use of striking illustrations and examples to maintain attention and help students to discern the critical features on which understanding depends, using lively and clear explanations. It is also crucial for the lecturer to "think out loud" in exemplifying the ways of thinking and practising in the subject, to show enthusiasm for the subject, and to demonstrate an alertness to difficulties that may emerge or explanations not understood, as well as a readiness to overcome them.

Face-to-face teaching is, however, just one facet of the whole teaching-learning environment, which includes the assessment procedures, the assignments set, the feedback provided to individual students, and the additional learning resources made available. And the social relationships that develop, among administrators, faculty, and students all affect the quality of the learning culture. Moreover, it has to be recognized that every element of the teaching-learning environment has to support the overall aims of the course and act synergistically with all the others—to be *congruent* with them. It is much easier to lead students into surface approaches to learning than it is to persuade them to engage actively in developing their own understanding of the subjects they are studying, so it is useful to review courses to detect any discordant elements, as was done in the ETL project. Indeed, the short version of the questionnaire used in that project (shown in Appendix 2) is one way of providing an evaluation that takes account of some of the most important features of a teaching-learning environment, if it is to support high-quality learning. But, because of *the inner logic of the subject and its pedagogy*, there will be other aspects that will need to be covered.

There is no question that the research suggests that faculty should endeavour to help students engage more deeply with the subject and become more actively responsible for their own learning, in the context of the goals of a particular institution, degree course, and group of students at a particular stage of their degree. And deciding what that involves is no small challenge!

References

Anderson, C. and D. Hounsell. 2007. Knowledge Practices "Doing the Subject" in Undergraduate Courses. *The Curriculum Journal* 18:463-78.

Ausubel, D.P., J.D. Novak, and H. Hanesian. 1978. *Educational Psychology: A Cognitive View,* 2nd edition. New York: Holt, Rinehart and Winston.

Barnett, R. 2007. *A Will to Learn: Being a Student in an Age of Uncertainty.* Berkshire: Open University Press and Society for Research into Higher Education.

Beaty, E., G. Gibbs, and A. Morgan. 1997. Learning Orientations and Study Contracts. In *The Experience of Learning,* 2nd edition, ed. F. Marton, D.J. Hounsell, and N.J. Entwistle, 72-88. Edinburgh: Scottish Academic Press. Out of print but available online at http://www.tla.ed.ac.uk/resources/EoL.html

Belenky, M.F., B.M. Clinchy, N.R. Goldberger, and J.M. Tarule. 1986. *Women's Ways of Knowing.* New York: Harper Collins.

Biggs, J.B. 1987. *Student Approaches to Learning and Studying.* Hawthorn, Victoria: Australian Council for Educational Research.

Biggs, J.B. 1993. From Theory to Practice: A Cognitive Systems Approach. *Higher Education Research and Development* 12:73-86.

Biggs, J.B. 1996. Enhancing Teaching through Constructive Alignment. *Higher Education* 32:1-18.

Biggs, J.B. 2007. *Teaching for Quality Learning at University,* 3rd edition. Buckingham: Open University Press and SRHE.

Bowden, J. and F. Marton. 1998. *The University of Learning: Beyond Quality and Competence in Higher Education.* London: Kogan Page.

Butler, A.C., J.D. Karpicke, and H.L. Roediger III. 2007. The Effect of Type and Timing of Feedback on Learning from Multiple-Choice Tests. *Journal of Experimental Psychology: Applied* 13(4):273-81.

Carnegie Foundation for the Advancement of Teaching. 2009. *Professional Preparation of Physicians: Medical Education Study.* Accessed 22 August 2009 at http://www.carnegiefoundation.org/programs/index.asp?key=1822

Cope, C. and M. Prosser. 2005. Identifying Didactic Knowledge: An Empirical Study of the Educationally Critical Aspects of Learning about Information Systems. *Higher Education* 49:345-72.

Dahllöf, U. 1991. Towards a New Model for the Evaluation of Teaching. In *Dimensions of Evaluation,* ed. U. Dahllöf, J. Harris, M. Shattock, A. Staropoli, and R. Veld. London: Jessica Kingsley.

Davies, P. and J. Mangan. 2007. Threshold Concepts and the Integration of Understanding in Economics. *Studies in Higher Education* 32:711-26.

Deary, I.J. 2000. *Looking Down on Human Intelligence: From Psychometrics to the Brain.* Oxford: Oxford University Press.

De Corte, E., L. Verschaffel, N.J. Entwistle, and J. van Merriënboer, eds. 2003. *Powerful Learning Environments: Unraveling Basic Components and Dimensions.* Oxford: Pergamon.

Donald, J.G. 1994. Science Students' Learning: Ethnographic Studies. In *Student Motivation, Cognition and Learning: Essays in Honor of Wilbert J. McKeachie,* ed. P.R. Pintrich, D.R. Brown, and C-E Weinstein, 79-112. Hillsdale, NJ: Lawrence Erlbaum.

Donald, J.G. 1995. Disciplinary Differences in Knowledge Validation. In *Disciplinary Differences in Teaching and Learning: Implications for Practice,* ed. N. Hativa and M. Marincovich. San Francisco: Jossey Bass.

Eizenberg, N. 1988. Approaches to Learning Anatomy: Developing a Programme for Preclinical Medical Students. In *Improving Learning: New Perspectives,* ed. P. Ramsden, 178-98. London: Kogan Page.

Entwistle, N.J. 1987. A Model of the Teaching-Learning Process. In *Student Learning: Research into Education and Cognitive Psychology,* ed. J.T.E. Richardson, M.W. Eysenck, and D. Warren-Piper, 13-28. Buckingham: SRHE and Open University Press.

Entwistle, N.J. 1998. Motivation and Approach to Learning: Motivation and Conceptions of Teaching. In *Motivating Students,* ed. S. Brown, S. Armstrong, and G. Thompson, 15-24. London: Kogan Page.

Entwistle, N.J. 2000. Approaches to Studying and Levels of Understanding: The Influences of Teaching and Assessment. In *Higher Education: Handbook of Theory and Research,* Vol. 15, ed. J.C. Smart. New York: Agathon Press.

Entwistle, N.J. 2007. Conceptions of Learning and the Experience of Understanding: Thresholds, Contextual Influences, and Knowledge Objects. In *Reframing the Conceptual Change Approach in Learning and Instruction,* ed. S. Vosniadou, A. Baltas, and X. Vamvakoussi, 123-44. Oxford: Elsevier.

Entwistle, N.J. 2009. *Teaching for Understanding at University: Deep Approaches and Distinctive Ways of Thinking.* Basingstoke, UK and New York: Palgrave Macmillan.

Entwistle, N.J. and A.C. Entwistle. 1997. Revision and the Experience of Under-standing. In *The Experience of Learning*, 2nd edition, ed. F. Marton, D.J. Hounsell, and N.J. Entwistle, 145-58. Edinburgh: Scottish Academic Press. Out of print but available online at http://www.tla.ed.ac.uk/resources/EoL.html

Entwistle, N.J. and D.M. Entwistle. 2003. Preparing for Examinations: The Inter-play of Memorising and Understanding, and the Development of Knowledge Objects. *Higher Education Research and Development* 22:19-42.

Entwistle, N.J. and V. McCune. 2004. The Conceptual Bases of Study Strategy Inventories. *Educational Psychology Review* 16:325-46.

Entwistle, N.J. and V. McCune. 2009. The Disposition to Understand for Yourself at University: Learning Processes, the Will to Learn, and Sensitivity to Context in Studying. In *Perspectives on the Nature of Intellectual Styles*, ed. L.-F. Zhang and R.J. Sternberg, 29-62. New York: Springer.

Entwistle, N.J., V. McCune, and J. Hounsell. 2003. Investigating Ways of Enhancing University Teaching-Learning Environments: Measuring Students' Approaches to Studying and Perceptions of Teaching. In *Powerful Learning Environments: Unravelling Basic Components and Dimensions*, ed. E. De Corte, L. Verschaffel, N. Entwistle, and J. van Merriënboer, 89-108. Oxford: Elsevier Science.

Entwistle, N.J., J. Nisbet, and A. Bromage. 2005. *ETL Project. Subject Overview Report: Electronic Engineering.* Accessed 7 January 2010 at http://www.etl.tla.ed.ac.uk//docs/EngineeringSR.pdf

Entwistle, N.J. and E.R. Peterson. 2004. Conceptions of Learning and Knowledge in Higher Education: Relationships with Study Behaviour and Influences of Learning Environments. *International Journal of Educational Research* 41:407-28.

Entwistle, N.J. and C.A. Smith. 2002. Personal Understanding and Target Under-standing: Mapping Influences on the Outcomes of Learning. *British Journal of Educational Psychology* 72:321-42.

Entwistle, N.J. and H. Tait. 1990. Approaches to Learning, Evaluations of Teach-ing, and Preferences for Contrasting Academic Environments. *Higher Education* 19:169-94.

Entwistle, N.J. and P. Walker. 2002. Strategic Alertness and Expanded Alertness within Sophisticated Conceptions of Teaching. In *Teacher Thinking, Beliefs and Knowledge in Higher Education*, ed. N. Nativa and P. Goodyear, 15-40. Dordrecht: Kluwer Academic Publishers.

Fyrenius, A., S. Wirell, and C. Silén. 2007. Student Approaches to Achieving Understanding – Approaches to Learning Revisited. *Studies in Higher Educa-tion* 32:149-65.

Gagne, R., L. Briggs, and W. Wager. 1992. *Principles of Instructional Design*, 4th edi-tion. Fort Worth, TX: HBJ College Publishers.

Gardiner, L.F. 1994. *Redesigning Higher Education: Producing Dramatic Gains in Student Learning.* Report No. 7. Washington, DC: Graduate School of Education and Human Development, The George Washington University.

Garrison, D.R. and H. Kanuka. 2004. Blended Learning: Uncovering Its Trans-formative Potential. *The Internet and Higher Education* 7:95-105.

Ginns, P. and R. Ellis. 2007. Quality in Blended Learning: Exploring the Relation-ships between Online and Face-to-Face Teaching and Learning. *The Internet and Higher Education* 10:53-64.

Greenfield, S. 2008. Networking Pays Off. *Times Educational Supplement Magazine*, 18 January, 36-7.

Habermas, J. 1986. *The Theory of Communicative Action*. Boston, MA: Beacon Press.

Hall, J. 2005. *Neuroscience and Education: What Can Brain Science Contribute to Teaching and Learning?* Spotlight, No. 92. Glasgow: University of Glasgow, SCRE Centre.

Hay, D.B. 2007. Using Concept Mapping to Measure Deep, Surface and Non-Learning Outcomes. *Studies in Higher Education* 32:39-57.

Hay, D.B. In press. Facilitating a Personal Understanding in Higher Education: The Role of Dialogic Concept-Mapping. *Psychological Journal (of Greece)*.

Haywood, J. 2004. *A Short Review of E-Learning in UK Higher Education*. Internal document, University of Edinburgh.

Hounsell, D. and J. Hounsell. 2007. Teaching-Learning Environments in Contemporary Mass Higher Education. In *Student Learning and University Teaching*. British Journal of Educational Psychology Monograph Series II, No. 4, ed. N.J. Entwistle and P.D. Tomlinson, 91-111. Leicester: British Psychological Society.

Hounsell, J. and N.J. Entwistle. 2005. *Shortened Experiences of Teaching and Learning Questionnaire*. ETL Project website at www.etl.ed.ac.uk/publications#measurement

Janssen, P.J. 1996. Studaxology: The Expertise Students Need to be Effective in Higher Education. *Higher Education* 31:117-41.

Land, R., J.H.F. Meyer, and J. Smith. 2008. *Threshold Concepts within the Disciplines*. Rotterdam: Sense Publishers.

Lave, J. 1988. *Cognition in Practice: Mind, Mathematics and Culture in Everyday Life*. Cambridge, UK: Cambridge University Press.

Lave, J. and E. Wenger. 1991. *Situated Learning: Legitimate Peripheral Participation*. Cambridge: Cambridge University Press.

Long, W.F. 2003. Dissonance Detected by Cluster Analysis of Responses to the Approaches and Study Skills Inventory for Students. *Studies in Higher Education* 28:21-36.

Lonka, K. and S. Lindblom-Ylänne. 1996. Epistemologies, Conceptions of Learning, and Study Practices in Medicine and Psychology. *Higher Education* 31:5-24.

Marsh, H.W. and M.J. Dunkin. 1997. Students' Evaluations of Teaching: A Multi-Dimensional Perspective. In *Effective Teaching in Higher Education: Research and Practice*, ed. R.P. Perry and J.C. Smart. New York: Agathon Press.

Marton, F. 1976. What Does It Take to Learn? Some Implications of an Alternative View of Learning. In *Strategies for Research and Development in Higher Education*, ed. N.J. Entwistle, 32-43. Amsterdam: Swets and Zeitlinger.

Marton, F. 2007. Towards a Pedagogical Theory of Learning. In *Student Learning and University Teaching*. British Journal of Educational Psychology Monograph Series II, No. 4, ed. N.J. Entwistle and P.D. Tomlinson, 19-30. Leicester: British Psychological Society.

Marton, F. and S. Booth. 1997. *Learning and Awareness*. Mahwah, NJ: Lawrence Erlbaum.

Marton, F., D.J. Hounsell, and N.J. Entwistle, eds. 1997. *The Experience of Learning: Implications for Teaching and Learning in Higher Education*, 2nd edition. Edinburgh: Scottish Academic Press. Out of print but available online at http://www.tla.ed.ac.uk/resources/EOL.html

Marton, F. and Säljö, R. 1997. Approaches to Learning. In *The Experience of Learning*, 2nd edition, ed. F. Marton, D.J. Hounsell, and N.J. Entwistle, 39-58. Edinburgh: Scottish Academic Press. Out of print, but available as above.

Marton, F. and A.B.M. Tsui. 2004. *Classroom Discourse and the Space of Learning.* Mahwah, NJ: Lawrence Erlbaum.

Mazur, E. 1997. Understanding or Memorization: Are We Teaching the Right Thing? In *Conference on the Introductory Physics Course,* ed. J. Wilson, 113-23. New York: Wiley.

Mazur, E. 2001. Peer Instruction: Ten Years of Experience and Results. *American Journal of Physics* 69:970-77.

Mentkowski and Associates. 2000. *Learning that Lasts: Integrating, Learning, Development, and Performance in College and Beyond.* San Francisco: Jossey-Bass.

Meyer, J.H.F. and R. Land. 2003. *Threshold Concepts and Troublesome Knowledge: Linkages to Ways of Thinking and Practising within the Disciplines.* ETL Project, Occasional Report 4. Accessed 8 January 2010 at http://www.etl.tla.ed.ac.uk/docs/ETLreport4.pdf

Meyer, J.H.F. and R. Land, eds. 2006. *Overcoming Barriers to Student Understanding: Threshold Concepts and Troublesome Knowledge.* London: Routledge.

O'Brien, M. 2008a. Teaching as Translation: An Investigation of University Teachers' Pedagogical Content Knowledge, Reasoning and Intention. PhD thesis, School of Education and Professional Studies, Griffith University, Queensland, Australia.

O'Brien, M. 2008b. Threshold Concepts for University Teaching and Learning: A Study of Troublesome Knowledge and Transformative Thinking in the Teaching of Threshold Concepts. In *Threshold Concepts in the Disciplines,* ed. J.H.J. Meyer, R. Land, and J. Smith, 289-306. Netherlands: Sense Publishers.

Pascarella, E.T. and P.T. Terenzini. 1991. *How College Affects Students: Findings and Insights from Twenty Years of Research.* San Francisco: Jossey-Bass.

Pascarella E.T. and P.T. Terenzini. 2005. *How College Affects Students: A Third Decade of Research.* San Francisco: Jossey-Bass.

Pask, G. 1988. Learning Strategies, Teaching Strategies and Conceptual or Learning Style. In *Learning Strategies and Learning Styles,* ed. R. Schmeck, 83-100. New York: Plenum Press.

Perkins, D. 2006. Constructivism and Troublesome Knowledge. In *Overcoming Barriers to Student Understanding: Threshold Concepts and Troublesome Knowledge,* ed. J.H.F. Meyer and R. Land, 33-47. London: Routledge.

Perkins, D.N. 2007. Theories of Difficulty. In *Student Learning and University Teaching.* British Journal of Educational Psychology Monograph Series II, No. 4, ed. N.J. Entwistle and P.D. Tomlinson, 31-48. Leicester: British Psychological Society.

Perkins, D.N. and R. Richhart. 2004. When in Good Thinking? In *Motivation, Emotion and Cognition: Integrative Perspectives on Intellectual Functioning and Development,* ed. D.Y. Dai and R.J. Sternberg, 351-84. Mahwah, NJ: Lawrence Erlbaum.

Perry, R.P. and J.C. Smart, eds.1997. *Effective Teaching in Higher Education: Research and Practice.* New York: Agathon Press.

Perry, W.G. 1970. *Forms of Intellectual and Ethical Development in the College Years: A Scheme.* New York: Holt, Rinehart and Winston.

Pintrich, P.R. and T, Garcia. 1994. Self-Regulated Learning in College Students: Knowledge, Strategies and Motivation. In *Student Motivation, Cognition and Learning. Essays in Honor of Wilbert J. McKeachie,* ed. P.R. Pintrich, D.R. Brown, and C-E. Weinstein. Hillsdale, NJ: Lawrence Erlbaum.

Pintrich, P.R., D.R. Brown, and C-E. Weinstein, eds. 1994. *Student Motivation, Cognition and Learning. Essays in Honor of Wilbert J. McKeachie.* Hillsdale, NJ: Lawrence Erlbaum.

Pratt, D.D., J.B. Collins, and S. Jarvis Selinger. 2001. *Development and Use of the Teaching Perspectives Inventory (TPI)*. AERA. Accessed 23 August 2009 at http://www.teachingperspectives.com/PDF/development1.pdf

Prosser, M., E. Martin, and K. Trigwell. 2007. Academics' Experiences of their Teaching and of their Subject Matter. In *Student Learning and University Teaching*. British Journal of Educational Psychology Monograph Series II, No. 4, ed. N.J. Entwistle and P.D. Tomlinson, 49-60. Leicester: British Psychological Society.

Prosser, M., E. Martin, K. Trigwell, P. Ramsden, and G. Lueckenhausen. 2005. Academics' Experiences of Understanding of their Subject Matter and the Relationship to their Experiences of Teaching and Learning. *Instructional Science* 33:137-57.

Prosser, M. and K. Trigwell. 1999. *Understanding Learning and Teaching: The Experience in Higher Education*. Buckingham: Open University Press and the Society for Research into Higher Education.

Reimann, N., R. Land, J.H.F. Meyer, and X. Rui. 2007. *ETL Project. Subject Overview Report: Economics*. Posted at http://www.etl.ed.ac.uk//docs/EconomicsSR.pdf

Richardson, J.T.E. 2000. *Researching Student Learning: Approaches to Studying in Campus-Based and Distance Education*. Buckingham: SRHE and Open University Press.

Richardson, J.T.E. 2007. Variations in Student Learning and Perceptions of Academic Quality. In *Student Learning and University Teaching*. British Journal of Educational Psychology Monograph Series II, No. 4, ed. N.J. Entwistle and P.D. Tomlinson, 61-72. Leicester: British Psychological Society.

Rodriguez, L. and F. Cano. 2007. The Learning Approaches and Epistemological Beliefs of University Students: A Cross-Sectional and Longitudinal Study. *Studies in Higher Education* 32:647-67.

Rogers, C. 1969. *Freedom to Learn: A View of What Education Might Become*, 1st edition. Columbus, Ohio: Charles Merill.

Rotter, J.B. 1954. *Social Learning and Clinical Psychology*. Engelewood Cliffs, NJ: Prentice-Hall.

Rotter, J.B., J.E. Chance, and E.J. Phares. 1972. *Applications of a Social Learning Theory of Personality*. New York: Holt, Rinehard & Winston.

Scheja, M. 2006. Delayed Understanding and Staying in Phase: Students' Perceptions of their Study Situation. *Higher Education* 52:421-45.

Schommer-Aikins, M. 2002. An Evolving Theoretical Framework for an Epistemological Belief System. In *Personal Epistemologies: The Psychology of Beliefs about Knowledge and Knowing*, ed. B.K. Hofer and P.R. Pintrich, 103-18. Mahwah, NJ: Lawrence Erlbaum.

Scouller, K. 1998. The Influence of Assessment Method on Students' Learning Approaches: Multiple Choice Question Examination Versus Assignment Essay. *Higher Education* 35:453-52.

Shulman, L.S. 1987. Knowledge and Teaching: Foundations of the New Reform. *Educational Researcher* 152:1-22.

Säljö, R. 1979. *Learning in the Learner's Perspective. I. Some Common-Sense Conceptions*, Report 76. Gothenburg: University of Gothenburg, Department of Education.

Skinner, B.F. 1953. *Science and Human Behavior*. New York: Macmillan.

Tait, H., N.J. Entwistle, and V. McCune. 1998. ASSIST: A Reconceptualisation of the Approaches to Studying Inventory. In *Improving Student Learning: Improving Students as Learners*, ed. C. Rust, 262-71. Oxford, UK: Oxford Centre for Staff and Learning Development, Oxford Brookes University.

Teaching and Learning Research Programme (TLRP). 2004. The Effectiveness of Problem Based Learning 1 – A Pilot Systematic Review and Meta-Analysis, *Research Briefing No. 8*. Accessed 14 December 2009 at http://www.tlrp.org/pub/research.html

Teaching and Learning Research Programme (TLRP). 2007. Learning and Teaching at University: The Influence of Subjects and Settings, *Research Briefing No. 31*. Accessed 14 December 2009 at http://www.tlrp.org/pub/documents/Hounsell%20RB%2031%20FINAL.pdf

Trowler, P. 2009. *Cultures and Change in Higher Education: Theories and Practice.* Houndmills, Basingstoke, Hampshire: Palgrave Macmillan.

Van Merriënboer, J.J.G., P.A. Kirschner, and L. Kester. 2003. Taking the Load Off a Learner's Mind: Instructional Design for Complex Learning. *Educational Psychologist* 38:5-13.

Vermunt, J.D. 1998. The Regulation of Constructive Learning Processes. *British Journal of Educational Psychology* 68:149-71.

Weinstein, C-E., S.A. Zimmerman, and D.A.Palmer. 1988. Assessing Learning Strategies: The Design and Development of the LASSI. In *Learning and Study Strategies: Issues in Assessment, Instruction, and Evaluation*, ed. C-E. Weinstein, E.T. Goetz, and P.A. Alexander. London: Academic Press.

Wenger, E. 1998. *Communities of Practice: Learning, Meaning, and Identity.* Cambridge: Cambridge University Press.

Wilson, E.O. 1998. *Consilience.* London: Little, Brown and Co.

Wiske, M.S., ed. 1998. *Teaching for Understanding: Linking Research with Practice.* San Francisco: Jossey-Bass.

Witkin, H.A., C.A. Moore, D.R. Goodenough, and P.W. Cox. 1977. Field-Dependent and Field-Independent Cognitive Styles and their Educational Implications. *Review of Educational Research* 47:1-64.

Zull, J.E. 2002. *The Art of Changing the Brain: Enriching the Practice of Teaching by Exploring the Biology of Learning.* Sterling, VA: Stylus Publishing.

APPENDIX 1

Factor Analysis of Scales and Inter-Correlations between Factors from the ETL Project[a]

Scales	Factor	Total sample (N = 4,538)				
		I	II	III	IV	V
Reasons for taking the degree						
Interest in the subject		.46				
Lack of purpose					.43	
Reasons for taking the module						
Interest in its content			.33			
Expected easiness					(.24)	(.28)
Prior general approaches to studying						
Deep approach		(.25)	.84			
Organised effort				.72		
Surface approach					.71	
Specific approaches to studying the actual module						
Deep approach			.49			
Organised effort				.81		
Surface approach					.57	(-.23)
Perceived demands within the module						
Prior knowledge easy						.49
Pace and difficulty level easy						.71
Experiences of teaching						
Aims and congruence		.64				
Choice allowed		.49				
Teaching for learning		.67				
Set work and feedback		.69				
Staff enthusiasm and support		.64				
Interest and enjoyment		.56				
Self-ratings on achievements						
Acquisition of knowledge and skills		.56				
General level of performance				(.22)		.40

Inter-correlation between factors	I	II	III	IV	V
I　Experiences of teach-learning environment	.--	.39	.35	-.20	.21
II　Deep approach		--	.41	-.31	.09
III　Organised effort			.--	-.26	.15
IV　Surface approach				.--	-.10
V　Self-rated achievement					--

Pattern matrix after maximum likelihood analysis with oblique rotation to simple structure

Variance extracted 51.9%　　Loadings > .40 are highlighted;　　< .30 omitted unless indicative

Notes: ETL = Enhancing Teaching and Learning.

[a] The word "staff" as it appears in this table is synonymous with "faculty," the more commonly used term in North America.

Source: Author's compilation.

APPENDIX 2A
Approaches and Study Skills Inventory for Students (ASSIST), Short Version

This questionnaire has been designed to allow you to describe, in a systematic way, how you go about learning and studying. The technique involves asking you a substantial number of questions which overlap to some extent to provide good overall coverage of different ways of studying. Most of the items are based on comments made by other students.

Please respond truthfully, so that your answers accurately describe your **actual** ways of studying, and work your way through the questionnaire quite **quickly**, making sure that you give a response to **every item**. In deciding your answers, think in terms of **this particular lecture course.**

It is also very important that you answer **all** the questions by circling a number: please check that you have.

5 *means agree* (√)   **4** = *agree somewhat* (√?)   **2** = *disagree somewhat* (x?)   **1** − *disagree* (x).

Try not to use **3** = *unsure* (??), *unless you really have to, or if it cannot apply to you or your course.*

	√	√?	??	x?	x
1. I often have trouble making sense of the things I have to remember.	5	4	3	2	1
2. When I'm reading an article or book, I try to find out for myself exactly what the author means.	5	4	3	2	1
3. I organise my study time carefully to make the best use of it.	5	4	3	2	1
4. There's not much work here that I find interesting or relevant.	5	4	3	2	1
5. I work steadily through the term or semester, rather than leave it all until the last minute.	5	4	3	2	1
6. Before tackling a problem or assignment, I first try to work out what lies behind it.	5	4	3	2	1
7. I'm pretty good at getting down to work whenever I need to.	5	4	3	2	1
8. Much of what I'm studying makes little sense: it's like unrelated bits and pieces.	5	4	3	2	1
9. I put a lot of effort into studying because I'm determined to do well.	5	4	3	2	1
10. When I'm working on a new topic, I try to see in my own mind how all the ideas fit together.	5	4	3	2	1
11. I don't find it at all difficult to motivate myself.	5	4	3	2	1
12. Often I find myself questioning things I hear in lectures or read in books.	5	4	3	2	1
13. I think I'm quite systematic and organised when it comes to revising for exams.	5	4	3	2	1
14. Often I feel I'm drowning in the sheer amount of material we're having to cope with.	5	4	3	2	1
15. Ideas in course books or articles often set me off on long chains of thought of my own.	5	4	3	2	1
16. I'm not really sure what's important in lectures, so I try to get down all I can.	5	4	3	2	1
17. When I read, I examine the details carefully to see how they fit in with what's being said.	5	4	3	2	1
18. I often worry about whether I'll ever be able to cope with the work properly.	5	4	3	2	1

Thank you very much for spending time completing this questionnaire: it is much appreciated.

If you would like to make any additional comments about your ways of studying, please use the back of this sheet.

Note: This questionnaire can be used freely with just an attribution of its origin.

Source: Author's compilation from Tait, Entwistle, and McCune (1998).

APPENDIX 2B
Scoring Key for ASSIST (Short Version)

Scoring procedure

The subscales are formed by adding together the responses on the items in that subscale and dividing the total by the number of items in that scale to give a score out of 5. For example, Deep approach = D02 + D06 +D10 + D12 +D15 + D17. The other two scale scores can then be formed in the same way. Scoring can be carried out by computer, using a program such as SPSS. Each item is set as a variable and then a subscale total is produced by creating a new variable by summing the items.

Deep Approach
D02   When I'm reading an article or book, I try to find out for myself exactly what the author means.
D06   Before tackling a problem or assignment, I first try to work out what lies behind it.
D10   When I'm working on a new topic, I try to see in my own mind how all the ideas fit together.
D12   Often I find myself questioning things I hear in lectures or read in books.
D15   Ideas in course books or articles often set me off on long chains of thought of my own.
D17   When I read, I examine the details carefully to see how they fit in with what's being said.

Strategic Approach
T03.   I organise my study time carefully to make the best use of it.
T05.   I work steadily through the term or semester, rather than leave it all until the last minute.
T07.   I'm pretty good at getting down to work whenever I need to.
T09.   I put a lot of effort into studying because I'm determined to do well.
T11.   I don't find it at all difficult to motivate myself.
T13.   I think I'm quite systematic and organised when it comes to revising for exams.

Surface Approach
S01.   I often have trouble making sense of the things I have to remember
S04.   There's not much work here that I find interesting or relevant.
S08.   Much of what I'm studying makes little sense: it's like unrelated bits and pieces.
S14.   Often I feel I'm drowning in the sheer amount of material we're having to cope with.
S16   I'm not really sure what's important in lectures, so I try to get down all I can.
S18.   I often worry about whether I'll ever be able to cope with the work properly.

Source: Author's compilation.

APPENDIX 3A
Experiences of Teaching and Learning Questionnaire (SETLQ), Short Version*

This questionnaire has been designed to allow you to describe, in a systematic way, your reactions to the course you have been studying and how you have gone about learning it. There are a series of questions, some of which overlap so as to provide good overall coverage of different experiences. Most of the items are based on comments made by other students. Please respond truthfully, so that your answers describe your **actual** experiences of **this particular course** or module, working your way through the questionnaire **quickly**. It is important that you respond to **every** item, even if that means using the "unsure" category. Please circle the appropriate number to indicate your response.

5 *means agree* (√)   **4** = *agree somewhat* (√?)   **2** = *disagree somewhat* (x?)   **1** = *disagree* (x).

Try not to use **3** = *unsure* (??), *unless you really have to, or if it cannot apply to you or your course.*

	√	√?	??	x?	x
Aims and congruence					
1. It was clear to me what I was supposed to learn in this course unit.	5	4	3	2	1
2. The topics seemed to follow each other in a way that made sense to me.	5	4	3	2	1
3. What we were taught seemed to match what we were supposed to learn.	5	4	3	2	1
4. The handouts and other materials we were given helped me to understand the unit.	5	4	3	2	1
5. I could see how the set work fit in with what we were supposed to learn.	5	4	3	2	1
Choice allowed					
6. We were given a good deal of choice over how we went about learning.	5	4	3	2	1
7. We were allowed some choice over what aspects of the subject to concentrate on.	5	4	3	2	1
Teaching and learning					
8. On this unit, I was prompted to think about how well I was learning and how I might improve.	5	4	3	2	1
9. The teaching encouraged me to rethink my understanding of some aspects of the subject.	5	4	3	2	1
10. This unit has given me a sense of what goes on "behind the scenes" in this subject area.	5	4	3	2	1
11. The teaching in this unit helped me to think about the evidence underpinning different views.	5	4	3	2	1
12. This unit encouraged me to relate what I learned to issues in the wider world.	5	4	3	2	1
Set work, feedback, and assessment					
13. It was clear to me what was expected in the assessed work for this course unit.	5	4	3	2	1
14. I was encouraged to think about how best to tackle the set work.	5	4	3	2	1
15. The feedback given on my work helped me to improve my ways of learning and studying.	5	4	3	2	1
16. Staff gave me the support I needed to help me complete the set work for this course unit.	5	4	3	2	1
17. The feedback given on my set work helped to clarity things I hadn't fully understood.	5	4	3	2	1
18. You really had to understand the subject to get good marks in this course unit.	5	4	3	2	1
19. To do well in this course unit, you had to think critically about the topics.	5	4	3	2	1

... continued

APPENDIX 3A
(Continued)

Staff enthusiasm and support from both staff and students	√	√?	??	x?	x
20. Staff tried to share their enthusiasm about the subject with us.	5	4	3	2	1
21. Staff were patient in explaining things which seemed difficult to grasp.	5	4	3	2	1
22. Students supported each other and tried to give help when it was needed.	5	4	3	2	1
23. Talking with other students helped me to develop my understanding.	5	4	3	2	1

Interest and enjoyment generated by the course					
24. I found most of what I learned in this course unit really interesting.	5	4	3	2	1
25. I enjoyed being involved in this course unit.	5	4	3	2	1

Demands made by the course or module

In this section, please tell us how easy or difficult you found different aspects of **this course unit**.

√ = *very easy*   √? = *fairly easy*   ?? = *unsure/not applicable*   x? = *fairly difficult*   x = *very difficult*

		√	√?	??	x?	x
a.	What I was expected to know to begin with.	5	4	3	2	1
b.	The rate at which new material was introduced.	5	4	3	2	1
c.	The ideas and problems I had to deal with.	5	4	3	2	1
d.	The skills or technical procedures needed in this subject.	5	4	3	2	1
e.	The amount of work I was expected to do.	5	4	3	2	1
f.	Working with other students.	5	4	3	2	1
g.	Organising and being responsible for my own learning.	5	4	3	2	1
h.	Communicating knowledge and ideas effectively.	5	4	3	2	1
i.	Tracking down information for myself.	5	4	3	2	1
j.	Information technology/computing skills (e.g. WWW, email, word processing).	5	4	3	2	1

What you have learned from this course or module

Now we would like to know how much you feel you have gained from studying **this course unit**.

√ = *a lot*   √? = *quite a lot*   ?? = *unsure/not applicable*   x? = *not much*   x = *very little*

		√	√?	??	x?	x
a.	Knowledge and understanding about the topics covered.	5	4	3	2	1
b.	Ability to think about ideas or to solve problems.	5	4	3	2	1
c.	Skills or technical procedures specific to the subject.	5	4	3	2	1
d.	Ability to work with other students.	5	4	3	2	1
e.	Organising and being responsible for my own learning.	5	4	3	2	1
f.	Ability to communicate knowledge and ideas effectively.	5	4	3	2	1
g.	Ability to track down information in this subject area.	5	4	3	2	1
h.	Information technology/computing skills (e.g. WWW, email, word processing).	5	4	3	2	1

Self-rating of academic progress

Finally, how well do you think you're doing in this course unit as a whole? Please try to rate yourself **objectively**, based on any marks, grades or comments you have been given.

very well	well	quite well	about average	not so well	rather badly
9	8	7	6	5	4	3	2	1

Please check back to make sure that you have answered every question.
Thank you very much for spending time completing this questionnaire; it is much appreciated.

Note: * This is only part of the SETLQ © SETLQ 2005, ETL Project, Universities of Edinburgh, Durham and Coventry. The full version is available at www.etl.ed.ac.uk/publications#measurement and either version can be used freely with an attribution.

Source: Hounsell and Entwistle (2005).

APPENDIX 3B
Scoring Procedure for SETLQ (Short Version)

For most of the items in the questionnaires, students respond on a 1-5 scale (5=high). The exception is the item asking about students' self-rating which has a 1-9 scale. Except for this last scale, the subscales are formed by adding together the responses on the items in that subscale and dividing the total by the number of items in that scale to give a score out of 5. Scoring can be carried out by computer, using a program such as SPSS. Each item is set as a variable and then a subscale total is produced by creating a new variable by summing the items.

For the set of items on the first page—experiences of teaching and learning—the scales are shown there. Scales for the second page are indicated below.

Perceived easiness of demands made

very easy = 5, fairly easy = 4, unsure/not applicable = 3, fairly difficult = 2, very difficult = 1

Prior knowledge
    a. What I was expected to know to begin with.
Pace
    b. The rate at which new material was introduced
Academic difficulty
    c. The ideas and problems I had to deal with
    d. The skills or technical procedures needed in this subject
Workload
    e. The amount of work I was expected to do
Generic skills
    f. Working with other students
    g. Organising and being responsible for my own learning
    h. Communicating knowledge and ideas effectively
Information skills
    i. Tracking down information for myself
    j. Information technology/computing skills (e.g. WWW, email, word processing)

Knowledge and learning acquired

a lot = 5, quite a lot = 4, unsure/not applicable = 3, not much = 2, very little = 1

Knowledge and subject-specific skills
    a. Knowledge and understanding about the topics covered
    b. Ability to think about ideas or to solve problems
    c. Skills or technical procedures specific to the subject.
Generic skills
    d. Ability to work with other students
    e. Organising and being responsible for my own learning
    f. Ability to communicate knowledge and ideas effectively
Information skills
    g. Ability to track down information in the subject area
    h. Information technology/computing skills (e.g. WWW, email, word processing)

Source: Hounsell and Entwistle (2005).

SECTION II

WHAT WE KNOW ABOUT STUDENT LEARNING

SECTION COMMENTARY

Alenoush Saroyan

The two chapters in this section are about what we know about student learning and how to enhance its quality, albeit from different perspectives. One tackles learning not just as a process waiting to be investigated and defined, but as a dynamic event that interacts with the context within which it occurs. The other considers it from the perspective of university faculty and their perceptions of why student learning can sometimes turn out to be less than optimal.

Sari Lindblom-Ylänne, an educational psychologist, presents a retrospective of her own research agenda, the thrust of which has been university students' approaches to learning and the consequences arising from the interaction of individual approaches with the real or perceived demands of the learning environment. In the process of describing her research findings, Dr. Lindblom-Ylänne elaborates on constructs such as deep and surface approaches to learning, study orchestration, and self-regulation. These elaborations are informative, particularly when placed within the context of the broader literature. What is more insightful, however, is the notion that developing coherent links between constructs internal to the individual as well as between the individual and the demands of the learning environment can have significant consequences on learning. Dr. Lindblom-Ylänne leaves the reader with the clear message that the more congruent the learner's framework with the environment, the more likely better learning will occur. Conversely, the more dissonant this relationship, the less likely it is that meaningful and sustained learning will occur.

Maryellen Weimer, professor emerita of biology and faculty developer, writes with the mission to improve the quality of student learning by lessening the gap between research and teaching practice. She develops her chapter on the premise that faculty have suppositions about why students do not get the most out of their learning experiences. These suppositions include a passive approach to learning, lack of confidence as learners, inadequate basic study skills, and the extrinsic motivation of grades rather than the intrinsic motivation of learning. Dr. Weimer asserts that faculty members often fail to see the connections between these deficiencies and their own teaching. She then draws on studies carried out by education specialists as well as those by disciplinary experts to generate specific and practical recommendations that faculty can incorporate into their teaching, in order to enhance the quality of student learning.

Both authors are clearly interested in the application of educational research, whether it is their own or the work of others, with a view to informing educators about important aspects that need to be taken into account when the goal is to design effective learning environments.

> *Exploring how the learning environment, self-regulation, and variation in study orchestrations influence student learning.*

3

STUDENTS' APPROACHES TO LEARNING AND THEIR PERCEPTIONS OF THE TEACHING-LEARNING ENVIRONMENT

Sari Lindblom-Ylänne

INTRODUCTION

This chapter presents a synthesis of findings from my own research and others concerning student approaches to learning and the interaction between students and their teaching-learning environments. It begins with a brief overview of the research on deep and surface learning approaches, which suggests that positive perceptions of the teaching-learning environment are positively related to the deep approach and that negative perceptions of the teaching-learning environment are related to the surface approach (e.g., Kreber 2003; Lawless and Richardson 2002; Richardson 2005). I also draw on research which demonstrates that the deep approach has been associated with higher-quality learning outcomes (e.g., Entwistle and Ramsden 1983; Lindblom-Ylänne and Lonka 1999; Nieminen, Lindblom-Ylänne, and Lonka 2004). Next, I introduce the concept of self-regulation—or the ability students have to regulate their own learning processes—which is also associated with deep learning. Finally, I focus on student "study orchestrations" or study approaches (Meyer 1991,

297). Empirical evidence suggests that dissonant study orchestrations are related to students' attempts to adapt to the learning environment. Thus, it is possible that the learning environment can force students to study in ways that do not correspond to their preferred approaches. An understanding of these dynamics—individually and collectively—is essential in our efforts to support student learning.

Approaches to Learning in Higher Education

Approaches to learning are at the core of research on student learning. They describe how students interpret and deal with different learning activities and how these interpretations direct their learning efforts (Ramsden 2003). Approaches to learning are dynamic and context-specific and can thus vary from one learning activity or situation to another (Marton and Säljö 1976, 1997). Research on approaches to learning provide both researchers and university teachers with important knowledge about student learning in different disciplines and in different phases of academic studies, about different objectives students set for their studying, and about variation in students' experiences of their teaching-learning environments. This knowledge is essential in support of efforts to improve the quality of student learning.

Approaches to learning may be roughly divided into two qualitatively different categories: a surface approach and a deep approach (e.g., Entwistle and Entwistle 1992; Entwistle and Ramsden 1983; Marton and Säljö 1976; Marton, Hounsell, and Entwistle 1997; Richardson 1994). A student applying a surface learning approach to a reading assignment concentrates on the text itself. A deep approach, on the other hand, is based on a genuine interest in the subject matter and the aim is in interpreting the meaning of the text (e.g., Biggs 1993; Entwistle, McCune, and Walker 2001). Previous research has shown that the deep approach to learning is more likely to be related to higher-quality learning outcomes than a surface approach (e.g., Entwistle and Ramsden 1983; Lindblom-Ylänne and Lonka 1999; Nieminen, Lindblom-Ylänne, and Lonka 2004).

An aspect somewhat independent of the surface and deep approaches to learning is the strategic approach. It refers to the ways in which students organise their studying in order to do well (Biggs 1985; Entwistle et al. 2001). Although students with a strategic approach may seek high grades by any means, be that a surface or a deep approach, there is empirical evidence suggesting that it is more effective to combine the strategic approach with the deep rather than the surface approach (e.g., Entwistle and Ramsden 1983; Lonka and Lindblom-Ylänne 1996). More recently, the strategic approach has also been referred to as organised studying and effort management (Entwistle and McCune 2004). According to Biggs (1993), only the deep approach may be called a natural approach. In comparison, surface and strategic approaches are institutional creations, shifting the focus from the task itself to ways of maximizing the rewards and minimizing the sanctions associated with successful or unsuccessful task completion. Adding further complexity to the distinction between deep and surface learning approaches, our recent study showed that in a large multidisciplinary sample of Finnish bachelor-level students, the deep approach was further divided into two separate dimensions: "one which concentrated on the intention to understand, and the other which was more analytical in nature" (Parpala et al. forthcoming).

Several potential explanations can be offered for this finding. One is the fact that the University of Helsinki is a highly research-intensive university with a strong emphasis on researcher education (Lindblom-Ylänne 2006). Thus, students are encouraged to develop their analytic and argumentative skills from the very beginning of their studies. These skills are also emphasized in the highly demanding entrance examinations in every discipline. Another possible explanation is that students' approaches to learning are closely related to their conceptions of learning and epistemological beliefs (e.g., Baxter Magolda 1999; Bendixen 2002; Entwistle and Walker 2000; Entwistle et al. 2000; Entwistle, McCune, and Hounsell 2003; Entwistle and Peterson 2004; Hofer 2002, 2004; King and Kitchener 2002; Kuhn and Weinstock 2002; Pintrich 2002; Schommer-Aikins 2002).

Regulation of Learning and Frictions that Arise

Another important dimension in understanding student learning comprises those activities—often referred to as "self-regulation"—which students use to monitor, plan, and control their processing strategies and their own learning processes (Vermunt 1998; Vermunt and van Rijswijk 1988). Self-regulation is defined here as self-generated thoughts, feelings, and actions aimed at attaining academic goals (Winne and Hadwin 1997; Zimmerman 1998). In their review, Puustinen and Pulkkinen (2001) compared different models of self-regulated learning and showed that while the models were rather different from each other, a common feature was that self-regulated learners actively and autonomously guide their own learning and update their knowledge whenever necessary.

According to Zimmerman (1998), self-regulatory models have a particular role in understanding academic studying from a student's perspective. Boekaerts (1997) defines it as a complex interactive process involving both cognitive and motivational self-regulation. Furthermore, she argues that cognitive self-regulation can be taught by providing adequate instructional support for the learner. Biggs' term meta-learning is closely related to self-regulation. It refers to students' awareness of task demands, to their intentions regarding how to meet those demands, and further, to a realistic assessment of their own cognitive resources (Biggs 1985).

In addition to self-regulation in learning, Vermunt and colleagues (Vermunt 1998; Vermunt and van Rijswijk 1988) distinguish between two other forms of regulation: external regulation and lack of regulation. These two forms are found in situations in which students do not have the opportunity, skills, or knowledge to regulate their own learning. External regulation refers to a situation where a teacher assumes control of the regulation activities. For example, the teacher sets the learning goals, directs student learning activities, and monitors the learning process instead of encouraging or allowing students to do this for themselves. Lack of regulation, on the other hand, reflects students' inability to self-regulate. It is often seen when students lack these skills or when they are unclear about the teacher's expectations, particularly with respect to learning objectives and activities.

Self-regulation in learning is most often related to the deep approach, whereas external regulation is more likely to be associated with the surface approach (e.g., Beishuizen, Stoutjesdijk, and van Putten 1994; Lonka and Lindblom-Ylänne 1996; Vermunt and van Rijswijk 1988). Further, the degree of self-regulation has been shown to be related to the degree of successful studying in medicine (Lonka and Lindblom-Ylänne 1993) and in many other domains (Vermunt and van Rijswijk 1988).

Regulation strategies in learning and teaching are in a constant interaction with one another. According to Vermunt and Verloop (1999), learning and teaching strategies are not always compatible. Teaching strategies may be seen in a broader sense as reflecting the goals and demands of the learning environment. Congruence occurs when teachers' teaching goals and strategies correspond with the learning goals and strategies of students. Friction occurs when there is a conflict between learning and teaching strategies. Vermunt and Verloop (1999) divide friction into two categories. Constructive friction challenges students to increase their use of learning strategies. Thus, the learning environment stimulates them to develop thinking approaches which they would not be inclined to develop on their own. Constructive friction is similar to Vygotsky's zone of proximal development (1962, 1978) because it emphasizes the importance of concentrating on the "buds" rather than the "fruits" of development during the process of becoming an expert learner.

The following interview excerpt provides an example of constructive friction.[1] This student was frustrated at the beginning of her studies, but ultimately changed her study strategies from a surface approach towards a deep approach and self-regulated learning (Lindblom-Ylänne and Lonka 1999):

There is a conflict between study habits and exams. The goal is to pass the exam. It should rather be to do your work as well as you can and to understand. Earlier I learned more by heart, now I study more for my future occupation, for my own sake, and my motivation has been aroused. (fifth-year medical student)

Destructive friction, on the other hand, may cause a decrease in learning or thinking skills. Students may not be able to use their existing skills or develop their skills to their fullest potential. The following interview excerpt illustrates destructive friction between a student and her learning environment. This student feels that destructive friction had severely affected her studies (Lindblom-Ylänne and Lonka 1999):

> I'm enormously disappointed with this organization; this has not suited me in any way. The way we learn and study has been very difficult for me, really. I could even say that this faculty hinders studying; this is the simple truth.... We learn by heart, studying is very school-like. There aren't any discussions about interesting subjects after lectures ... we do not go anywhere to talk about unclear things. There isn't any sense in the way they teach us.... The content is not difficult, only the way we study. There is this conflict ... if I had my own goals, I couldn't achieve them in this system, because the conflict is huge.... You're better to adapt to the system's goals, i.e., pass the exams and other things.... At least I haven't got the strength to wonder if I will become a good physician after learning this and this ... I buried my own goals a long time ago. (fifth-year medical student)

Having discussed the importance of deep learning, self-regulation, and constructive friction, next, I explore the concept of student study profiles or orchestrations.

Study Orchestrations as Individual Combinations of Different Aspects of Learning

The study orchestration concept was introduced at the beginning of the 1990s by Meyer who defined it as a "conceptualised study approach adopted by individual students or groups of students" (1991, 297). The concept recognizes three important aspects of student learning: the existence of qualitative individual differences in the manner in which students approach and engage in learning tasks, the influence of the teaching-learning environment on such engagement, and differing conceptions of learning and personal epistemology among individual students (Meyer 1991). The verb "orchestrate" captures the current emphasis on self-directed learning and focuses on the different ways students direct their resources in specific learning contexts.

The term "study orchestration" refers to an event or a process rather than a state. Further, the term orchestration is helpful in examining student learning because it is precisely defined and embraces the concept of self-regulation. A comparison of two concepts, "approaches to learning" and "study orchestration," shows that both depend on the context, the content, and the demands of the learning task, but approaches to learning describe a more specific component of learning than study orchestration.

In general, a study orchestration is expected to exhibit a considerable degree of conceptual coherence or consonance. This means that it should be recognisable and interpretable in terms of our emerging understanding of how students vary in their conceptualization and engagement of learning (Meyer 2000a). However, study orchestrations may also involve degrees of conceptual incoherence or dissonance. This means that the expected theoretically coherent linkages between some or all of the more common sources of explanatory variation in contextualised learning behaviour fail to appear in a readily recognisable and interpretable form. A dissonant study orchestration is characterized by an atypical combination of aspects of studying, which do not theoretically fit together (Meyer 2000a).

Meyer and colleagues showed that study orchestrations of "at-risk" students were dominated by learning style pathologies (Meyer, Parsons, and Dunne 1990a, 1990b; Entwistle, Meyer, and Tait 1991), and that different orchestrations were also respectively related to different degrees of study success (Meyer et al. 1990a, 1990b). According to Meyer, Parsons, and Dunne (1990a), a coherent meaning orchestration was related to academic success, whereas its absence, or dissonant orchestration, was associated with academic failure.

Variation in Study Orchestrations. Combining survey and student interview data in earlier work, I found clear differences among the study orchestrations of law students in terms of coherence and dissonance; students' study orchestrations varied from clearly coherent to clearly dissonant (Lindblom-Ylänne 2003). In this study, the inventory applied was RoLI (Reflections on Learning Inventory, Meyer 2000b) which consisted of 75 items comprising 15 subscales (see Table 1).

Figure 1 shows an example of a coherent study orchestration. The profile presented in Figure 1 may be described as a good profile. There is an extremely clear difference between the mean scores of the surface scales and those of the deep scales. This student scored highly on all the deep scores, and highest on *memorising with understanding* (MWU). Furthermore, the student scored low on all the surface scores, including *repetition aids understanding* (RAU).

During an interview, this student analyzed his RoLI inventory results (Meyer 2000a) in the following way:

> This looks fine! I don't like to read the text many times. It was only when I studied for the entrance examination that I read the books many times. When I study for examinations, I don't have time to read many times. For me it's very good that I'm able to study in different kinds of learning environments.

I'm able to change my study strategies according to the demands of the learning environment. In the army, I often wondered why I didn't remember the things they taught me. Their way of teaching wasn't the right way. We had to study minor details, which weren't related to anything. Of course, I'm able to learn individual facts by heart, but it's not motivating or wise. (Student no. 43, a second-year law student, Lindblom-Ylänne 2003)

TABLE 1
Summary of the KOLI Scales with Item Examples

Scale	Item example
Scales measuring "surface" dimensions of learning	
FAC=Learning is fact-based	"Learning means collecting all the facts that need to be remembered."
MAR= Memorising as rehearsal	"I learn things that don't make sense to me by reading them over and over until I can remember them."
MBU= Memorising before understanding	"I need to commit something to memory before I can make meaning out of it."
KDF= Knowledge discrete and factual	"Knowledge really just consists of pieces of information."
DRP= Detail-related pathology	"I have difficulty in fitting together facts and details to form an overall view of something."
FRA=Fragmentation	"Much of what I have learned seems to consist of unrelated bits and pieces of information."
RAU= Repetition aids understanding	"Repetition helps me to remember things by creating a deeper impression."
Scales measuring "deep" dimensions of learning	
SDI= Seeing things differently	"I believe that learning involves seeing things from a new perspective."
IND= Thinking independently	"I know I have learned something when I can form counter arguments of my own."
RID= Relating ideas	"In learning new concepts or ideas I relate them as far as possible to what I already know."
"Neutral" scales, i.e., not clearly measuring either surface or deep dimensions	
LBE= Learning by example	"My learning has developed as a result of emulating other people's examples."
RER= Re-reading a text	"When re-reading a text I add to the meaning of what I already know about it."
DUT= Learning experienced as duty	"When I am learning I feel as if I am fulfilling an obligation."

Source: Author's compilation.

FIGURE 1
An Example of a Coherent Study Orchestration

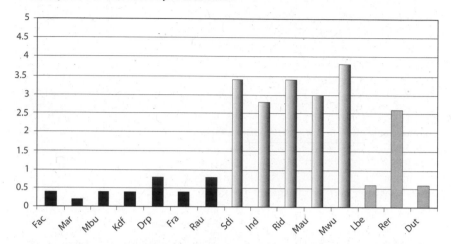

Notes: The scales measuring the surface dimensions of learning are shown on the left and the deep dimensions in the middle. The more neutral dimensions are shown on the right. These dimensions are separated from each other by applying different patterns.
Source: Adapted from Lindblom-Ylänne (2003).

The example in Figure 2 represents a clear dissonant study orchestration. This profile contains high scores on both the surface and deep scales. This student scores high on deep scales such as *thinking independently* (IND) and *memorising with understanding* (MWU) and, further, high on surface scales, such as *memorising as rehearsal* (MAR) and *memorising before understanding* (MBU).

In the interview, this student expressed difficulties in developing a new method of study. However, the student seemed to be aware that his current way of studying was not efficient for university studies:

> I should have developed another kind of study strategy in high school already. I shouldn't repeat things so many times. I should be able to read only once and still remember. I'm used to repetition. I should think more about the idea of the text when reading. Now at the Faculty of Law, I have tried to keep a list of concepts in my mind when reading a book. I hope this helps me. I should develop a way of studying in which reading once is enough. I got used to reading the material many times in high school. I should have done it differently then. Even my school friends told me that you don't have to read the material many times. (Student no. 40, a first-year law student, Lindblom-Ylänne 2003)

Between these two "extremes of the continuum" or, more precisely, between clearly coherent and clearly dissonant study orchestrations, there

FIGURE 2
An Example of a Dissonant Study Orchestration

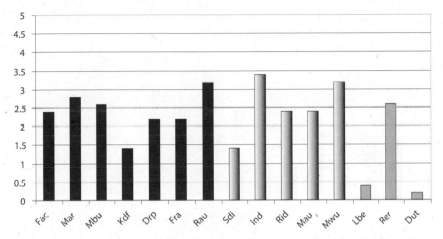

Notes: The scales measuring the surface dimensions of learning are shown on the left and the deep dimensions in the middle. The more neutral dimensions are shown on the right. These dimensions are separated from each other by applying different patterns.
Source: Adapted from Lindblom Ylänne (2003).

were students whose study orchestrations were diagnosed as slightly dissonant (see Figure 3). These students' study orchestrations were dominated by elements either from a deep profile or from a surface profile, but at the same time they also contained theoretically atypical combinations of scale scores. Thus, these orchestrations were "spoiled" by one or two high-scale scores that did not fit the overall profile.

This student scored high on most of the deep scales and generally low on the surface scales. However, his score on KDF was so high that it was not possible to diagnose his orchestration as coherent. Furthermore, he scored quite highly on MAR. In the interview, he expressed destructive friction between his conceptions of learning and the way the learning environment forced him to study:

> I think the results correspond very well to my own conceptions of myself as a student. I answered this questionnaire on the basis of my own conceptions.... On the other hand, here at the Faculty of Law I have to do differently in order to succeed. Unfortunately, I have to use memorising more than I would spontaneously do. That's the way to achieve good results. However, I'm not able to remember if there is no sense in what I'm studying. I have to understand. (Student no. 42, a second-year law student, Lindblom-Ylänne 2003)

Thus, even though these orchestrations were not severely dissonant, they reflected problems in the students' study practices and frictions in

FIGURE 3
An Example of a Slightly Dissonant Study Orchestration

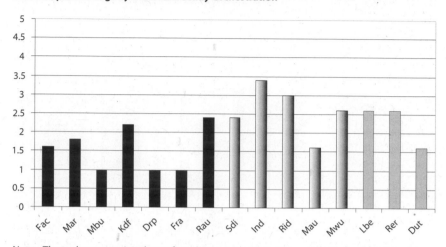

Notes: The scales measuring the surface dimensions of learning are shown on the left and the deep dimensions in the middle. The more neutral dimensions are shown on the right. These dimensions are separated from each other by applying different patterns.
Source: Adapted from Lindblom-Ylänne (2003).

relation to their learning environment. Many students who were expressing slightly dissonant study orchestrations reported that their learning environment forced them to study more superficially than they would normally do. This reflects a destructive friction between the students and their learning environment.

The Effect of the Learning Environment on Study Orchestrations. Dissonance is an extremely interesting phenomenon because, in addition to illuminating theoretically atypical combinations of different approaches to learning, it reflects problematic relationships between individual students and their learning environments, particularly their perceptions of their environments (e.g., Lindblom-Ylänne 2003; Lindblom-Ylänne and Lonka 1999). However, dissonance is not related to any particular approach to learning, but is rather developed through interaction among students' approaches to learning, factors such as their learning experiences and regulatory skills, and the learning environment (Lindblom-Ylänne 1999). Lindblom-Ylänne and Lonka (1999) analysed the dissonance of advanced medical students' study orchestrations. It appeared that the learning environment in medical school forced some students to study in a way not typical of them. The dissonant study orchestrations seemed to be a result of the conflict between the requirements of the learning environment and the students' individual study practices. As Boekaerts (1997) pointed out, the goals that teachers set may not be congruent with those generated and defined by the students. This confusion may manifest itself as either constructive or destructive friction (Vermunt 1996) in the perception of the learning environment.

However, a constant mismatch does not always increase the probability of a dissonant study orchestration. In my work with Lonka (Lindblom-Ylänne and Lonka 1999; Lonka and Lindblom-Ylänne 1995), I found that some students who did not try to adapt to the learning environment were able to maintain their coherent way of studying despite the constant mismatch between their learning practices and the teacher's teaching practices. This was the case with advanced medical students expressing a coherent meaning orchestration. They were the most successful in their studies, even though their orchestrations were not supported by the teaching practices in the traditional medical curriculum. Thus, the students who expressed coherent study orchestrations seemed to be "immune" to the demands of the learning environment (Lindblom-Ylänne and Lonka 1999, 2000; Lonka and Lindblom-Ylänne 1995). For example, these students did not study in order to succeed in the examinations, but instead, in order to learn as well as possible and to become good physicians, as the following extract shows:

> I always try to understand and to relate new knowledge to my previous knowledge. Some of the examination books require much memorising. However, it is possible to read these kinds of books by reasoning, not by learning by heart. I don't study by heart, but instead, choose the main things by underlining and write, on the basis of the text underlined, my own summary of the exam material, which I study carefully. (Student no. 20, a fifth-year medical student, Lindblom-Ylänne and Lonka 2001)

My 2003 study confirmed my earlier findings (Lindblom-Ylänne and Lonka 1999, 2000; Lonka and Lindblom-Ylänne 1995), showing that law students who expressed coherent study orchestrations were also immune to the demands of the learning environment and continued to search for meaning even when they studied materials that consisted of a great deal of facts.

The results of our 1999 study (Lindblom-Ylänne and Lonka 1999) showed that half of the medical students expressing dissonant orchestrations had problems with their study practices. They also lacked the metacognitive skills to evaluate their study practices and quality of learning. On the other hand, the other half of the medical students expressing dissonant study orchestrations noticed a change in their study practices during their studies. These students applied good study strategies and practices, which were "broken down" because of the destructive friction between these students and their traditional learning environment.

Analyses of the individual ways in which advanced medical students orchestrated their studying indicated that a conflict between students' own goals and those of their learning environment somehow broke down the regulation activities that they were used to. Despite these students' ability to use metacognitive regulation activities, they were unable to regulate their studies. As their studies proceeded, these students were no longer sure who was responsible for the regulation: themselves as self-regulated learners or the curriculum teachers as external regulators. This implies that high-achieving students expressing a dissonant orchestration may not lack regulation abilities. It may rather be a case of the externally regulated learning environment forcing students to change their study practices and to adopt a more externally regulated learning style, a process which may lead to the development of a dissonant orchestration. Active and self-regulated students may not be satisfied with their studying in the traditional learning environment. Severe conflicts may arise, because the demands of the learning environment and the students' personal goals are not congruent. However, as mentioned earlier, some meaning-oriented medical students were shown to be immune to the mismatch between the demands of the learning environment and their own study practices. These students were different in that they continued to study in a way they thought would be the best for them regardless of their perceptions of the learning environment.

As this study demonstrates, research on study orchestrations of university students can be extremely fruitful at an individual level, even though it is also possible to look at the study orchestrations of groups of students. Research on dissonant study orchestrations at the individual level is particularly valuable because it deepens our understanding of problems related to the relationship between the student and the learning environment, and to low academic achievement. These results can be used to inform teaching practice and also be applied to student counselling, and in this way may enhance the quality of student learning. Next, I look at the interaction of students and their perceptions of teaching-learning environments at the departmental and disciplinary level.

Students' Perceptions of Their Teaching-Learning Environments

There is evidence that the teaching-learning environment affects student learning. Students' perceptions of teaching, assessment, and course content, as well as of structure within the natural setting of academic departments, influence their learning. Assessment has an important role in determining what and how students learn. According to Biggs (2003), good teaching is based on constructive alignment, which refers to teaching where the objectives are appropriate and clear to the students, and the teaching methods and assessment tasks support student engagement in learning activities in order to gain desired skills and understanding. Teaching, learning, and assessment are strongly related and their alignment has always been crucial for achieving the goals of education. Inappropriate assessment and a heavy workload have been shown to push students toward a surface approach to learning (e.g., Pellegrino 2002; Shepard 2000).

Perceptions of good teaching influence students to move toward a deep approach to learning (Lizzio, Wilson, and Simons 2002). Entwistle and colleagues (2000) emphasize the role of teaching in supporting high-quality learning. According to them, good teaching can be defined as an extended awareness of the relationship between learning and teaching. There is a relationship between teachers' approaches to teaching and students' approaches to learning (Kember and Gow 1994; Prosser and Trigwell 1999). In particular, there is evidence that student-centred teachers seem to support their students in adopting a deep approach to learning (Trigwell, Prosser, and Waterhouse 1999).

Given this, it is not surprising that research has shown that approaches to learning are related to students' perceptions of their learning environments. Students' positive perceptions of their learning environment are positively related to a deep approach to learning and negatively to a surface approach to learning (Kreber 2003; Lawless and Richardson 2002; Richardson 2005; Richardson and Price 2003; Sadlo and Richardson 2003). The link between a deep approach to learning and student perception of the learning environment has been found in different educational contexts and different subject areas (Entwistle, Tait, and McCune 2000; McCune 2003; Parpala et al. forthcoming).

Furthermore, there is evidence of disciplinary variation in approaches to learning (e.g., Entwistle and Ramsden 1983; Lonka and Lindblom-Ylänne 1996; Smith and Miller 2005). Students from the sciences or applied sciences are more inclined to adopt a surface approach to learning, whereas students from the humanities or social sciences tend to adopt a deep approach. Building on these results, our recent study (Parpala et al. forthcoming) showed that the analytical and argumentative approach to learning was the most common among the students of behavioural and social sciences and theology. Thus, there is evidence that norms concerning the production of knowledge, as well as communication norms, vary by discipline, and students tacitly learn these norms during their study years (Parry 1998; Ylijoki 2000). Disciplines have their own categories of thought which provide members with shared concepts, theories, methods, techniques, and problems (Ylijoki 2000).

Challenges for Future Research

The challenges of research in higher education focus mainly on the fact that most research takes place in real-life settings. So many factors affect student learning and teaching in a specific situation that it is impossible to control for all of them. In addition, ethical considerations are among the most important to be thoroughly considered, in particular, when research takes place in courses which students are taking in order to achieve a degree.

Different dimensions of student learning in higher education have been explored extensively during the last forty years. There is ample research on approaches to learning, self-regulation of learning, epistemological beliefs of students, self-efficacy beliefs, and motivation. In addition, there is empirical evidence that all these aspects are related to successful studying at university. Furthermore, more and more research is being conducted on university teachers, for example, on their approaches to teaching, self-efficacy beliefs, and the scholarship of teaching and learning.

However, what is most needed is additional research on the interrelations between different aspects of teaching and learning in higher education. For example, more research is needed on how teachers' approaches to teaching and their teaching practices affect students' approaches to learning and the quality of their learning outcomes. Trigwell, Prosser, and Waterhouse (1999) found a relationship between approaches to teaching adopted by a teacher and approaches to learning adopted by his/her students. The results of that study showed that if a teacher adopts a teacher-centred approach to teaching, the students are more likely to adopt a surface approach to learning. Conversely, if a teacher adopts a more student-centred approach to teaching, the students are more likely to adopt a deep approach to learning. However, the study was limited to self-reports of Australian first-year chemistry and physics students and their teachers. More research is therefore needed on the interaction of teaching and learning in higher education by applying mixed-method approaches and by using large multidisciplinary samples. Furthermore, more follow-up studies are needed on the development of approaches to learning and teaching, and on students' perceptions of their teaching-learning environments throughout their university studies.

In order to enhance the quality of student learning in university, more research is also needed on discipline-specific approaches to teaching and learning and on disciplinary variation. There is a body of research on students of some disciplines, such as medicine and psychology, but we know much less about challenges in teaching and studying, for example, in history, philosophy, or law.

Research on higher education has many important practical implications. Research results can be applied in order to develop more effective teaching and assessment methods and to help students develop their study strategies and practices. Research results can also foster the development of student counselling and supervising practices. In order to encourage greater dissemination and uptake of these results, faculty and educational developers need to be better informed of research findings and researchers need to be more cognizant of their dissemination practices.

NOTE

[1] The following excerpts are taken from a study that was conducted in Finland. Student quotes have been translated from Finnish.

REFERENCES

Baxter Magolda, M.B. 1999. *Creating Contexts for Learning and Self-Authorship: Constructive-Developmental Pedagogy.* Nashville, TN: Vanderbilt University Press.

Beishuizen, J., E. Stoutjesdijk, and K. van Putten. 1994. Studying Textbooks: Effects of Learning Styles, Study Task, and Instruction. *Learning and Instruction* 4:151-74.

Bendixen, L.D. 2002. A Process Model of Epistemic Belief Change. In *Personal Epistemology: The Psychology of Beliefs about Knowledge and Knowing,* 1st edition, ed. B.K. Hofer and P.R. Pintrich, 191-208. Mahwah, New Jersey: Lawrence Erlbaum Associates, Inc.

Biggs, J. 1985. The Role of Metalearning in Study Processes. *British Journal of Educational Psychology* 55:185-212.

Biggs, J. 1993. What Do Inventories of Students' Learning Processes Really Measure? A Theoretical Review and Clarification. *British Journal of Educational Psychology* 63:3-19.

Biggs, J. 2003. *Teaching for Quality Learning at University.* 2nd edition. Buckingham: The Society for Research into Higher Education & Open University Press.

Bockaerts, M. 1997. Self-Regulated Learning: A New Concept Embraced by Researchers, Policy Makers, Educators, Teachers, and Students. *Learning and Instruction* 2:161-86.

Entwistle, A. and N. Entwistle. 1992. Experiences of Understanding in Revising for Degree Examinations. *Learning and Instruction* 2:1-22.

Entwistle, N.J. and V. McCune. 2004. The Conceptual Base of Study Strategies Inventories in Higher Education. *Educational Psychology Review* 164:325-45.

Entwistle, N., V. McCune, and J. Hounsell. 2003. Investigating Ways of Enhancing University Teaching-Learning Environments: Measuring Students' Approaches to Studying and Perceptions of Teaching. In *Powerful Learning Environments: Unravelling Basic Components and Dimensions,* 1st edition, ed. E. De Corte, L. Verschaffel, N. Entwistle, and J. van Merriënboer, 89-108. Amsterdam: Pergamon.

Entwistle, N., V. McCune, and P. Walker. 2001. Conceptions, Styles, and Approaches within Higher Education: Analytic Abstractions and Everyday Experience. In *Perspectives on Thinking, Learning, and Cognitive Styles,* ed. R.J. Sternberg and L.F. Zhang, 197-226. Mahwah, NJ: Lawrence Erlbaum.

Entwistle, N.J., J.H.F. Meyer, and H. Tait. 1991. Student Failure: Disintegrated Patterns of Study Strategies and Perceptions of the Learning Environment. *Higher Education* 21:249-61.

Entwistle, N. and E.R. Peterson. 2004. Conceptions of Learning and Knowledge in Higher Education: Relationships with Study Behaviour and Influences of Learning Environments. *International Journal of Educational Research* 416:407-28.

Entwistle, N. and P. Ramsden. 1983. *Understanding Student Learning.* London: Croom Helm.

Entwistle, N., D. Skinner, D. Entwistle, and S. Orr. 2000. Conceptions and Beliefs about Good Teaching: An Integration of Contrasting Research Areas. *Higher Education Research & Development* 191:5-26.

Entwistle, N., H. Tait, and V. McCune. 2000. Patterns of Response to Approaches to Studying Inventory Across Constracting Groups and Contexts. *European Journal of Psychology of Education* 16:33-48.

Entwistle, N. and P. Walker. 2000. Strategic Alertness and Expanded Awareness within Sophisticated Conceptions of Teaching. *Instructional Science* 285:335-61.

Hofer, B.K. 2002. Personal Epistemology as a Psychological and Educational Construct: An Introduction. In *Personal Epistemology: The Psychology of Beliefs about Knowledge and Knowing*, 1ˢᵗ edition, ed. B.K. Hofer and P.R. Pintrich, 3-14. Mahwah, New Jersey: Lawrence Erlbaum Associates, Inc.

Hofer, B.K. 2004. Epistemological Understanding as a Metacognitive Process: Thinking Aloud During Online Searching. *Educational Psychologist* 391:43-55.

Kember, D. and L. Gow. 1994. Orientations to Teaching and Their Effect on the Quality of Student Learning. *Journal of Higher Education* 65:58-73.

King, P.M. and K.S. Kitchener. 2002. The Reflective Judgement Model: Twenty Years of Research on Epistemic Cognition. In *Personal Epistemology: The Psychology of Beliefs about Knowledge and Knowing*, 1ˢᵗ edition, ed.B.K. Hofer, and P.R. Pintrich, 37-61. Mahwah, New Jersey: Lawrence Erlbaum Associates, Inc.

Kreber, C. 2003. The Relationship between Students' Course Perception and Their Approaches to Studying in Undergraduate Science Courses: A Canadian Experience. *Higher Education and Development* 22:57–70.

Kuhn, D. and M. Weinstock. 2002. What is Epistemological Thinking and Why Does It Matter? In *Personal Epistemology: The Psychology of Beliefs about Knowledge and Knowing*, 1ˢᵗ edition, ed. B.K. Hofer and P.R. Pintrich, 121-44. Mahwah, New Jersey: Lawrence Erlbaum Associates, Inc.

Lawless, C. and J.T.E. Richardson. 2002. Approaches to Studying and Perceptions of Academic Quality in Distance Education. *Higher Education* 44:257-82.

Lindblom-Ylänne, S. 1999. *Studying in a Traditional Medical Curriculum – Study Success, Orientations to Studying and Problems that Arise. Academic dissertation.* Helsinki: Helsinki University Printing House.

Lindblom-Ylänne, S. 2003. Broadening an Understanding of the Phenomenon of Dissonance. *Studies in Higher Education* 28(1):63-77.

Lindblom-Ylänne, S. 2006. Enhancing the Quality of Teaching in Higher Education in Finland – the Case of the University of Helsinki. In *International Policy Perspectives on Improving Learning with Limited Resources*, ed. C. Kreber, 63-72. San Francisco: Jossey-Bass/Wiley.

Lindblom-Ylänne, S. and K. Lonka. 1999. Individual Ways of Interacting with the Learning Environment – Are They Related to Study Success? *Learning and Instruction* 9:1-18.

Lindblom-Ylänne, S. and K. Lonka. 2000. Dissonant Study Orchestrations of High Achieving University Students. *European Journal of Educational Psychology* 15: 19-32.

Lindblom-Ylänne, S. and K. Lonka. 2001. Students' Perceptions of Assessment Practices in a Traditional Medical Curriculum. *Advances in Health Science Education* 6:121-40.

Lizzio, A., K. Wilson, and R. Simons. 2002. University Students' Perceptions of the Learning Environment and Academic Outcomes: Implications for Theory and Practice. *Studies in Higher Education* 271:27-52.

Lonka, K. and S. Lindblom-Ylänne. 1993. Study Strategies, Learning From Text, and Success in Medical School. A paper presented at EARLI invited symposium "Improving the Quality of Student Learning in Higher Education: Research Using Psychological Concepts and Research Methods" for the European Congress of Psychology, Tampere, Finland, 5-9 July 1993.

Lonka, K. and S. Lindblom-Ylänne. 1995. Epistemologies, Conceptions of Learning, and Study Success in Two Domains: Medicine and Psychology. A paper presented at the 6th EARLI conference, Nijmegen, The Netherlands, 26-31 August 1995.

Lonka, K. and S. Lindblom-Ylänne. 1996. Epistemologies, Conceptions of Learning, and Study Practices in Medicine and Psychology. *Higher Education* 31:5-24.

Marton, F., D. Hounsell, and N. Entwistle, eds. 1997. *The Experience of Learning* 2nd edition. Edinburgh, UK: Scottish Academic Press.

Marton, F. and R. Säljö. 1976. On Qualitative Differences in Learning: I. Outcome and Process. *British Journal of Educational Psychology* 46:4-11.

Marton, F. and R. Säljö. 1997. Approaches to Learning. In *The Experience of Learning* 2nd edition, ed. F. Marton, D. Hounsell, and N. Entwistle, 39-58. Edinburgh, UK: Scottish Academic Press.

McCune, V. 2003. Promoting High-Quality Learning: Perspectives from the ETL project. Paper presented at the 14th Conference on University and College Pedagogy of the Norwegian Network in Higher Education, Fredrikstad, 22-23 October 2003.

Meyer, J.H.F. 1991. Study Orchestration: The Manifestation, Interpretation and Consequences of Contextualised Approaches to Studying. *Higher Education* 22:297-316.

Meyer, J.H.F. 2000a. The Modelling of Dissonant Study Orchestration in Higher Education. *European Journal of Psychology of Education* 15:5-18.

Meyer, J.H.F. 2000b. An Overview of the Development and Application of the Reflections on Learning Inventory RoLI. Paper presented at the *RoLI Symposium*, Imperial College, London, 25 July.

Meyer, J.H.F., P. Parsons, and T.T. Dunne. 1990a. Study Orchestration and Learning Outcome: Evidence of Association over Time among Disadvantaged Students. *Higher Education* 20:245-69.

Meyer, J.H.F., P. Parsons, and T.T. Dunne. 1990b Individual Study Orchestrations and Their Association with Learning Outcome. *Higher Education* 20:67-89.

Nieminen, J., S. Lindblom-Ylänne, and K. Lonka. 2004. The Development of Study Orientations and Study Success in Students of Pharmacy. *Instructional Science* 32:387-417.

Parpala, A., S. Lindblom-Ylänne, E. Komulainen, T. Litmanen, and L. Hirsto. forthcoming. Students' Approaches to Learning and Experiences of Their Teaching-Learning Environment in Different Disciplines. *British Journal of Educational Psychology*.

Parry, S. 1998. Disciplinary Discourse in Doctoral Theses. *Higher Education* 36:273-99.

Pellegrino, J.W. 2002. Knowing What Students Know. *Issues in Science & Technology* 192:48-52.

Pintrich, P.R. 2002. Future Challenges and Directions for Theory and Research on Personal Epistemology. In *Personal Epistemology: The Psychology of Beliefs about Knowledge and Knowing*, 1st edition, ed. B.K. Hofer and P.R. Pintrich, 389-414. Mahwah, New Jersey: Lawrence Erlbaum Associates, Inc.

Prosser, M. and K. Trigwell. 1999. *Understanding Learning and Teaching: The Experience in Higher Education*. Buckingham: The Society for Research into Higher Education & Open University Press.

Puustinen, M. and L. Pulkkinen. 2001. Models of Self-Regulated Learning: A Review. *Scandinavian Journal of Educational Research* 453:269-86.

Ramsden, P. 2003. *Learning to Teach in Higher Education*, 2nd edition. London: Routledge.

Richardson, J.T.E. 1994. Cultural Specificity of Approaches to Studying in Higher Education: A Literature Survey. *Higher Education* 27:449-68.

Richardson, J.T.E. 2005. Students' Perceptions of Academic Quality and Approaches to Studying in Distance Education. *British Educational Research Journal* 31:7-27.

Richardson, J.T.E. and L. Price. 2003. Approaches to Studying and Perceptions of Academic Quality in Electronically Delivered Courses. *British Journal of Educational Technology* 34:45-56.

Sadlo, G. and J.T.E. Richardson. 2003. Approaches to Studying and Perceptions of the Academic Environment in Students Following Problem-Based and Subject-Based Curricula. *Higher Education Research and Development* 22:253–274.

Schommer-Aikins, M. 2002. An Evolving Theoretical Framework for an Epistemological Belief System. In *Personal Epistemology: The Psychology of Beliefs about Knowledge and Knowing*, 1st edition, ed. B.K. Hofer and P.R. Pintrich, 103-18. Mahwah, New Jersey: Lawrence Erlbaum Associates, Inc..

Shepard, L.A. 2000. The Role of Assessment in a Learning Culture. *Educational Researcher* 297:4-14.

Smith, S. and R. Miller. 2005. Learning Approaches: Examination Type, Discipline of Study, and Gender. *Educational Psychology* 251:43-53.

Trigwell, K., M. Prosser, and F. Waterhouse. 1999. Relations between Teachers' Approaches to Teaching and Students' Approaches to Learning. *Higher Education* 37:57-70.

Vermunt, J.D.H.M. 1996. Metacognitive, Cognitive and Affective Aspects of Learning Styles and Strategies: A Phenomenographic Analysis. *Higher Education* 31:25-50.

Vermunt, J.D.H.M. 1998. The Regulation of Constructive Learning Processes. *British Journal of Educational Psychology* 68:149-171.

Vermunt, J.D.H.M. and F.A.W.M. van Rijswijk. 1988. Analysis and Development of Students' Skill in Self-Regulated Learning. *Higher Education* 170:647-82.

Vermunt, J.D.H.M. and N. Verloop. 1999. Congruence and Friction between Learning and Teaching. *Learning and Instruction* 9:257-80.

Vygotsky, L.S. 1962. *Thought and Language*. Cambridge, MA: Harvard University Press.

Vygotsky, L.S. 1978. *Mind in Society. The Development of Higher Psychological Processes*. Cambridge, MA: Harvard University Press.

Winne, P.H. and A.F. Hadwin. 1997. Studying as Self-Regulated Learning. In *Metacognition in Educational Theory and Practice*, ed. D.J. Hacker, J. Dunlosky, and A.C. Graesser. Mahwah, NJ: Lawrence Erlbaum Associates, Inc.

Ylijoki, O.H. 2000. Disciplinary Cultures and the Moral Order of Studying – A Case Study of Four Finnish University Departments. *Higher Education* 39:339-62.

Zimmerman, B.J. 1998. Academic Studying and the Development of Personal Skill: a Self-Regulatory Perspective. *Educational Psychologist* 33:73-86.

> *Building bridges between what faculty know about student learning and their teaching practice — through scholarship, application, and breaking the rules.*

4

TAKING STOCK OF WHAT FACULTY KNOW ABOUT STUDENT LEARNING

Maryellen Weimer

INTRODUCTION

Most of what faculty know about student learning they have learned from first-hand, classroom observation. Their observations confirm that problems do exist, but most do not recognize that teaching can contribute to these problems. Furthermore, most would not look to educational research for an understanding of the etiology of learning problems or as a source of solutions for those problems. This paper explores the unfortunate disconnect between teaching practice and the research on student learning, and some ways of better connecting the two.

If asked, what would most faculty say about students as learners? Based on my own experience as an educational developer, I believe that chances are good they would identify one or several of these four problems. First, *students are passive*. They want to sit back and have education "done unto them," and they hope the experience will be pleasant and painless. This means they do not want to be called on unless they volunteer and they do not volunteer unless absolutely certain they know the right answer. They do not want to generate examples (questions, theories, or anything else), particularly in groups with other students. They want the teacher to write the material on the board, or better yet show it on a PowerPoint

Taking Stock: Research on Teaching and Learning in Higher Education, ed. J. Christensen Hughes and J. Mighty. Montreal and Kingston: McGill-Queen's University Press, Queen's Policy Studies Series. © 2010 The School of Policy Studies, Queen's University at Kingston. All rights reserved.

presentation that can be conveniently downloaded. They really like it when teachers provide complete sets of notes from class.

Next, *students lack confidence as learners*. They do not like it when they have to make decisions related to learning. They want teachers to spell out exactly what they should to do. Teachers should specify paper length, appropriate fonts, margin size, and the number of references for the bibliography. Students want to know whether they should write in the first person, or include examples or quotations. They want teachers to "go over" what will be on the test, detailing those sections of the text that should be the focus of in-depth study. Sometimes they find it difficult to say for sure whether or not they understand something.

Third, faculty might observe that *many students lack the basic study skills necessary to succeed in college*. They struggle to read technical material, even texts that have become simpler and better organized than they used to be. They depend on a limited repertoire of study strategies—flash cards, recopying notes, and underlining material in texts. If those strategies fail, students still use them, thinking that the only option is to use them more. Often they write and calculate poorly.

Finally, faculty might complain that *the only thing that motivates students are grades, points, and marks*. Students rarely demonstrate any intellectual curiosity. They will volunteer but only if the learning opportunity involves points, even just a few of them. They engage in intellectual dialogue with passion only when the argument involves the possibility of more points or an increase in partial credit.

Research on student learning has much to say about each of these characteristics—both in terms of explaining why students so regularly demonstrate them, and in terms of offering solutions to faculty who want to help students become better learners. An analysis of each area illustrates what faculty could learn from research on student learning.

Why Are Students So Passive and What Can Teachers Do to Effectively Engage Them in the Learning Process?

Students are passive in part because instruction continues to be so didactic. A survey of 172,000 faculty in the US (nearly one out of every three) found that 76 percent list the lecture as their primary instructional method (Finkelstein, Seal, and Schuster 1998). Lectures can be engaging, but most encourage passivity with excessive amounts of teacher talk. In Nunn's (1996) observational study of participation in college classrooms, on average less than 6 percent of class time involved student interaction. That's three minutes of student talk per 50 minutes of class time.

So if teachers lectured less, what would students be doing in class? They could be learning from and with each other. The viability of group work, especially co-operative learning structures, is well documented by educational research. In the post-secondary arena, Springer, Stanne, and Donnovan's (1999) meta-analysis of studies on group work in math, science, and engineering disciplines showed these collective learning experiences positively affected academic achievement and persistence in college. Often, the case for students learning from and with each other is a hard sell in heavily content-oriented disciplines, but the evidence from research on student learning conducted in those fields verifies more generic findings. For example, in chemistry (and even though these studies were conducted within non-educational disciplines, they are well-designed and carefully executed educational studies), McCreary, Golde, and Koeske (2006) found that students in labs led by students (who had successfully completed the lab previously and were trained in conducting the labs) learned more than students in labs taught by instructors. Lewis and Lewis (2005) found that when one chemistry lecture per week was replaced by a guided discussion facilitated by peers, students in the discussion sections did not learn less (as measured by final exam scores), causing the researchers to conclude: "Fears that students who had less exposure to lecture would learn less proved to be groundless in this study" (139).

The case for active learning in general is made across a patchwork of different studies done by educational researchers as well as faculty researchers based in the disciplines. The diversity of the approaches used to study those methods that engage students makes them difficult to compare but Prince (2004) has done a masterful job of organizing and integrating this work. He concluded that "… there is broad but uneven support for the core elements of active, collaborative, co-operative and problem-based learning" (223). This support is not just for involvement in activity per se but substantiates that the various kinds of student engagement explored in these studies results in better learning—whether that is longer retention of content, greater facility in applying what has been learned, or a deeper understanding of the content.

In sum, the propensity of students to sit back and have education "done unto them" is reinforced by the continued reliance on didactic instruction. Educational research of various sorts verifies that any number of different methods can successfully engage and involve students in learning. Use of these active learning approaches does not automatically sacrifice content knowledge or dilute the intellectual currency of a course.

Why are Students Such Dependent Learners and What Can Teachers Do to Develop Their Confidence and Empower Them as Learners?

It is faculty who decide what students will learn (as in the content of courses), faculty who decide what learning and assessment activities students will participate in (writing papers, taking exams, doing labs, completing projects, participating in class), faculty who establish and enforce the terms and conditions under which learning will take place (attendance policies, late paper penalties, rules for classroom behaviors, etc.), faculty who determine the pace (by setting and following the course calendar), and finally it is faculty who decide if students have learned and how well. Some of the decisions in each of these areas legitimately belong to faculty, but in each area control has been extended beyond what is good for learners.

Some of this teacher control derives from tradition. Most of it is well-intentioned. As students arrive at college with fewer skills, less focus, and a propensity to make poor decisions about learning, faculty have intervened. If students do not know what they need to do to succeed in college (and life), faculty will make those decisions for them. They set about requiring those behaviors associated with success (knowing when to have your cell phone off, meeting deadlines, speaking when called on, arriving on time, and not leaving early).

This approach does solve the problem in the short term. Unfortunately, it has serious long-term consequences. When faculty make all the learning decisions, students never learn how to make them on their own and this negatively impacts learner self-confidence.

Educational research underscores this point. Take, for example, the work of Perry (1997) who has studied the extent to which students believe they can or cannot control events. If students perceive a loss of control, that orientation strongly affects their academic performance to the extent that they are not even ameliorated by effective instruction and highly rated teachers.

Pintrich's (2003) work on motivation and his comprehensive review of research on the topic affirms that beliefs about self-efficacy and competence as well as beliefs about control influence motivation. Students are likely to be motivated when they believe in themselves and feel as though they can control at least some of the issues related to their learning. Knowing this (in addition to the use of active learning approaches) can help teachers who are confronted with disengaged and passive students. In *Learner-Centered Teaching* (Weimer 2002), I propose ways students can be involved in decisions about their learning in five areas of classroom instruction.

The positive impact of a whole range of inductive teaching methods (discovery learning, inquiry-based learning, problem-based learning, project-based learning, case-based teaching, and just-in-time teaching) has been documented by Prince and Felder (2006) who conclude "the collective evidence favoring inductive teaching over traditional deductive pedagogy is conclusive" (135). All of the inductive methods explored in this review are notable for the way they involve students and for the extent to which students have at least some control over the learning processes. Faculty may believe that by controlling how students learn, they improve the chances of success, when in fact this approach likely creates more problems than it solves.

Why Are Students Missing Basic Learning Skills, and What Can Teachers Do to Expand Their Repertoire of Learning Strategies?

The easy response to this question blames previous educational experiences. The tougher answer points the finger at college and university teachers and their continued emphasis on covering content. A false yet common assumption seems to be that more is always better when it comes to content, and the commitment to coverage only grows as students continue through the educational system. Into this focus on content have been woven issues of course and instructor credibility. Courses develop reputations by being difficult, as in containing lots of complicated content for students to master. As information explodes, teachers have more and more content to teach to students who are less and less prepared to handle its rigors. Getting the course content covered reduces the time that can be devoted to learning skill acquisition.

Historically, students have been expected to develop sophisticated learning skills automatically, simply by being exposed to those skills. In the process of learning chemistry or French, political science or plant pathology, students learn the content and as they acquire content knowledge they come to a tacit understanding of how to learn that particular kind of content. If a student sees how the teacher solves a problem without any explicit instruction, the student may learn problem-solving skills. Learning by modeling does occur. The problem is that understanding acquired this way becomes intuitive knowledge. The processes are understood implicitly. Without explicit knowledge, what is known is less easily manipulated and less effectively controlled and directed toward other learning.

Woods' (1987) study on engineering students illustrates the problem. Woods estimated that during a four-year course of study, students observed faculty solving something close to 1,000 problems. Those students were also assigned something like 3,000 homework problems. Woods discovered that "… despite all this activity, they showed negligible improvement in problem solving skills….What they acquired was a set of memorized procedures for about 3,000 problem situations that they could, with varying degrees of success, recall" (Woods 1987, 59). Bottom line: teachers should teach learning skills explicitly, using (as opposed to covering) the content to help students expand their repertoire of strategies and develop a more detailed understanding of themselves as learners.

Studies far too numerous to list establish how quickly students forget course content, even under the best circumstances like an upper division, major course. For example, using an interesting longitudinal design, Bacon and Stewart (2006) found that after two years, marketing majors who had taken a junior-level consumer behavior course had lost virtually all the content from that course.

Educational research offers an interesting explanation as to why students fail to retain course content. Kember and Gow (1994), for example, found that teaching methods have a direct impact on the strategies students opt to use. If the course is full of content which the teacher moves to cover efficiently, primarily by lecturing, then students tend to rely on surface-learning approaches, like memorization. Memorization may result in good exam performance, but if students have memorized material without really understanding it, shortly after the exam the material is gone.

In this age of exploding knowledge and enhanced technology, expectations for lifelong learning will grow. Post-secondary education should be offering students the opportunity to develop learning skills and an awareness of themselves as learners to the same level it offers opportunities to develop content knowledge.

Why Are Students Not Intrinsically Motivated, and What Can Teachers Do to Cultivate Their Innate Curiosity and Love of Learning?

Nowhere is the case against excessive reliance on extrinsic motivators made more convincingly than in Kohn's (1993) book, *Punished by Rewards: The Trouble with Gold Stars, Incentive Plans, A's, Praise and Other Bribes*. Kohn cites all sorts of research that establishes how effectively extrinsic motivators squelch the intrinsic motivation learners need to truly excel. Consider one concrete example. Students come to class not having done the reading. The teacher tries to make them come prepared with unannounced pop quizzes. Students report that those quizzes keep them up with the reading. But unannounced pop quizzes do not teach students the value of reading, or show them how much can be learned from reading, or make them understand why reading is a part of virtually all professional positions. No, students are doing something because they have to and that orientation makes it very difficult for them to see the value of what they are doing.

Candy's (1991) compilation of work on self-directed learning shows how motivation increases when learners are in charge of their own learning. His appendix lists 13 research-generated characteristics of self-directed learners. They profile a learner that stands in stark contrast to the very dependent, unmotivated student that end up being the majority of learners in most post-secondary classrooms.

Teachers must work to create classroom climates that are conducive to learning—climates where the need to know motivates action the same way a change in temperature motivates people to take off or put on clothing.

Building Bridges and Crossing Divides

The discussion of each of these beliefs illustrates how much faculty could learn from educational research—be it done by educational researchers or by faculty involving discipline-based educational inquires. However, the disconnect between practice in the post-secondary classroom and educational research is wide. Both may be worlds in the same universe but travel between them is difficult and almost never occurs.

Who is to blame? In reality, fingers point in both directions. Educational research (like research in most fields) is written to inform subsequent research. To do that, articles must use specialized language, and describe research methods and results in excruciating detail. Application of findings to practice is not the main concern of those working to push back the frontiers of what is known about learning. On the other hand, those who teach at the post-secondary level still receive little or no pedagogical training and few professional norms expect them to grow and develop as pedagogues the way they are expected to grow and develop knowledge of a discipline. As a result, their knowledge is experientially derived and not usually submitted to rigorous evidentiary tests.

However, prolonged consideration of who's to blame sidetracks the needed efforts at bridge building and divide crossing. What might be used to construct bridges able to span this divide? What might those bridges look like and who is available to construct them? The following sections describe potential building materials, identify models, and discuss what makes this particular construction project so challenging.

Scholarship that Integrates

Faculty practitioners do not need nor do they benefit from traditional reviews of research pieces that establish the knowledge landscape within certain domains. That scholarship guides those currently at work or about to start work within that area. Practitioners need reviews that are much more functional. They need to know what topics researchers have considered, what is known about each, how they relate to each other, and what implications for practice the findings hold. Here are two examples that illustrate this kind of functional integrative scholarship.

Prince (2004) reviewed research on the most common forms of active learning. The piece starts with clear definitions (in a domain that is loosely and variously defined). Those definitions do exclude certain strategies and techniques, so it is not a comprehensive review but it is a clearly focused review of most of the major categories of active learning. A wide range of research evidence for each kind of active learning is considered and described briefly, with non-technical language. The piece makes clear where the weight of the evidence lays and what the implications for practice are. I have shared this article with many, many faculty and although some remain unconvinced of the power of active learning, they uniformly respond positively to the format and acknowledge that the article considers the evidence fairly and in potentially useful ways.

More recently, Prince joined forces with Felder (2006) to review a variety of instructional approaches they label "inductive teaching and learning methods" (123). Here again the definitions are clear, an expansive view of the literature is taken, findings are summed succinctly, and the case is made. It is interesting that these innovatively formatted but imminently useful reviews were put together by engineers, both noted pedagogical scholars, but still the work was done in a field far removed from education.

Even though this is precisely the kind of work that could be used to promote evidence-based practice, this particular building material remains in short supply and for good reasons. First, this is not easy scholarship and not all attempts to do it are successful. It is easy to oversimplify both the process and the results. It is easy to overgeneralize the findings. Different lines of inquiry (active learning exemplifies the wide diversity of research questions and methodological approaches) have not been examined collectively and so those surveying these knowledge domains are often assembling pieces that have not been put together previously. Good integrative scholarship does not dilute the intellectual integrity of what is known. It is the difference between examining a painting close up where all the details, colors, and techniques can be seen from inches away, and looking at the painting from across the room. It is the same painting, just seen from two different perspectives. Close-up descriptions may be more detailed but those from across the room are not easier to construct nor are they inherently less accurate.

Besides the intellectual challenge required to do integrative scholarship well, there are few incentives to build these knowledge blocks. Despite Boyer's (1990) widely acclaimed calls for broader definitions of scholarship, integrative scholarship is not generally rewarded or recognized institutionally or within disciplines, as Braxton, Luckey, and Hellend's (2002) research documents.

Finally, the location of this kind of work remains problematic. If this is not scholarship of particular interest to those pushing back knowledge frontiers in education, then doing the scholarship falls to practitioners or those who work with them (like educational developers). Outlets for the work of those scholars exist mostly within the disciplines. The two examples cited earlier were published in the *Journal of Engineering Education*, obviously to the great benefit of that field but of no benefit to those in other fields who have no reason to read this particular pedagogical periodical. The integrative scholarship that could do much to make practice evidence-based transcends the disciplines but there are few cross-disciplinary publication outlets and those that do exist are not widely read.

Scholarship that Applies

In addition to work that integrates research in ways that make clear what is known about the basic elements of practice (like pedagogical methods, for example), practitioners also need work that explores how established knowledge should be applied in practice. Once again, this is not generally a task of interest to those doing the research. As a result, those applications rarely appear in the educational research literature. Here as well, the task falls to others.

The practitioner's pedagogical literature (mostly written by faculty within disciplines) is replete with articles that offer advice and tell faculty what should be done about various aspects of instruction. So far, the qualifications of those offering the advice and the bases on which the advice rests (individual or collective experience, or quantitative or qualitative analyses) have not been addressed in the literature. This means a lot of what is recommended is not as evidence–based as it ought to be.

Nonetheless, there are some fine examples in the literature. Based on her extensive knowledge of educational psychology, Svinicki (1998) helps students (and their teachers) understand grades. She offers concrete advice on constructing grading systems, includes illustrations, and proposes how grades and grading should be discussed with students. The principles proposed in the article can help faculty in every discipline deal with this challenging aspect of instruction. Van Gelder (2005) draws lessons from the cognitive sciences and proposes a set of principles for teaching students to think critically. This is a super piece that not only helps faculty better understand the processes involved, it enables them to put some perspective around the frustration and discouragement that often accompany efforts. Van Gelder's first lesson is: "critical thinking is hard" (42).

As with scholarship that integrates, good application scholarship requires intellectual effort. Just like scholarship that integrates, scholarship that applies is not generally rewarded or recognized. And finally, as before, the location of the work is also problematic, although perhaps less so. Both the Svinicki and van Gelder examples were published in *College Teaching*, a cross-disciplinary journal (with a very small circulation given its broad intended audience). The principles that should govern good grading practices do transcend disciplines—no discipline-specific application is needed. That is less true when the topic is critical thinking. What students are being asked to think about influences thinking processes. The van Gelder piece has value because it provides the broad context, the general principles out of which more specific applications can be derived. However, no article that I know of takes those principles and applies them within a variety of specific contexts. If more specific applications are made, they are done by individual readers.

Scholarship that Breaks the Rules

Beyond scholarship that integrates and scholarship that applies, we also need scholarship that breaks the rules. For the most part, academic scholarship is disseminated via books, refereed journal articles, and at conferences. Even though those venues are familiar to faculty and have credibility, so far they haven't been particularly effective mechanisms for communicating the evidence needed to inform practice in the classroom.

Part of this failure is not related to the literature itself but is the result of the absence of norms and expectations for instructional growth for those who teach at the post-secondary level. Under the current system, at least in most North American contexts, there are few negative consequences if a faculty member opts not to read, study, or participate in any other kind of professional-development activity. In this very fundamental way, teaching is devalued by the way it is practised.

Given the absence of norms expecting the professional development of faculty, the literature must command attention on its own. The rules governing academic publication make this difficult to do. The writing doesn't make for good reading and article formats preclude author involvement and reader engagement.

In my book on pedagogical scholarship (Weimer 2006), I explore the characteristics of pedagogical literature that practitioners might be motivated to read. The work needs to address topics that are relevant, address questions that practitioners are asking, and offer concrete, specific suggestions. It also needs to be written in a style that engages readers. This does not mean it is work without intellectual integrity. We need high standards for pedagogical scholarship, but they should not be the same standards used to assess research work. This work fills a different need and should be measured by standards that reflect its purpose and goals.

If we allow that this scholarship can break the rules, we can consider other venues and formats; venues like newsletters, blogs, and other vehicles for the electronic exchange of information. We can let authors take positions and argue against current aspects of practice—like Kohn does so ably in both his books; one that takes on teachers' over reliance on extrinsic motivators (1993), and an earlier work that goes after the role of competition in learning environments (1986). These books point fingers and poke sticks at common beliefs that are reflected in widespread practices. They do not always convince faculty to change but they motivate reflection, analysis, and genuine discussion. They are the kind of books faculty can be persuaded to read.

Conclusion

It is a tragedy that classroom practice at the post-secondary level is generally not evidence-based, not informed by what is known. The absence of that evidence is one of the most significant ways in which teaching is devalued, even by those committed to excellent practice. Until practice becomes evidence-based, teaching at the post-secondary level will not gain the status it deserves as a profession.

REFERENCES

Bacon, D.R. and K.A. Stewart. 2006. How Fast Do Students Forget What They Learned in Consumer Behavior? A Longitudinal Study. *Journal of Marketing Education* 28:181-92.

Boyer, E.L. 1990. *Scholarship Reconsidered.* Lawrenceville, NJ: Princeton University Press.

Braxton, J.M., W. Luckey, and P. Helland. 2002. *Institutionalizing a Broader View of Scholarship Through Boyer's Four Domains.* ASHE-ERIC Higher Education Report 29(2). San Francisco: Jossey-Bass.

Candy, P.C. 1991. *Self-Direction for Lifelong Learning.* San Francisco: Jossey-Bass.

Finkelstein, M.J., R.K. Seal, and J. Schuster. 1998. *The New Academic Generation: A Profession in Transformation.* Baltimore: The Johns Hopkins University Press.

Kember, D. and L. Gow. 1994. Orientations to Teaching and Their Effect on the Quality of Student Learning. *Journal of Higher Education* 65(1):58-74.

Kohn, A. 1986. *No Contest: The Case Against Competition.* Boston: Houghton Mifflin.

Kohn, A. 1993. *Punished by Rewards.* Boston: Houghton Mifflin.

Lewis, S.E. and J.E. Lewis. 2005. Departing from Lectures: An Evaluation of a Peer-Led Guided Inquiry Alternative. *Journal of Chemical Education* 82(1):135-39.

McCreary, C.L., M.F. Golde, and R. Koeske. 2006. Peer Instruction in General Chemistry Laboratory: Assessment of Student Learning. *Journal of Chemical Education* 83(5):804-10.

Nunn, C.E. 1996. Discussion in the College Classroom: Triangulating Observational and Survey Results. *Journal of Higher Education* 67(3):243-66.

Perry, R.P. 1997. Perceived Control in College Students: Implications for Instruction in Higher Education. In *Effective Teaching in Higher Education: Research and Practice,* ed. R.P. Perry and J.C. Smart. New York: Agathon Press.

Pintrich, P.R. 2003. A Motivational Perspective on the Role of Student Motivation in Learning and Teaching Contexts. *Journal of Educational Psychology* 95(4):667-86.

Prince, M. 2004. Does Active Learning Work? A Review of the Research. *Journal of Engineering Education* 93(3):223-31.

Prince, M. and R. Felder. 2006. Inductive Teaching and Learning Methods: Definitions, Comparisons, and Research Bases. *Journal of Engineering Education* 95(2):123-38.

Springer, L., M.E. Stanne, and S.S. Donovan. 1999. Effects of Small-Group Learning on Undergraduates in Science, Mathematics, Engineering, and Technology: A Meta-Analysis. *Review of Educational Research* 69(1):21-51.

Svinicki, M.D. 1998. Helping Students Understand Grades. *College Teaching* 46(3):101-05.

van Gelder, T. 2005. Teaching Critical Thinking: Some Lessons from Cognitive Science. *College Teaching* 53(1):41-6.

Weimer, M. 2002. *Learner-Centered Teaching: Five Key Changes to Practice.* San Francisco: Jossey-Bass.

Weimer, M. 2006. *Enhancing Scholarly Work on Teaching and Learning.* San Francisco: Jossey-Bass.

Woods, D.R. 1987. How Might I Teach Problem Solving? In *Developing Critical Thinking and Problem-Solving Abilities,* No. 30 in the New Directions for Teaching and Learning Series, ed. J.E. Stice. San Francisco: Jossey-Bass.

Appendix to References

Bacon, D.R. and K.A. Stewart 2006: interesting longitudinal design which shows that after two years, marketing majors in a consumer behavior course had lost virtually all the content from that course.

Boyer, E.L. 1990: seminal work proposing a redefinition of scholarship that broadens its scope and purpose.

Braxton, J.M., W. Luckey, and P. Helland 2002: survey research that looks at the extent to which institutions are using Boyer's broader definitions of scholarship in their assessments of faculty work, finding that the preeminence of discovery-based scholarship still prevails.

Candy, P.C. 1991: a wonderful compilation of work on independent, self-directed learning; a great appendix contains 13 research-identified characteristics of autonomous, self-regulated learners who bear little resemblance to the students most regularly seen in class.

Finkelstein, M.J., R.K. Seal, and J. Schuster 1998: a giant survey of US faculty that looks at a wide range of personal and professional characteristics; documenting that three-quarters list the lecture as their primary instructional method.

Kember, D. and L. Gow 1994: early work in a now established line of research documenting that teaching methods affect approaches taken to learning; a strong content orientation that focuses on coverage makes it more likely that students will use surface approaches.

Kohn, A. 1986; Kohn, A. 1993: both of Kohn's books make strong cases against current educational practices; in the first book he takes on competition, and in the second it's extrinsic motivation used in grades and points. Both books are extremely well written and effectively encourage reflection and discussion.

Lewis, S.E. and J.E. Lewis 2005: in this study, one lecture per week was replaced by a guided discussion; students in the guided-discussion sections scored as well on a comprehensive final as those students who listened to a full complement of lectures.

McCreary, C.L., M.F. Golde, and R. Koeske 2006: in this study, students (who had taken the lab previously and been trained) led lab sections and in several ways students taking those lab session performed at higher levels than students in conventionally run labs; in no area measured by the researchers did they perform less well.

Nunn, C.E. 1996: a study of participation in college classrooms; documenting that in most classrooms, very little time is devoted to student interaction.

Perry, R.P. 1997: part of a line of research showing that when students perceive a loss of control, that orientation affects academic achievement; even when taught by an effective teacher, those effects were not ameliorated.

Pintrich, P.R. 2003: a well-organized, comprehensive review of research on motivation; noteworthy also because it spells out implications for practice based on the findings.

Prince, M. 2004: a marvelously functional review of research that offers clear definitions, succinct and nontechnical summaries of research findings, and implications for practice; this is the article to share with faculty still unconvinced that active learning makes a difference.

Prince, M. and R. Felder 2006: inductive methods reviewed here include inquiry learning, problem-based learning, project-based learning, case-based teaching, discovery learning, and just-in-time teaching; another well-organized and useful review of research with implications for practice clearly spelled out.

Springer, L., M.E. Stanne, and S.S. Donovan 1999: a meta-analysis of studies that looks at the effects of small-group learning experiences in undergraduate science, math, engineering, and technology courses; finding that small-group experiences promote greater academic achievement, more favorable attitudes toward learning, and increased persistence in these courses.

Svinicki, M.D. 1998: uses educational research to identify viable grading systems and proposes ways to discuss grading issues with students; a great example of scholarship that integrates and applies educational research.

van Gelder, T. 2005: extrapolates from research a series of lessons that should guide efforts to teach critical thinking skills; a great example of scholarship that integrates and applies educational research.

Weimer, M. 2002: describes aspects of current practice that need to change in order for teaching to become more learning- and learner-centred.

Weimer, M. 2006: looks at practitioner pedagogical scholarship that is published mostly within disciplines; describes its characteristics, identifies examples, proposes standards, and suggests what this scholarship contributes to instructional practice.

Woods, D.R. 1987: research showing that solving problems does not necessarily develop an explicit understanding of problem-solving skills.

> *How research on student learning can enhance the learning environment.*

5

RESEARCH ON STUDENT LEARNING: CONVERGING AND DIVERGING MESSAGES

Alenoush Saroyan

INTRODUCTION

The two chapters in this section are about enhancing the quality of teaching and learning. They are explicit demonstrations, albeit different in nature, of how research can inform teaching practice and more importantly, enhance the process of student learning.

Sari Lindblom-Ylänne's chapter is written from the perspective of an educational psychologist whereas Maryellen Weimer's is written from the perspective of a professor of biology, turned faculty developer. Dr. Lindblom-Ylänne describes the trajectory of a research agenda that has unfolded in the manner of design experiments (Brown 1992; Collins 1992) which aim at "develop[ing] a class of theories about both the process of learning and the means that are designed to support that learning" at every level, from the individual student to the larger system (Cobb et al. 2003, 10). True to this definition, over the years Dr. Lindblom-Ylänne has attempted to contribute to the theoretical literature on student approaches to learning. Moreover, she has studied the influence of learning environments, including the disciplinary community, on learning in Finnish post-secondary education in general and at the research-intensive University of Helsinki in particular.

A central characteristic of design experiments is "involving both researcher and practitioner in the process [of learning and designing learning environments] ... to bring about meaningful change in the context of practice" (The Design-Based Research Collective 2003, 6). Thus, Dr. Weimer's scholarship can also be considered to be in the same genre although her partnership with educational researchers and practitioners has not been in the traditional sense. Her significant contribution to improving teaching practice has been through the "translation" of research findings from the educational as well as disciplinary research literature into practical and concrete recommendations and making these accessible to and usable by professors from every discipline.

What are the key messages that these two chapters convey and in what ways do these messages converge or diverge? How comprehensive are the presented points of views and in what ways can they be complemented? What are the implications of this type of research in general for improving the quality of post-secondary education? What pressing issues need to be addressed in light of the discussed findings as we forge ahead in the 21st century? These questions frame the discussion presented in this chapter.

Synthesis of Key Messages: Converging Messages

Approaches to Learning. A salient message that both Sari Lindblom-Ylänne and Maryellen Weimer convey is that students' learning styles or their approaches to learning influence the way they learn and the extent to which they can retain the learned material and transfer that learning to new and different contexts.

One aspect of Dr. Lindblom-Ylänne's research concerns deep and surface learning, concepts first introduced by Marton and Säljö (1976) and subsequently elaborated on by Entwistle and Ramsden (1983) and Biggs (1985). Surface learning is associated with memorizing isolated facts, accepting disseminated information without questioning, and developing superficial understanding of concepts that does not last long. In contrast, deep learning involves the ability to critically analyze new ideas, create links between newly learning material and prior knowledge, retain knowledge, and transfer and apply it in new and different contexts (Houghton 2004). The distinction between these two types of learning is somewhat similar to the levels of learning reflected in taxonomies such as those developed by Bloom (1956), and LaSere Erickson and Weltner Strommer (1991). Both represent levels of learning in sequenced hierarchies: the former in terms of six levels—knowledge, understanding, application, analysis, synthesis, and evaluation; and the latter in terms of three levels—knowing, understanding, and thinking.

Sari Lindblom-Ylänne also links her discussion of learning approaches to regulation activities and study orchestrations. Both concepts underscore the agency of the learner; the ability to position oneself vis-à-vis the learning task, and take control of and responsibility for learning if one has a repertoire of strategies from which to draw.

Maryellen Weimer's discussion of similar concepts is framed by the notion of passive and active approaches to learning. She asserts that faculty's perception of most students is that they remain passive and uninvolved in class, soak in disseminated information, and regurgitate it back without meaningful understanding. While Dr. Weimer does not present empirical evidence to determine the prevalence of this view of the learner among faculty, there are other references in the literature that characterize students as passive learners who do not actively engage in the learning process either because they do not want to or are incapable of invoking higher-order regulatory mechanisms. For instance, in their taxonomy of teaching methods, Schank and Jona (1991) refer to the "sponge method" where the student is perceived to have no agency or volition in the learning process and is fed information. Others (see, e.g., Kember 1997) have characterized passivity not just by the role assumed by the student but in terms of other factors that reinforce this passivity. These factors or dimensions include: the "teacher" who is cast in the role of presenter of information; "teaching", which is depicted as transfer of knowledge; "content," which is considered to be restricted because of curricular boundaries; and "knowledge," which is depicted as a construct possessed only by the lecturer (262).

Learning and the Environment. A second theme common in both chapters pertains to the influence of the broader learning environment, including teaching methods, on the strategies and approaches that students adopt in the learning process. Both authors are right on the mark in identifying the environment as an important factor in enhancing student learning. Menges and Austin (2001), in their seminal review chapter on teaching in higher education which appeared in the *Handbook of Research on Teaching (Fourth Edition)*, identified the teaching and learning environment as "... the most important area—the one from which research will be most revealing and will have the greatest effect—[and] ... where explicit attention is given simultaneously to learners, to teachers, and to content" (1122).

Dr. Lindblom-Ylänne refers to findings from her own research regarding the compatibility between the individual and the environment. She asserts that congruence between the students' approaches to learning and environmental factors (e.g., approaches to teaching, assessment, academic-program demands) can influence the nature and quality of learning positively. Conversely, friction between the students' approaches to learning and environmental factors can influence learning negatively. She cites Biggs (1985) in support of the argument that surface and deep approaches to learning are institutional creations. The interpretation of her findings from students in her own institution is that contextual factors, perhaps inadvertently, may influence students to select strategies and goals that are less likely to yield meaningful learning.

Dr. Weimer presents a similar view. She concurs with the assertion that learning approaches can be a reaction to the environment. She frames her chapter within the context of perceptions that faculty might have about problems associated with student learning and makes the case that these problems can be reinforced by non-optimal approaches to teaching. She further asserts that by manipulating various aspects of the environment, students can be rendered more active, become more confident as learners, develop basic study skills, and become more intrinsically motivated and passionate about learning.

In addition to the two themes highlighted above, the two chapters cross paths, albeit indirectly, on a number of other constructs. One such construct is self-regulation and the extent to which students take responsibility for their own learning and engage in processes and actions that lead them to attaining their academic goals. While Dr. Lindblom-Ylänne describes degrees of self-regulation, Dr. Weimer focuses on the absence of self-regulation and uses terms such as "dependency" and lack of "learner confidence" to emphasize the power of external factors (e.g., professor, curriculum) in controlling and directing student learning. She asserts that educational contexts today promote greater levels of dependency because almost everything is outside the control of students—from the selection of content, to in-class activities, to participation and assessment. This leaves little time and opportunity for students to develop independent study habits and higher-order cognitive abilities.

The constructs, characterizing ways of learning and the role and agency of the student in the process, described in the two chapters are a reminder to educators that student learning is not just about content learning. It is also about learning how to learn, and being able to invoke strategies that will lead to the development of complex cognitive functions such as critical thinking and problem solving. These and similar skills ought to be transferable from one context to the next and applicable in a lifetime. They comprise the "knowledge" that would be usable in the future unlike some content knowledge that is likely to become obsolete with time.

Synthesis of Key Messages: Diverging Messages

The diverging messages conveyed in the two chapters are partly due to the differing perspectives of the authors. Sari Lindblom-Ylänne's chapter is a retrospective of a personal research agenda, the focus of which has been student learning and ways in which it can be enhanced. Maryellen Weimer's, on the other hand, is written from the perspective of a consumer of educational research. The chapter captures her passion about teaching. It highlights her scholarship spanning more than two decades, aimed at making sense of educational research on teaching and learning in higher education, synthesizing it, and disseminating it to faculty across disciplines. She asserts that faculty practitioners neither need nor benefit from a traditional review of research pieces that "establish the knowledge landscape within certain domains." What they need instead is a synthesis of research, explained in layman's terms so that they can utilize the information in their own teaching.

Not surprisingly, the literature these two authors cite is disparate with only one common citation (Kember and Gow 1994) shared between the two. Dr. Lindblom-Ylänne draws on the work of primarily European, including British, higher-education researchers. Dr. Weimer casts a wider net for her references and includes among them authors, researchers, and teachers outside mainstream educational-research circles. For instance, she includes Kohn's (1986) compilation of empirical studies on competition as well as studies on teaching and learning carried out by subject-matter experts: Bacon and Stewart (2006) in marketing; McCreary, Golde, and Koeske (2006) in chemistry; Prince (2004) in engineering.

Together these complementary chapters represent a valuable set of readings for researchers and practitioners alike. They demonstrate that teaching and learning are two sides of the same coin and both need to be considered if the aim is to gain insight into ways in which teaching can enhance student learning.

Complementary Perspectives

Educational researchers are notorious for two things. One is conducting research that practitioners do not find useful (Lagemann and Shulman 1999). The second is conducting research in silos. Even those who investigate the same phenomena at different levels (e.g., K-12 versus tertiary) typically do not cross reference one another (Entwistle et al. 2000) or "take full advantage of these research findings" (Kane, Sandretto, and Heath 2002, 343), regardless of how relevant findings in one context can be to another.

The authors of the preceding two chapters are clearly not culpable insofar as the application of research to practice is concerned. Dr. Lindblom-Ylänne has built her career intertwining research with development. Her investigations about study orchestration, and self-regulatory habits of medical and law students and variations in approaches to learning in different disciplines such as medicine, law, social sciences, and theology have been carried out within the context of her institution with a view to enhancing learning. Similarly, Dr. Weimer has dedicated her career to synthesizing and disseminating what she considers useful findings from various domains in a language that is comprehensible to the broader academic community. There is room, however, within this discussion to introduce complementary research from other contexts.

Clearly, there are differences between teaching and learning in higher education and teaching and learning at the school level—e.g., differences in the roles and missions of schools versus universities (Menges and Austin 2001); differences in identity—teacher versus subject-matter expert (Altbach and Lewis 1996); and differences in the range of disciplines and the relevance of pedagogical content knowledge in teaching (Shulman 1987). However, there is likely to be as much in common across levels as there are variations (Entwistle and Walker 2000), and it is in this regard that additional perspectives are suggested.

Many of the constructs presented in Sari Lindblom-Ylänne's chapter have been the topic of recent seminal publications in psychology and educational psychology. Among these is work on self-regulation by Zimmerman (2008), Bandura's (2008) work on the influence of different contexts on personal agency, and the comprehensive review of self-regulated learning (SRL) models by Finnish researchers Puustinen and Pulkkinen (2001). The SRL models included in the latter review are distinguished on the basis of the theories they are based on and as a consequence of the definition they attach to SRL: goal-oriented definition, as is the case of Boekaert's (1999), Pintrich's (2000), and Zimmerman's (1989a, b) models; and metacognitively monitored process, as is the case of Winne's (1996) and Borkowski, Chan, and Muthukrishna's (2000) models. These different theoretical lenses are particularly complementary to Dr. Lindblom-Ylänne's research.

Dr. Lindblom-Ylänne's work also references epistemic beliefs as an important influence on the way in which students understand and participate in the learning act. Recent publications on the topic by Muis (2007), and Schommer-Aikins, Duell, and Hutter (2005), and the seminal work of Hofer and Pintrich (1997, 2002) on the development of epistemological theories as well as Schommer's (1998) research reiterate that "… epistemic beliefs affect achievement mediated through self-regulation … [this model] accounts for how students design their approaches to learning and adapt those approaches as feedback about progress becomes available (Muis 2007, 173).

Dr. Lindblom-Ylänne's acknowledgment of assessment as a significant factor in leading students to make choices in the learning strategies they adopt is also notable. The seminal work of Shepard (2000), Bransford (see, e.g., Bransford and Brown 2001) and Pellegrino (see, e.g., Pellegrino, Baxter, and Glaser 1999) are extremely valuable in that they provide thoughtful insights on the implications of understanding how students learn from curriculum design, instruction, and assessment.

Much of the literature cited above is also complementary to Dr. Weimer's chapter. A logical extension to Dr. Weimer's work, for example, could be a discussion of faculty conceptions of teaching. Epistemic beliefs, conception, or views on teaching (Ramsden 1992) lead faculty to the choices they make in their teaching approaches (Saroyan 2000; Saroyan,

Dagenais, and Zhou 2008). Gow and Kember (1993) found that in addition to teaching methods, conceptions strongly influenced how the learning task was defined and what the corresponding assessment and workload demands were (69).

Ramsden's (1992) classification of teaching conceptions or, in his words, "theories of teaching," is often illuminating to faculty because it makes them realize that their actions are firmly grounded in their beliefs. His first theory depicts teaching as the "transmission of authoritative content or the demonstration of procedures," casting students as "passive recipients of the wisdom of a single speaker" (111). His second theory conceptualizes teaching as organizing student activity; "activity in students is regarded as panacea" (113). Students' active role is seen as the end and not a means to intended learning. His third theory casts teaching as making learning possible, and faculty as facilitators of that learning. The implication of this view is that faculty need to make intentional efforts to create optimal learning environments for all students and to engage them in activities aligned with goals of learning and assessment. "Teaching involves finding out about students' misunderstandings, intervening to change them, and creating a context of learning which encourages students actively to engage with the subject matter" (114).

Just as the literature on student epistemic beliefs is providing insight into approaches to learning, so too is the literature on conceptions of teaching (Kane, Sandretto, and Heath 2002; Pajares 1992). Knowing about the influence of personal beliefs on approaches to teaching is likely to be an eye-opener for Dr. Weimer's target audience: the subject-matter expert professor. It is also the first step if a change is to be made in one's teaching approach. Changing entrenched beliefs, however, is not an easy feat. Several researchers (Block and Hazelip 1995; Kagan 1992; Pajares 1992) have asserted that teachers' belief systems are grounded in their personal experiences and are, therefore, highly resistant to change. Herein lays a second complementary section to this chapter; the notion of change, and conditions under which it is more likely to happen.

In this regard, the work of two researchers from disparate areas comes to mind. The first is Windschitl's (2002) framework of dilemmas, elaborated specifically within the context of school teaching and, more specifically, school reforms and the adoption of constructivist approaches by school teachers. He discusses four dilemmas, the first of which is conceptual. This is the case when the teacher (or professor) lacks a conceptual understanding of the "philosophical, psychological, epistemological underpinnings" (132) of the approach. Drawing from Maryellen Weimer's and Sari Lindblom-Ylänne's chapters, a faculty member not having specific knowledge about deep and surface, or active and passive, learning or self-regulation would be an example of a conceptual dilemma. Representative questions of concern for professors might be: Which definition of deep and surface approach is appropriate for my course? Do all self-regulated activities lead to deep learning? What does active learning involve?

The second is a pedagogical dilemma. This implies the ability to design learning environments, activities, and curricula to correspond with a specific orientation, or philosophical and/or theoretical perspective. Representative questions of concern for professors might be: What does it mean for me to facilitate the development of independent learners? How can I engage students in active learning that is meaningful and leads to the development of higher-order thinking skills?

The third is a cultural dilemma, representing the roles assigned to or adopted by the student and the teacher/professor and ensuing expectations in the teaching and learning context. Representative questions of concern for professors might be: How can I trust students to assume responsibility for their own learning? Will I be comfortable with not being the "sage on stage" and relegating a more prominent role to students?

Finally, the fourth is a political dilemma and this implies reconciling with other stakeholders or system demands to teach for understanding. Representative questions of concern for professors in this regard might be: Will my students be prepared for the next course if I do not teach all the content I have planned to teach? Would teaching for understanding disadvantage students who are headed to graduate school and need to take GREs or other exams?

Closer to the higher-education context is the work of Centra (1993), in particular his model for change, articulated within the context of faculty development and formative evaluation. He suggests that in order for change to occur, four conditions need to be met. The first is that the person (i.e., faculty member) seeking knowledge must perceive the knowledge to be important and valid such that it would provide insight into one's strengths and weaknesses as a teacher. The second is that the source that provides the knowledge is credible. The third is being able to make effective change in light of the new knowledge gained. Finally, the fourth condition is a motivation component, extrinsic or intrinsic, so that faculty would be enticed to invest time and resources in embracing teaching improvement.

Understanding what potential obstacles might hinder change and what conditions need to be present in order to facilitate change are important concepts for faculty. Windschitl's (2002) dilemmas framework and Centra's (1993) model for change are interesting complements to Dr. Weimer's chapter for two reasons. First, they highlight teaching and the teacher and the significant role they play with respect to student learning. Second, they offer theoretical insight into why professors may not readily embrace or enact change directives. Specifically, they suggest that in addition to the observations made by Dr. Weimer, we must also consider the extent to which (a) faculty agree that these problems may have something to do with their teaching, and (b) they are capable of making changes to their teaching approach.

Finally, the findings and recommendations presented by Sari Lindblom-Ylänne and Maryellen Weimer are consistent with the current learning-sciences perspective, summarized concisely by Sawyer (2006) under the following subheadings:

- The importance of deeper conceptual understanding;
- Focusing on learning in addition to teaching;
- Creating learning environments;
- The importance of building on learners' prior knowledge;
- The importance of reflection.

Future Research on Student Learning

The 21st century is a new era with formidable challenges and unparalleled opportunities. The necessity to make the most out of diminishing resources has never been as profound. Corresponding pressures are being felt across the board, even in the resource-rich Ivy League institutions (see The Economist 2009). Student diversity and increase in enrollments, both of which are likely to further grow with the current economic downturn, behoove all educators to develop a more profound understanding of learning and the range of student needs. Global competition necessitates that, as Canadian institutions, we maintain our competitive edge and remain cognizant of major international developments beyond our borders; in particular, those shepherded by the Bologna process in the European Union, the Programme on Institutional Management in Higher Education (IMHE), and the Forum on Higher Education of the Organization for Economic Co-operation and Development (OECD). It also necessitates that we keep an open mind and ear to what competencies are required for our students to be successful as life-long learners and professionals anywhere they choose to fulfill their aspirations.

We have known for a while that higher-order thinking skills (e.g., problem-solving, critical and analytical thinking) are competencies that university graduates need to develop in addition to subject matter knowledge. But today's employers demand more. The Conference Board of Canada highlights three skill sets in its 2000+ bulletin (The Conference Board of Canada 2000). These include fundamental skills (e.g., communicate, manage information, use numbers, think, and solve problems), personal management skills (demonstrate positive attitudes and behaviours, be responsible, be adaptable, learn continuously, and work safely), and teamwork skills (work with others, participate in projects and tasks). A survey of US employers concerning weaknesses they perceive in Ph.D. holders highlight other issues (cited in Nicolas 2008). These include:

- Fear of risk taking;
- Not valuing time;

- Not establishing priorities;
- Not seeing the big picture;
- Poor "people skills;"
- Failing to move beyond personal curiosity;
- Lacking openness to other problems and needs;
- Poor project management.

What implications do these demands have on the ways we teach and the ways our students learn? What are we doing now that is different from what we did before, in an era where many of the parameters were different? What are the most pressing and precipitous research questions that we still need to answer about teaching and learning in order to address these needs and improve quality?

There is evidence that these new demands are having some impact on teaching and learning practices. The increase in the number of problem-based learning (PBL) programs across disciplines, the reconceptualization of doctoral programs (see, e.g., the Carnegie Initiative on the Doctorate [The Carnegie Foundation for the Advancement of Teaching 2009]), and the pervasive use of technology in teaching and learning are all evidence of change in curricula, modes of delivery, and learning experiences of students. The basis on which these and other changes are made ought to be rigorous research. In other words, research is fundamental to advancing our knowledge about university teaching and learning but it will not be sufficient to change practice if findings are disseminated to only a very limited group of scholars who have similar interests and, as a result, remain obscure and shelved in databases and libraries.

CONCLUSION

In order to effect change for the better, we (as practicing or aspiring educational researchers, educational developers, administrators, or policy makers) need to ask ourselves: In what ways can we contribute to the educational debates that are shaping the world around us? In Berliner's (2003) words: "... entering policy debates may be an obligation of members of a profession, an obligation that goes right along with the rights and privileges that are granted to professionals, particularly those that belong to the professoriate...." (3). We each need to ask ourselves: In what ways can research inform policy regarding specifically those factors that influence teaching and learning? We need to make sure that research findings are brought to bear and that our voices are heard when decisions are made about: increasing class sizes, the systematic pedagogical development of faculty, the integration of technology in teaching and learning, the choice of one type of curriculum versus another (e.g., PBL versus traditional), and on modes of assessment. A small step is being taken to this end. There is an initiative underway, spearheaded by the provosts of Canada's research-intensive universities (G13 Research), the aim of which is to create a repository of research on higher education with potential policy implications that can inform senior university administrators about decisions they make regarding teaching and learning.

Educational research can further be associated with practice if it can account for the influence of contexts, the emergent and complex nature of outcomes that the 21st century demands, and the incompleteness of knowledge about which factors are relevant for prediction (Robinson 1998). One way to do this is to use design-based research methodologies which enable us to study a *"learning ecology*—a complex, interacting system involving multiple elements of different types and levels—by designing its elements and by anticipating how these elements function together to support learning" (Cobb et al. 2003, 9). Both Drs. Lindblom-Ylänne and Weimer advocate developing an understanding of the complete picture by suggesting that teaching and learning ought not be studied as isolated phenomena but as complementary constructs mediated by the environment. An even more holistic view is to broaden the environment to include the system within which teaching and learning happens. Examining a system (e.g., an institution) from a Cultural Historical Activity Theory (CHAT)[1] perspective could afford the possibility to gain insight into the contradictions that exist in the system and which may impede teaching and learning in different ways. Existing policies and resources are examples of factors that may negatively affect teaching and learning regardless of how perfectly all other factors are lined up. Taking these factors into account is fundamental to understanding why teachers teach in a particular way, why the environment is laid out in the way it is, and what the roles and responsibilities of each stakeholder are in the process of teaching and learning.[2]

Research questions from this perspective would address Berliner's (2003) concern about our role as professionals in guiding policy decisions and the possibility of considering the "learning ecology" as espoused by Cobb et al. (2003). Potential questions posed within the context of design-experiment methodology would "emphasize function in a realized context," contribute to the advancement of both practice and theory, and be applicable to a range of settings including teacher-experimenter and student, classroom experiments, faculty and educational development initiatives, institutional restructuring, and the like (Cobb et al. 2003, 9). The holistic perspective of design-experiments would satisfy Dr. Lindblom-Ylänne's concern about studying learning and teaching separately. The pragmatic aspect would address Dr. Weimer's concern about the relevance and use of research findings to practice. Most importantly, this type of systematic research would contribute to the development of theories in higher education in domain-specific areas and, in so doing, would engage professors from fields other than education in collaborative investigations to improve the quality of teaching and learning.

Notes

[1] This theory was first developed by Vygotsky (1986) and elaborated upon further by his colleagues and students, Leont'ev (1978) and Luria (1981). CHAT provides a comprehensive framework for investigating everyday work (Engeström 1987). The theoretical terms of the activity system include agent (subject), object/outcome, tools used (means of production), division of labor, community, and rules.

[2] An elaboration of the application of this theory to studying teaching and learning in universities can be found in the research proposal by Saroyan (2008), funded by the Social Sciences and Humanities Research Council of Canada.

References

Altbach, P.G. and L.S. Lewis. 1996. The Academic Profession in International Perspective. In *The International Academic Profession: Portraits from Fourteen Countries*, ed. P.G. Altbach, 3-48. Princeton, NJ: Carnegie Foundation for the Advancement of Teaching.

Bacon, D.R. and K.A. Stewart. 2006. How Fast Do Students Forget What They Learned in Consumer Behavior? A Longitudinal Study. *Journal of Marketing Education* 28:181-92.

Bandura, A. 2008. Reconstrual of "Free Will" From the Agentic Perspective of Social Cognitive Theory. In *Are We Free? Psychology and Free Will*, ed. J. Baer. Oxford Scholarship Online. doi: 10.1093/acprof:oso/9780195189636.001.0001

Berliner, D.C. 2003. Educational Psychology as a Policy Science: Thoughts on the Distinction Between a Discipline and a Profession. *Canadian Journal of Educational Administration and Policy* 26(April). Accessed 4 January 2010 at http://www.umanitoba.ca/publications/cjeap/articles/miscellaneousArticles/berliner.html

Biggs, J. 1985. The Role of Metalearning in Study Processes. *British Journal of Educational Psychology* 55:185-212.

Block, J.H. and K. Hazelip. 1995. Teachers' Beliefs and Belief Systems. In *International Encolpaedia of Teaching and Teacher Education*, ed. L.W. Anderson, 25-8. New York, NY: Pergamon Press.

Bloom, B.S. 1956. *Taxonomy of Educational Objectives. Handbook I: The Cognitive Domain*. New York: David McKay Co. Inc.

Boekaerts, M. 1999. Self-Regulated Learning: Where We Are Today. *International Journal of Educational Research* 31:445-57.

Borokowski, J.G., L.K.S. Chan, and N. Muthukrishna. 2000. A Process-Oriented Model of Metacognition: Links between Motivation and Executive Functioning. In *Issues in the Measurement of Metacognition*, ed. G. Shraw and J. Impara. Lincoln, Nebraska: Buros Institute of Mental Measurements, University of Nebraska.

Bransford, J. and A. L. Brown, eds. 2001. *How People Learn*. Washington, DC: National Academy Press.

Brown, A.L. 1992. Design Experiments: Theoretical and Methodological Challenges in Creating Complex Interventions in Classroom Settings. *Journal of the Learning Sciences* 2:141-78.

The Carnegie Foundation for the Advancement of Teaching. 2009. Professional and Graduate Education. Accessed 1 May 2009 at http://www.carnegiefoundation. org/previous-work/professional-graduate-education

Centra, J.A. 1993. *Reflective Faculty Evaluation: Enhancing Teaching and Determining Faculty Effectiveness*. San Francisco: Jossey-Bass.

Cobb, P., J. Confrey, A. diSessa, R. Lehrer, and L. Schauble. 2003. Design Experiments in Educational Research. *Educational Researcher* 32(1):9-13.

Collins, A. 1992. Toward a Design Science of Education. In *New Directions in Educational Technology*, ed. E. Scanlon and T. O'Shea. New York: Springer-Verlag.

The Conference Board of Canada. 2000. *Employability Skills 2000+*. Accessed 17 December 2009 at http://www.conferenceboard.ca/topics/education/ learning-tools/employability-skills.aspx

The Design-Based Research Collective. 2003. Design-Based Research: An Emerging Paradigm for Educational Inquiry. *Educational Researcher* 32(1).5-8.

The Economist. 2009. December 13th-19th. Ivory Tower Infernos. *The Economist* 389:88.

Engeström, Y. 1987. *Learning by Expanding: An Activity-Theoretical Approach to Developmental Research*. Helsinki, Finland: Orienta-Konsultit.

Entwistle, N. and P. Ramsden. 1983. *Understanding Student Learning*. London: Croom Helm.

Entwistle, N., D. Skinner, D. Entwistle, and S. Orr. 2000. Conceptions and Beliefs About Good Teaching. An Integration of Contrasting Research Areas. *Higher Education Research and Development* 19(1):5-26.

Entwistle, N. and P. Walker. 2000. Strategic Alertness and Expanded Awareness within Sophisticated Conceptions of Teaching. *Instructional Science* 28(5):335-61.

G13 Research. Accessed 4 September 2009 at https://g13research.dabbledb.com/ page/g13research/cJtvzodG

Gow, L. and D. Kember. 1993. Conceptions of Teaching and Their Relationship to Student Learning. *British Journal of Educational Psychology* 63:20-33.

Hofer, B. and P.R. Pintrich. 1997. The Development of Epistemological Theories: Beliefs about Knowledge and Knowing and their Relation to Learning. *Review of Educational Research* 67(1):88-140.

Hofer, B. and P.R. Pintrich, eds. 2002. *Personal Epistemology: The Psychology of Beliefs about Knowledge and Knowing*. Mahwah, NJ: Lawrence Erlbaum.

Houghton, W. 2004. *Engineering Subject Centre Guide: Learning and Teaching Theory for Engineering Academics*. Loughborough: HEA Engineering Subject Centre.

Kagan, D.1992. Implications of Research on Teacher Belief. *Educational Psychologist* 27(1):65-90.

Kane, R., S. Sandretto, and C. Heath. 2002. Telling Half the Story: A Critical Review of Research on the Teaching Beliefs and Practices of University Academics. *Review of Educational Research* 72(2):177-228.

Kember, D. 1997. The Reconceptualization of the Research into University Academics' Conceptions of Teaching. *Learning and Instruction* 7(3):255-75.

Kember, D. and L. Gow. 1994. Orientations to Teaching and Their Effect on the Quality of Student Learning. *Journal of Higher Education* 65(1):58-74.

Kohn, A. 1986. *No Contest: The Case against Competition*. Boston: Houghton Mifflin.

Lagemann, E.C. and L.S. Shulman, eds. 1999. *Issues in Education Research: Problems and Possibilities*. San Francisco: Jossey-Bass, 1999.

LaSere Erickson, B., and D. Weltner Strommer. 1991. *Teaching College Freshmen*. San Francisco: Jossey Bass.

Leont'ev, A.A. 1978. *Activity, Consciousness and Personality*. Englewood Cliffs, NJ: Prentice Hall.

Luria, A.R. 1981. *Language and Cognition*. New York, NY: John Wiley.

Marton, F. and R. Säljö. 1976. On Qualitative Differences in Learning: Outcomes and Processes. *British Journal of Educational Psychology* 46:4-11.

McCreary, C.L., M.F. Golde, and R. Koeske. 2006. Peer Instruction in General Chemistry Laboratory: Assessment of Student Learning. *Journal of Chemical Education* 83(5):804-10.

Menges, R.J. and A.E. Austin. (2001). Teaching in Higher Education. In *Handbook of Research on Teaching*, ed. V. Richardson, 1122-56. Washington, DC: American Educational Research Association.

Muis, K. 2007. The Role of Epistemic Beliefs in Self-Regulated Learning. *Educational Psychologist* 42(3):173-90.

Nicolas, J. 2008. Researchers for Tomorrow. *University Affairs*, 7 January.

Pajares, M.F. 1992. Teachers' Beliefs and Educational Research: Cleaning up a Messy Construct. *Review of Educational Research* 62(3):307-32.

Pellegrino, J., G. Baxter, and R. Glaser, eds. 1999. *Addressing the "Two Disciplines" Problems: Linking Theories of Cognition and Learning with Assessment and Instructional Practice*, Vol. 24, Review of Research in Education, ed. A. Iran-Nejad and P.D. Peterson. Washington, DC: American Educational Research Association.

Pintrich, P.R. 2000. The Role of Goal Orientation in Self-Regulated Learning. In *Handbook of Self-Regulation*, ed. M. Boekaerts, P.R. Pintrich, and M. Zeidner, 451-502. San Diego, CA: Academic.

Prince, M. 2004. Does Active Learning Work? A Review of the Research. *Journal of Engineering Education* 93(3):223-31.

Puustinen, M. and L. Pulkkinen. 2001. Models of Self-Regulated Learning: A Review. *Scandinavian Journal of Educational Research* 45(1):269-86.

Ramsden, P. 1992. *Learning to Teach in Higher Education*. London: Routledge.

Robinson, V. 1998. Methodology and the Research-Practice Gap. *Educational Researcher* 27(1):17-26.

Saroyan, A. 2000. The Lecturer: Working with Large Groups. In *Teaching Alone/ Teaching Together: Transforming the Structure of Teams for Teaching*, ed. J. Bess, 87-107. San Francisco: Jossey-Bass.

Saroyan, A. 2008. *University Teaching from an Activity Systems Perspective*. Research Proposal. Montreal: Social Sciences and Humanities Research Council of Canada. Accessed 7 December 2009 at http://herg.mcgill.ca/SSHRC_Activity_systems_proposal.html

Saroyan, A., J. Dagenais and Y. Zhou. 2008. Graduate Students' Conceptions of University Teaching and Learning: Formation for Change. *Instructional Science*. doi: 10.1007/s11251-008-9071-8

Sawyer, R.K. 2006. The New Science of Learning. In *The Cambridge Handbook of the Learning Sciences*, ed. R.K. Sawyer, 1-16. New York: Cambridge University Press.

Schank, R. and M. Jona. 1991. Empowering the Student: New Perspectives on the Design of Teaching Systems. *Journal of the Learning Sciences* 1(1):7-35.

Schommer, M. 1998. The Role of Adults' Beliefs About Knowledge in School, Work, and Everyday Life. In *Adult Learning and Development: Perspectives from Educational Psychology*, ed. M.C. Smith and T. Pourchot, 127-43. Mahwah, NJ: Lawrence Erlbaum Associates.

Schommer-Aikins, M., O.K. Duell, and R. Hutter. 2005. Epistemological Beliefs, Mathematical Problem-Solving, and Academic Performance of Middle School Students. *The Elementary School Journal* 105:289-304.

Shepard, L. 2000. The Role of Assessment in a Learning Culture. *Educational Researcher* 29(7):4-14.

Shulman, L.S. 1987. Knowledge of Teaching: Foundations of the New Reform. *Harvard Educational Review* 57(1):1-22.

Vygotsky, L. 1986. *Mind in Society: The Development of Higher Psychological Processes*. Translated by A. Kozulin, ed. Original work published in 1934. Cambridge, MA: MIT.

Windschitl, M. 2002. Framing Constructivism in Practice as the Negotiation of Dilemmas: An Analysis of the Conceptual, Pedagogical, Cultural, and Political Challenges Facing Teachers. *Review of Educational Research* 77(2):131-75.

Winne, P.H. 1996. A Metacognitive View of Individual Differences in Self-Regulated Learning. *Learning and Individual Differences* 8:327-53.

Zimmerman, B.J. 1989a. A Social Cognitive View of Self-Regulated Academic Learning. *Journal of Educational Psychology* 81:329-39.

Zimmerman, B.J. 1989b. Goal Setting: A Key Proactive Source of Academic Self-Regulation. In *Motivation and Self-Regulated Learning: Theory, Research, and Applications*, ed. D.H. Schunk and B.J. Zimmerman, 267-95. Mahwah, NJ: Lawrence Erlbaum Associates.

Zimmerman, B.J. 2008. Goal Setting: A Key Proactive Source of Academic Self-Regulation. In *Motivation and Self-Regulated Learning: Theory, Research, and Applications*, ed. D.H. Schunk and B.J. Zimmerman, 267-95. Mahwah, NJ: Lawrence Erlbaum Associates.

SECTION III

WHAT WE KNOW ABOUT HOW TEACHING AND LEARNING IMPACT ONE ANOTHER

SECTION COMMENTARY

W. Alan Wright

This section addresses the state of our knowledge about how teaching and learning impact one another, drawing on the vast research accomplishments and experiences of a stellar international trio of contributors: Keith Trigwell of the University of Sydney, Michael Prosser of the University of Hong Kong, and Jillian Kinzie of the Center for Postsecondary Research, National Survey of Student Engagement (NSSE) Institute.

Dr. Trigwell's chapter, an essential contribution to this book, highlights over three decades of research on the central question of how variation in approaches to teaching impact variation in student approaches to learning. Of note, he delineates a number of "teacher-focused" and "student-focused" approaches to teaching, and relates these to both teacher characteristics and teacher perceptions of the learning context. Dr. Trigwell also reviews helpful studies of seven characteristics of good university teaching, touches on Canadian parallel transcript research providing insight into teacher-learner relations, and pinpoints the need for studies invoking causality and further research. Dr. Trigwell concludes that there is hope as the research clearly demonstrates that teachers' approaches to teaching and students' approaches to learning can be changed!

Keith Trigwell's research collaborator, Michael Prosser, makes a unique contribution in the second chapter of this section. His research categorizes academics in terms of the way they experience teaching, the way they experience research, and the way they experience their subject matter. The originality of this chapter lies, in part, in Dr. Prosser's investigation of how what one might consider the more evolved or sophisticated views of teaching align with the more evolved or holistic views of research and subject matter. Dr. Prosser concludes that we can learn from these findings and influence the quality of teaching by reaching teachers—coaxing and stimulating them to improve their approach to teaching—through their subject matter and their research interests. These findings have implications for educational development programs and practices as well as institutional and national higher-education policies designed to foster effective pedagogy.

Finally, Jillian Kinzie of the NSSE Institute provides an expert view regarding student engagement and learning as they play out in hundreds of post-secondary education institutions in the US and Canada. She begins by briefly restating the need to develop higher-quality learning environments to accommodate the diverse needs of a student population that is growing and changing. She then describes the student-engagement framework and the "positive relationship" between student engagement and student learning and growth, concluding that student engagement is "an intermediate outcome and a robust proxy for student success." Dr. Kinzie's chapter identifies four propositions arising from research and study on the impact of college on students. These recommendations for teaching and engagement involve strategies that institutions can adopt to help students achieve intended learning outcomes: providing students with high expectations, stimulating and highly significant educational experiences, and total learning environments, as well as recognizing that what faculty stress as important will influence student behaviours and actions. The author concludes with some observations regarding the need for institutions to implement practices which will focus the academic community on what enhances student learning in higher education.

The three chapters which follow review the research concerning the relationship between teaching and learning, emphasizing what we know about the ways in which the conceptualization of one's teaching, and even one's views of the subject matter and research, can impact the student learning experience. Together, these chapters place the research findings into context: they remind the reader of key factors in establishing a positive teaching and learning relationship.

> *Demonstrating the relationship between faculty approaches to teaching (information transmission, teacher-focus and conceputal change, student-focus) and student approaches to learning (surface and deep).*

6

TEACHING AND LEARNING: A RELATIONAL VIEW

Keith Trigwell

INTRODUCTION

If there is not a positive relationship between the quality of teachers' teaching and the quality of their students' learning, why do we make such an effort to improve teaching? If there is such a relationship, where is the evidence for it?

In his comprehensive account of teaching and learning research in post-secondary education in this volume, Noel Entwistle has provided an overview of the history of the field and the key contributions to it. Most of this chapter focuses on one small part of that field: the relational research that has explored teachers' approaches to teaching and how variations in those approaches are related to variations in students' approaches to learning. While elements of this field of study have numerous contributors, very few have provided evidence of direct relations between teaching and learning. Four accounts of such research are included below.

Taking Stock: Research on Teaching and Learning in Higher Education, ed. J. Christensen Hughes and J. Mighty. Montreal and Kingston: McGill-Queen's University Press, Queen's Policy Studies Series. © 2010 The School of Policy Studies, Queen's University at Kingston. All rights reserved.

The Experience of Teaching and Learning

The student approach to learning perspective is not new. Since the idea first appeared some 30 years ago, it has contributed to a significant change in the direction and application of student-learning research (Marton, Hounsell, and Entwistle 1997). The key features of this perspective are first, that students' approaches to learning are seen to be more a relation between student and context than characteristics of the student, and that student learning may be influenced by changing the context or students' perceptions of it. Second, variation in approach to learning is related to variation in the quality of the outcomes of learning. An overview of this research, and descriptions of the two qualitatively different approaches to student learning (deep and surface) that form the key elements of departure in this research, have already been provided by Entwistle (Chapter 2) and elaborated upon by Sari Lindblom-Ylänne (Chapter 3).

The study of university teaching from this perspective is more recent, with the first substantive publications appearing from studies conducted in the early 1990s. Interview-based studies with university teachers have provided considerable consensus in describing qualitative variation in approaches to teaching (Martin and Balla 1991; Samuelowicz and Bain 1992, 2001; Trigwell and Prosser 1996a; Kember 1997). The extremes of this variation are illustrated in the following two quotations taken from interviews with Australian university science teachers:

> Teacher A: So in preparing for an hour lecture I decide what I want the students to get out of this lecture, specifically what I want them to be able to do as a result of this lecture. So that is one of the first parts of planning my list if you like, planning my lecture. I also plan them in a way so that I know the notes that I want the students to get. I'll write my notes in such a way so that the students don't have to decide when to take notes, I tell them to. I'll dictate to them, I have handouts prepared, I have gaps in them that they fill in and I take that decision away from the students about when and how to take notes.

> Teacher E: I think, more explicitly what I want to achieve with, eh, buzz sessions and the questions, and stuff [in lectures] is confronting students with their pre-conceived ideas about the subject which quite often conflict with what we're talking about, the official dogmas as it were. Um, so you've got to bring out that conflict and make the people aware that what they already know may not be what is the official line, as it were. (Prosser and Trigwell 1999, 139, 141)

In the phenomenographic study which yielded these quotations (Trigwell, Prosser, and Taylor 1994), five qualitatively different approaches to teaching were constituted (Figure 1).

FIGURE 1
Five Qualitatively Different Approaches to Teaching

Approach A:	**Teacher-focused strategy with the intention of transmitting information to students** The focus of the transmission in this approach is on facts and skills. The prior knowledge of students is not considered to be important and it is assumed that students do not need to be active in the teaching process—they will learn by receiving the transmitted material.
Approach B:	**Teacher-focused strategy with the intention that students acquire the concepts of the discipline** This approach is one in which the teacher adopts a teacher-focused strategy, with the intention of helping their students acquire the concepts of the discipline and the relationships between them. They assume, however, that their students can learn this information by being told about the concepts and their relationships. Like Approach A, they do not seem to see that their students need to be active for the teaching-learning process to be successful.
Approach C:	**A teacher-student interaction strategy with the intention that students acquire the concepts of the discipline** This approach is one in which the teachers adopt a teacher-student interaction strategy to help their students acquire the discipline-based concepts and the relationships between them. Like Approaches A and B, students are not seen to construct their own knowledge but, unlike Approaches A and B, they are seen to gain this disciplinary knowledge through actively engaging in the teaching-learning process.
Approach D:	**A student-focused strategy aimed at students developing their conceptions** This approach is one in which the teachers adopt a student-focused strategy to help students further develop their worldview or conceptions already held. A student-focused strategy is assumed to be necessary because it is the students who have to construct their knowledge in order to change their conceptions.
Approach E:	**A student-focused strategy aimed at students changing their conceptions** This approach is one in which teachers adopt a student-focused strategy to help their students change their worldviews or conceptions of the phenomena they are studying. Like Approach D, students are seen to have to construct their own knowledge, and so the teacher has to focus on what the students are doing in the teaching-learning situation. A student-focused strategy is assumed to be necessary because it is the students who have to re-construct their knowledge to produce a new worldview or conception. The teacher understands that he/she cannot transmit a new worldview or conception to the students.

Source: Trigwell, Prosser, and Taylor (1994).

What characterizes this set of descriptions, and distinguishes it from other sets of teaching styles, forms, theories, and perspectives are that:

1. It contains descriptions of approaches to teaching made in response to perceptions by the teachers from a particular context;
2. Any one description is not a complete description of that approach to teaching. The focus in this set is on what constitutes the aspects of variation in a group of teachers' experience of teaching, and not on the common experience of that group of teachers;
3. It is a hierarchically inclusive set: Approach B includes elements of A, and Approach C includes elements of A and B, and so on;
4. It does not necessarily contain developmental stages. The approach used to constitute this outcome involves a snapshot in time of variation in a group, not the way an individual changes over time. As noted above, a teacher may use aspects of Approach D in one context (say, Ph.D. supervision) and aspects of Approach B with none of D in another (say, first-year teaching). Teachers who develop more sophisticated approaches may shift from Approach A to Approach E without "passing through" Approaches B-D.

The quote from Teacher E illustrates Approach E, called a Conceptual Change/Student-Focused (CCSF) approach. In adopting this approach, teachers have a student-focused strategy with the aim of changing (challenging) students' conceptions of the subject matter. The least inclusive approach, called an Information Transmission/Teacher-Focused (ITTF) approach (illustrated in the quote from Teacher A), involves a strategy aimed at transmitting content to students. Transmission elements of the ITTF approach are included in the CCSF approach, but the student-focused element of a CCSF approach is not a part of the ITTF approach. Because of this inclusivity, a CCSF approach is considered to be a more sophisticated or complete approach than the more limiting ITTF approach.

When qualitative variation of this sort was described and replicated in a range of contexts, an immediate question of interest to most researchers was whether this variation in teaching was associated with any differences in student learning. And if it was, could the association be measured? In the early 1990s, Prosser and Trigwell embarked on a project to investigate these relations quantitatively.

Relations between Teaching and Learning

Studies that show relations between what teachers do and what their students do are uncommon in higher education. One exception (Greeson 1988) reported research on activities in two classes; one student-centred and the other teacher-centred. Each class contained 16 students and one lecturer who served as the instructor for both classes. The results showed that although the outcome of the two classes was not statistically differ-ent, the overall student experience in the student-centred class was more favourable. The student-centred / student self-directed method of teach-ing was rated consistently higher by the students than the traditional teacher-centred approach. For example, higher values were recorded on variables such as organisation and direction, interest and enthusiasm, and presentation and clarity. This study suggested that student-centred approaches are more desirable, though the small numbers of classes and the unknown contribution from the one lecturer meant that the results had to be considered tentative.

Similar results were found in Hong Kong by Kember and Gow (1994) at the departmental level. Using the university department as the unit of analysis, they found substantial relations between teachers' orientation to teaching (learning facilitation or knowledge transmission) and the ap-proaches to learning of students (deep or surface) in the same department.

Using the outcomes of the phenomenographic study referred to above, an inventory designed to capture large-scale self-reports of qualitative variation in approaches to teaching at the level of courses making up a degree program was developed (Trigwell, Prosser, and Ginns 2005; Prosser and Trigwell 2006). The Approaches to Teaching Inventory (ATI) now includes 11 items in each of two scales (CCSF and ITTF) (Appendix 1) and focuses on a particular teaching context. The five research studies described below made use of the original 16-item version (Trigwell and Prosser 2004).

Studies of the relations among students' approaches to learning, percep-tions of their learning environment, prior experience, and outcomes of learning (Figure 2a) were conducted in the 1970s and 1980s (Marton and Saljo 1976; van Rossum and Schenk 1984; Entwistle and Ramsden 1983). The availability of a teaching-approaches inventory enabled a similar in-vestigation of the teaching context (Figure 2b) as well as an exploration of the relations between teachers' approaches to teaching and the approaches to learning of students in the classes of those teachers (Figures 2a and b).

At least five studies in quite different contexts have now been conducted on the relations between teaching and learning using the ATI and an indicator of student approaches to learning (such as the Study Process Questionnaire (Biggs 1987a, 1987b; Biggs, Kember, and Leung 2001). The original study (Trigwell, Prosser, and Waterhouse 1999) involved 46 university science teachers in 48 classes with 3,956 students. A factor analysis of the 48 cases yielded one factor with a negative loading on the surface approach to learning (-0.66) and ITTF approach to teaching (-0.31) variables, and high positive loading on the deep approach to learning (0.80) and CCSF approach to teaching (0.69) variables.

A second, larger-scale study (Trigwell et al. 1999) replicated the meth-odology of the first, but covered a broader range of disciplines, and involved 55 large first-year courses taught by six to 12 teachers in each

FIGURE 2a
Model of Student Learning

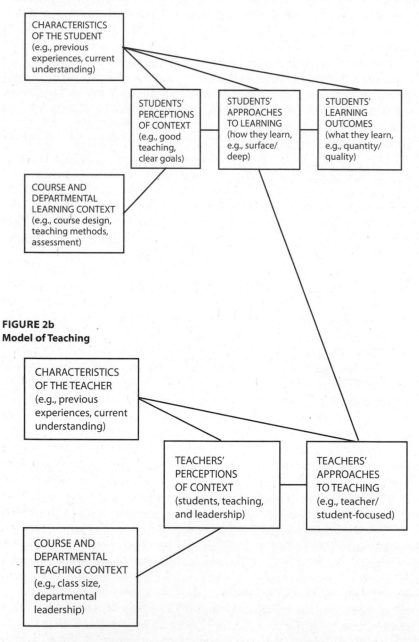

FIGURE 2b
Model of Teaching

Source: Author's compilation.

course. Feedback was received from 408 teachers and 8,829 students in the classes of those teachers. The correlations between approaches to teaching and approaches to learning from this study are shown in Table 1.

TABLE 1
Correlation Coefficients (Pearson, R) between Teachers' Approach to Teaching and Students' Approach to Learning Variables

Variable	Deep	Surface	CCSF	ITTF
		Variable		
Deep approach to learning	-	-.22	.38*	-.15
Surface approach to learning		-	-.48*	.38*
CCSF approach to teaching			-	-.30
ITTF approach to teaching				-

Notes: *p<.05; n=55; CCSF = Conceptual change/student-focused; ITTF = Information transmission/teacher-focused.
Source: Author's compilation.

Together these results indicate, with classes as the unit of analysis, that an information transmission / teacher-focused approach to teaching is strongly and positively associated with surface and non-deep approaches to learning, and that a conceptual change / student-focused approach to teaching is positively associated with deep and non-surface approaches to learning. When teachers report that their focus is on what they do in their teaching, when they believe students have little or no prior knowledge of the subject they are teaching, when they do little more than transmit facts so that students will have a good set of notes (ITTF approach), their students are more likely to adopt surface approaches to learning. Conversely, when teachers report that they have the student as the focus of their activities, where it matters more to them what the student is doing and learning than what the teacher is doing or covering, where the teacher is one who encourages self-directed learning, who makes time (in formal "teaching" time) for students to interact and to discuss the problems they encounter, where the teacher assesses conceptual change, where the teacher provokes debate, uses a lot of time to question students' ideas and to develop a "conversation" with students in lectures (CCSF approach), then his or her students are less likely to adopt a surface approach and more likely to adopt a deep approach.

Two studies in other contexts show similar results. Kek (2006), in a study of teaching and learning in a Malaysian private university found that "to achieve high deep approaches to learning it was beneficial to be in classes with teachers who employed more CCSF approaches." Her study went further and looked at relations between the teacher and student approaches and the student-learning outcomes. She noted that "students had lower academic achievement scores when they were in the classes of teachers who employed mainly ITTF approaches." Similarly, students in the US studying at a distance adopted deeper approaches to learning when taught by teachers who described using a CCSF approach in their online courses (Kim and Branch 2002).

Gibbs and Coffey used the ATI to explore changes in teaching approach among teachers who are engaged in university-teaching development programs (2004). Their sample of 230 teachers completed the ATI along with other inventories, including one designed to capture information on their teaching methods, at the beginning of their courses. They reported finding positive relations between a Conceptual Change/Student-Focused (CCSF) approach to teaching and the size of the "armoury" of teaching methods of which the teacher was aware. They noted that their sample, when compared with a control group, showed no change in ITTF scores but increases in CCSF scores over the life of the program, and the latter were associated with changes in their students' approaches to learning.

The relations observed in the studies described in this paper are signifi- cant because they show connections between teaching and outcomes of learning that point to ways to improve student learning through teaching, and therefore help to define good teaching. Numerous studies have con- tributed to the growing evidence that surface approaches to learning are related to lower-quality outcomes of learning as noted earlier. In the new studies described above, a pathway connecting variation in approach to *teaching* and the quality of student learning outcomes has been established.

This connecting pathway assists in the development of programs to improve student learning. Research by Entwistle and Ramsden (1983), which indicated that student perceptions of their learning environment are related to their approaches to learning, was a source of information used in attempts to improve learning. By focusing on changing students' perceptions of those aspects of the learning environment described by students to be related to their approaches to learning, it is possible to improve the quality of learning. The results from the teaching/learning relations studies described above highlight the importance in these at- tempts of also working with academic staff to encourage the adoption of CCSF approaches to teaching. In order to change the way teachers ap- proach their teaching (to focus more on their students rather than their own performance and the content they are teaching), it may be necessary to address conceptions of teaching and learning (Trigwell 1995; Trigwell and Prosser 1996b). Where teachers conceive of learning as information accumulation to meet external demands, and conceive of teaching as trans- mitting course content to students, they approach their teaching in terms of teacher-focused strategies. On the other hand, where teachers conceive of learning as developing and changing students' conceptions, they conceive of teaching in terms of helping students to develop and change their conceptions and approach their teaching in a student-focused way.

Teaching that is student-focused, that encourages self-directed learning, that includes time (in formal "teaching" time) for students to interact and to discuss the problems they encounter, that uses assessments to reveal conceptual change, that provokes debate, that uses a lot of time to question students' ideas and to develop a "conversation" with students in lectures, is teaching that is related to student learning. These CCSF approaches to teaching might be added to the elements of good university teaching identified through a literature review by Ramsden et al. (1995):

- Good teachers are also good learners; for example, they learn through their own reading, by participating in a variety of professional-development activities, by listening to their students, by sharing ideas with their colleagues, and by reflecting on classroom interactions and students' achievements. Good teaching is therefore dynamic, reflective, and constantly evolving;
- Good teachers display enthusiasm for their subject, and a desire to share it with their students;
- Good teachers recognise the importance of context, and adapt their teaching accordingly; they know how to modify their teaching strategies according to the particular students, subject matter, and learning environment;
- Good teachers encourage learning for understanding and are concerned with developing their students' critical thinking skills, problem-solving skills, and problem-approach behaviours;
- Good teachers demonstrate an ability to transform and extend knowledge, rather than merely transmitting it; they draw on their knowledge of their subject, their knowledge of their learners, and their general pedagogical knowledge to transform the concepts of the discipline into terms that are understandable to their students. In other words, they display "pedagogical-content knowledge;"
- Good teachers set clear goals, use valid and appropriate assessment methods, and provide high-quality feedback to their students;
- Good teachers show respect for their students; they are interested in both their professional and their personal growth, encourage their independence, and sustain high expectations of them.

Where to from Here?

In this analysis, no mention has been made of causality or the direction of causality in describing the relations observed between teaching approaches and learning approaches. The studies were not designed to yield such information and, in any event, the issue of causality is problematic. For example, the context established by a teacher using a conceptual change/student-focused approach may influence students to adopt a deep approach, but it may be equally likely that some teachers adapt their approach to teaching in response to the requests of students to, for example, go through problems in a transmission/teacher-focused manner. Such issues need to be the focus of continuing qualitative studies in which students and teachers articulate the influences upon their approaches.

The research described in this paper has focused on the relations between self-reports of teachers and self-reports of students on the approaches they adopt. In their review of this type of research, Kane, Sandretto, and Heath (2002) were critical of studies that relied totally on self-reports. Studies that investigate the relations between teaching and outcomes of learning are the next logical step and one example is a project being conducted at King's College London (UK). It will use concept mapping and interview techniques to measure cognitive change in students' understandings of specific disciplines, and it will assess lecturers' approaches to teaching as a consequence of participation in an accredited teaching-development program. The members of the research team have developed this concept-mapping method to make learning visible and to measure learning quality through the tracking of cognitive change. The study is being conducted in eight disciplines.

Another possibility pertains to pedagogic resonance, which at the level of the individual student has been described as the connection between the act of teaching and the act of learning (Trigwell and Shale 2004). As the bridge between teacher knowledge and student learning, pedagogic resonance may be one way to provide the qualitative information needed to clarify some of the quantitative results described in this paper. Canadian research on parallel transcripts (McAlpine and Weston 2002) provides such an insight into teacher-learner relations. A video of a lecture is watched by the lecturer and, separately, by students who attended the lecture. Each provides a commentary linked to timing points in the lecture: the lecturer on what they were trying to teach, and the students on where they felt they were learning. The transcripts of these interviews are then analysed in parallel to capture those moments when teacher and students, on reflection, considered that they were on the "same wavelength."

The results from this one Canadian study suggest that pedagogic resonance is rare in a one-hour lecture. Face-to-face teaching and lectures are not usually designed to facilitate learning, and to expect so is to place unrealistic expectations on them. However, it may be possible to extend this type of research to contexts more likely to facilitate learning, and to move away from teaching acts and more towards teaching approaches as a way of defining the more generic elements of teaching that contribute to learning. What is apparent is that much more research is needed if the effects on learning, of those aspects of teaching designed to lead to learning, are to be understood.

CONCLUSION

The major outcomes of the research described in this paper are that: teachers who themselves report adopting more of a transmission/teacher-focused approach to teaching have students in their classes who themselves report adopting a more surface approach to learning; and teachers who report adopting more of a conceptual change/student-focused approach to teaching have students who report adopting a deeper approach to learning. Without a result such as this, much of the previous research from the student-learning perspective on teaching and learning in higher education would be for nought. These relations help define those aspects of teaching that are likely to enhance student learning, and are therefore seen as a means through which learning might be enhanced. This is the legacy of the relational research approach.

NOTE

Much of the original work described in this paper was conducted by the author in collaboration with Michael Prosser, whose contribution is acknowledged.

REFERENCES

Biggs, J.B. 1987a. *The Study Process Questionnaire (SPQ) Users' Manual.* Hawthorne, Victoria: Australian Council for Educational Research.

Biggs, J.B. 1987b. *Student Approaches to Learning and Studying.* Melbourne: Australian Council for Educational Research.

Biggs, J., D. Kember, and D.Y.P. Leung. 2001. The Revised Two-Factor Study Process Questionnaire: R-SPQ-2F. *British Journal of Educational Psychology* 71:133-49.

Entwistle, N. and P. Ramsden. 1983. *Understanding Student Learning.* London: Croom Helm.

Greeson, L.E. 1988. College Classroom Interaction as a Function of Teacher- and Student-Centered Instruction. *Teaching and Teacher Education* 4:305-15.

Gibbs, G. and M. Coffey. 2004. The Impact of Training of University Teachers on their Skills, their Approach to Teaching and the Approach to Learning of their Students. *Active Learning* 5:87-100.

Kane, R., S. Sandretto, and C. Heath. 2002. Telling Half the Story: A Critical Review of Research on the Teaching Beliefs and Practices of University Academics. *Review of Educational Research* 72:177-228.

Kek, Y.C. 2006. Individual Characteristics, Family, Self-Efficacy, Curriculum, University and Classroom Learning Environments, Teaching Approaches and Teacher Factors, Learning Approaches, and Student Outcomes in a Malaysian Private University: A Mixed Research Study. Unpublished Ph.D., University of Adelaide, Adelaide.

Kember, D. 1997. A Reconceptualisation of the Research in Academics' Conceptions of Teaching. *Learning and Instruction* 7:255-75.

Kember, D. and L. Gow. 1994. Orientations to Teaching and their Effect on the Quality of Student Learning. *Journal of Higher Education* 65:59-74.

Kim, D. and R.M. Branch. 2002. The Relationship between Teachers' Approach to Teaching, Students' Perceptions of Course Experiences and Students' Approaches to Studying in Electronic Distance-Learning Environments. Paper presented at the annual meeting of the American Educational Research Association, New Orleans, April.

Martin, E. and M. Balla. 1991. Conceptions of Teaching and Implications for Learning. *Research and Development in Higher Education* 13:298-304.

Marton, F. and R. Säljö. 1976. On Qualitative Differences in Learning. I. Outcome and Process. *British Journal of Educational Psychology* 46:4-11.

Marton, F., D. Hounsell, and N.J. Entwistle, eds. 1997. *The Experience of Learning: Implications for Teaching and Studying in Higher Education,* 2nd edition. Edinburgh: Scottish Academic Press.

McAlpine, L. and C. Weston. 2002. Parallel Transcripts. Paper presented at the annual meeting of the American Educational Research Association, New Orleans, April.

Prosser, M. and K. Trigwell. 1999. *Understanding Learning and Teaching: The Experience in Higher Education.* Buckingham, UK: SRHE and Open University Press.

Prosser, M. and K. Trigwell. 2006. Confirmatory Factor Analysis of the Approaches to Teaching Inventory. *British Journal of Educational Psychology* 76:405-19.

Ramsden, P., D. Margetson, E. Martin, and S. Clarke. 1995. *Recognizing and Rewarding Good Teaching.* Canberra: Australian Government Printing Services.

Samuelowicz, K. and J.D. Bain. 1992. Conceptions of Teaching Held by Teachers. *Higher Education* 24:93-112.

Samuelowicz, K. and J.D. Bain. 2001. Revisiting Academics' Beliefs about Teaching and Learning. *Higher Education* 41:299-325.

Trigwell, K. 1995. Increasing Faculty Understanding of Teaching. In *Successful Faculty Development Strategies,* ed. W.A. Wright, 76-100. Boston: Anker Publishing Co.

Trigwell, K. and M. Prosser. 1996a. Congruence between Intention and Strategy in Science Teachers' Approach to Teaching. *Higher Education* 32:77-87.

Trigwell, K. and M. Prosser. 1996b. Changing Approaches to Teaching: A Relational Perspective. *Studies in Higher Education* 21:275-84.

Trigwell, K. and M. Prosser. 2004. Development and Use of the Approaches to Teaching Inventory. *Educational Psychology Review* 16(4):409-24.

Trigwell, K. and S. Shale. 2004. Student learning and the scholarship of university teaching. *Studies in Higher Education* 29:523-36.

Trigwell, K., M. Prosser, and P. Ginns. 2005. Phenomenographic Pedagogy and a Revised Approaches to Teaching Inventory. *Higher Education Research and Development* 24(4):349-60.

Trigwell, K., M. Prosser, and P. Taylor. 1994. Qualitative Differences in Approaches to Teaching First Year University Science. *Higher Education* 27:75-84.

Trigwell, K., M. Prosser, and F. Waterhouse. 1999. Relations between Teachers' Approaches to Teaching and Students' Approach to Learning. *Higher Education* 37:57-70.

Trigwell, K., M. Prosser, P. Ramsden, and E. Martin. 1999. Improving Student Learning through a Focus on the Teaching Context. In *Improving Student Learning,* ed. C. Rust, 97-103. Oxford: Oxford Centre for Staff and Learning Development.

van Rossum, E.J. and S.M. Schenk. 1984. The Relationship between Learning Conception, Study Strategy and Learning Outcome. *British Journal of Educational Psychology* 54:73-83.

APPENDIX 1
Approaches to Teaching Inventory-R

This inventory is designed to explore a dimension of the way that academics go about teaching in a specific context or subject or course. This may mean that your responses to these items in one context may be different to the responses you might make on your teaching in other contexts or subjects. For this reason we ask you to describe your context.

Please name the subject/course of your response: . . . .

For each item please circle one of the numbers (1-5). The numbers stand for the following responses:

    1 - this item was **only rarely or never** true for me in this subject.
    2 - this item was **sometimes** true for me in this subject.
    3 - this item was true for me **about half the time** in this subject.
    4 - this item was **frequently** true for me in this subject.
    5 - this item was **almost always or always** true for me in this subject.

Please answer each item. Do not spend a long time on each: your first reaction is probably the best one.

	only rarely			almost always	
1. In this subject students should focus their study on what I provide them.	1	2	3	4	5
2. It is important that this subject should be completely described in terms of specific objectives that relate to formal assessment items.	1	2	3	4	5
3. In my interactions with students in this subject I try to develop a conversation with them about the topics we are studying.	1	2	3	4	5
4. It is important to present a lot of facts to students so that they know what they have to learn for this subject.	1	2	3	4	5
5. I set aside some teaching time so that the students can discuss, among themselves, key concepts and ideas in this subject.	1	2	3	4	5
6. In this subject I concentrate on covering the information that might be available from key texts and readings.	1	2	3	4	5
7. I encourage students to restructure their existing knowledge in terms of the new way of thinking about the subject that they will develop.	1	2	3	4	5
8. In teaching sessions for this subject, I deliberately provoke debate and discussion.	1	2	3	4	5
9. I structure my teaching in this subject to help students to pass the formal assessment items.	1	2	3	4	5
10. I think an important reason for running teaching sessions in this subject is to give students a good set of notes.	1	2	3	4	5
11. In this subject, I provide the students with the information they will need to pass the formal assessments.	1	2	3	4	5

... continued

APPENDIX 1
(Continued)

	only rarely				almost always
12. I should know the answers to any questions that students may put to me during this subject.	1	2	3	4	5
13. I make available opportunities for students in this subject to discuss their changing understanding of the subject.	1	2	3	4	5
14. It is better for students in this subject to generate their own notes rather than copy mine.	1	2	3	4	5
15. A lot of teaching time in this subject should be used to question students' ideas.	1	2	3	4	5
16. In this subject my teaching focuses on the good presentation of information to students.	1	2	3	4	5
17. I see teaching as helping students develop new ways of thinking in this subject.	1	2	3	4	5
18. In teaching this subject it is important for me to monitor students' changed understanding of the subject matter.	1	2	3	4	5
19. My teaching in this subject focuses on delivering what I know to the students.	1	2	3	4	5
20. Teaching in this subject should help students question their own understanding of the subject matter.	1	2	3	4	5
21. Teaching in this subject should include helping students find their own learning resources.	1	2	3	4	5
22. I present material to enable students to build up an information base in this subject.	1	2	3	4	5

Thank you.

Source: Trigwell, Prosser, and Ginns (2005).

> How the potential relationship between faculty approaches to research and teaching may affect student learning.

7

FACULTY RESEARCH AND TEACHING APPROACHES: EXPLORING THE RELATIONSHIP

Michael Prosser

INTRODUCTION

The relationship between teaching and research quality in higher education is a contentious one. Most academics subscribe to the view that there is a relationship between the two, yet empirical research correlating quantitative performance indicators of teaching and research suggests otherwise. In this chapter, which draws extensively on a paper recently published in *Instructional Science* (Prosser et al. 2008), it is argued that there is support for the existence of a relationship between teaching and research; not between indicators of performance, but more in the way faculty understand and experience these two primary facets of their work. Research evidence suggests that the way faculty experience their research is related logically and empirically to the way they experience their teaching and their subject matter. The main contribution of this work is the suggestion that student-focused teaching (and hence student learning) is associated with the extent to which faculty focus their research on the development of the theoretical and conceptual understandings of their fields. This finding provides additional insight into the challenges and potential approaches associated with promoting student-focused teaching strategies in support of student learning.

Background

Research on student learning in higher education has been an active area of research for over 30 years. In that time, research on student learning, from a student-learning perspective, has described key variations in the way students approach their studies in higher education, how those approaches relate to teaching and learning contexts and perception of those contexts, and to student-learning outcomes. That research has shown that students adopt fundamentally different approaches to study, focusing either on short-term reproduction to meet immediate demands (surface approach) or longer-term understanding and engagement (deep approach). Furthermore, the approach adopted is not a stable character- istic of individual students but is related to students' prior experiences of teaching and learning, and to their perceptions and understanding of the (present) teaching and learning context. An individual student approach may vary between tasks, within subjects, and between subjects. In turn, these approaches are found to relate to quality, and to a lesser extent, quantity of learning outcomes. The focus of this work is on the context and how that relates to students' learning experiences and outcomes, rather than on variation in students' characteristics. That is not to say that variation in students' characteristics is not important, but simply that it is not the focus of this work.

About 15 years ago, my colleague Keith Trigwell and I began research- ing teaching in higher education from a student-learning perspective. In that work, we have described how teachers in higher education ap- proach their teaching and how those approaches relate to how students approach their learning. As demonstrated by Dr. Trigwell in the preced- ing chapter, that work has shown that teachers approach their teaching from fundamentally different perspectives. At one end of the spectrum, teachers adopt what we have termed information transmission, or teacher- focused (ITTF) approaches, and at the other end, conceptual change and development, or student-focused (CCSF) approaches. The key distinction found was more to do with the underlying intention of teaching, between information transmission and conceptual change and development, rather than the strategies, teacher-focused or student-focused.

The most important aspect of this work has been the identification of the relationship between the way teachers approach their teaching in higher education and the way their students approach their learning. We have shown in a series of studies that teachers who report adopting more information transmission and teacher-focused approaches have students who report adopting more surface approaches to learning; while teach- ers who report adopting more conceptual change and student-focused approaches have students who report adopting deeper approaches to learning.

In recent years, questions concerning the relationship between teaching and research in higher education have also been increasing. Some have suggested that there is a positive relationship between teaching and research, i.e., better researchers are also better teachers (Neumann 1993; Brew and Boud 1995; Rowland 1996; Jenkins et al. 1998; Brew 1999), while others have suggested that there is little or no evidence to support this claim (Ramsden and Moses 1992; Hattie and Marsh 1996). Here, drawing on the work of Elton (2000), Glassick, Huber, and Maeroff (1997), and Martin and Ramsden (2000), I argue that this lack of a statistically significant relationship may be misinterpreted; academics' conceptions of their experiences "may form the basis for an explanation of the existence or absence of a link between the discovery of new knowledge and the sharing of existing knowledge" (Prosser et al. 2008, 4).

In a recent study, I explored this relationship with my colleagues Martin, Trigwell, Ramsden, and Middleton (for a full account of the study, see Prosser et al. 2008). Drawing upon our previous research, we hypothesized that rather than finding a relationship between teaching and research-performance outcomes, the relationship might have more to do with the way teaching and research are experienced, and that the relationship may be mediated by the way in which the subject matter is understood.

For this study, we interviewed 37 academic staff across a range of disciplines and fields of study. We used semi-structured interviews to investigate their experiences of teaching, research, and understanding of subject matter, and a phenomenographic approach in the analysis of the transcripts. Furthermore, rather than including in our sample both research and non-research faculty—as is the case in most educational studies—we decided to focus, in the first instance, on research-active faculty only, and on the qualitative variation in the ways they experienced their research, subject matter, and teaching.

Findings

Our results produced categories of description for how faculty experienced their teaching (see Appendix 1), their subject matter (see Appendix 2), and their research (see Appendix 3). For teaching, six categories of experience were identified (similar to those found by Prosser and Trigwell 1999). The key difference among the teaching categories was that A to D captured teacher-focused pedagogies and subject matter that focused on "parts relating to other parts or parts relating to wholes" (Prosser et al. 2008, 7). In categories E and F, teaching was student-focused and the subject matter focused "on wholes (either constituted in terms of parts or relating to greater or new wholes)" (7).

Five categories were also identified for how faculty experience their subject matter. "Structurally, the key difference between these categories is that categories A, B, and C focus on parts" (i.e., the internal structure of the subject matter with a focus on facts and techniques or concepts, issues and procedures), "while categories D and E focus on wholes," (the relationship between the subject matter and the field of study including underpinning theories and conceptions) (8).

Finally, four categories were identified as to how faculty experience their research. Categories A and B focused on the internal structure of the field and included self-contained or independent problem-focused projects; whereas categories C and D focused on the relationship between the field and its constituent parts, and other fields, and were concerned with such issues as the development of the field and changing understanding of the field.

Once classified, a 3 x 3 matrix was formed and tested for statistical significance. As hypothesized, a strong empirical relationship was found between the Experience of Research and the Experience of Understanding the Subject Matter (as reported in Prosser et al. 2008, Somers' $d=.71$, $p<.001$). In fact, of all of the interviewees who experienced their subject matter either in parts, or parts related to other parts, none experienced their research in terms of wholes. Similarly, of all who experienced their research in terms of parts, none experienced their understanding of their subject matter in terms of wholes.

Furthermore, a moderately strong empirical relationship was found between the Experience of Understanding the Subject Matter and the Experience of Teaching (as reported in Prosser et al. 2008, Somers' $d=.67$, $p<.001$). Again, it can be noted that of the interviewees who experienced their subject matter either in parts, or parts related to other parts, none experienced their teaching in terms of a focus on student conceptions, developing or changing them. Similarly, of the interviewees who experienced their teaching in terms of a focus on transferring parts to students, none experienced their understanding of their subject matter in terms of wholes.

Finally, a moderately strong empirical relationship was also found between the Experience of Research and the Experience of Teaching (as reported in Prosser et al. 2008, Somers' $d=.47$, $p<.001$). As such, these findings provide an important alternative explanation for the nature of this relationship.

Implications

The results suggest that there is a relationship between the way research faculty experience their research, their subject, and their teaching. Those whose research focused on wholes demonstrated more student-focused conceptual change and development forms of teaching, rather than information transmission and teacher-focused forms. The converse was also true. Given that the former is associated with higher-quality learning outcomes than the latter, the issue is not that faculty are active or not-active researchers, but whether those that are active are focused more on overall conceptual understanding and development rather than just on individual isolated problems. As we concluded, "All this suggests that it is not the quantity of research that is associated with quality of teaching, but how the field as a whole is maintained and developed that is important. This may apply equally to non-research active as well as to research-active faculty" (Prosser et al. 2008, 13).

Conclusion

This research raises a number of important policy issues at both institutional and national levels. The key issue at the institutional level concerns the development of faculty. If more student-focused approaches to teaching are associated with more coherent and broadly based understandings of subject matter and research, then in trying to develop more student-focused approaches, subject matter and research may well need to be addressed. At both the national and institutional levels, from a teaching and learning perspective, these results raise issues about the sorts of research activities faculty should engage in or be encouraged to engage in. One-off projects aimed at addressing short-term practical issues may not be the sort of research which further develops an academic's understanding of their subject matter. Longer-term, more theoretically based research may be more appropriate to the development of teaching and learning, and contribute to the enhancement of the teaching and learning culture overall.

References

Brew, A. 1999. Research and Teaching: Changing Relationships in a Changing Context. *Studies in Higher Education* 24:291-301.

Brew, A. and D. Boud. 1995. Teaching and Research: Establishing the Vital Link with Research. *Higher Education* 29:261-73.

Elton, L.R.B. 2000. Turning Academics into Teachers: A Discourse on Love. *Teaching in Higher Education* 5:257-60.

Glassick, C., M. Huber, and G. Maeroff. 1997. *Scholarship Assessed: Evaluation of the Professoriate*. San Francisco: Jossey-Bass.

Hattie, J. and H.W. Marsh. 1996. The Relationship between Research and Teaching: A Meta-Analysis. *Review of Educational Research* 66:507-42.

Jenkins, A., T. Blackman, R. Lindsay, and R. Paton-Saltzberg. 1998. Teaching and Research: Student Perspectives and Policy Implications. *Studies in Higher Education* 23:127-42.

Martin, E. and P. Ramsden. 2000. Introduction to Scholarship in Teaching. *Higher Education Research and Development* 19:133-37.

Neumann, R. 1993. Research and Scholarship: Perceptions of Senior Academic Administrators. *Higher Education* 25:97-110.

Prosser, M. and K. Trigwell. 1999. *Understanding Learning and Teaching: The Experience in Higher Education*. Buckingham: Open University Press.

Prosser, M., E. Martin, K. Trigwell, P. Ramsden, and H. Middleton. 2008. University Academics' Experiences of Research and Its Relationship to their Experience of Teaching. *Instructional Science* 36:3-16.

Ramsden, P. and I. Moses. 1992. Associations between Research and Teaching in Australian Higher Education. *Higher Education* 23:273-95.

Rowland, S. 1996. Relationship between Teaching and Research. *Teaching in Higher Education* 1:7-20.

APPENDIX 1
Six Qualitatively Different Conceptions of Teaching

Category A:	Teaching is teacher-focused with the intention of transferring information to students. Subject matter is concrete, taken for granted, and seen as independent parts or topics.
Category B:	Teaching is teacher-focused student activity with the intention of transferring information to students. Subject matter is concrete, taken for granted, and seen as a series of related topics or as parts being related to other parts.
Category C:	Teaching is teacher-focused student activity with the intention of students acquiring the concepts of the discipline. Subject matter is a concrete and connected structure of topics with parts being related to other parts.
Category D:	Teaching is teacher-focused student activity with the intention of students acquiring the concepts of the discipline. Subject matter Is a concrete and connected structure within a discipline or field, with parts being related to the field as a whole.
Category E:	Teaching is student-focused student activity with the intention of students developing their conceptions. Subject matter is relational, as in the relationship between teachers' understanding and students' experience; it is seen in terms of a whole made up of constituent parts.
Category F:	Teaching is student-focused student activity with the intention of students changing their conceptions. Subject matter is relational, as in the relation between teachers' worldviews and students' worldviews, which are open to change; it is seen in terms of wholes related to other wholes.

Source: Prosser, Martin, Trigwell, Ramsden, and Middleton (2008, 6-7).

APPENDIX 2
Five Qualitatively Different Conceptions of Subject Matter

Category A:	A series of facts and/or techniques; with an awareness that the subject matter sits within one or more fields of study, but the focus is on individual internal facts and processes pertaining to the subject matter.
Category B:	A series of individual concepts or topics; with an awareness that the subject matter sits within one or more fields of study, but the focus is on individual internal concepts and issues pertaining to the subject matter.
Category C:	A series of concepts, issues, or procedures, which are linked and integrated to form a whole with a coherent structure and meaning; with an awareness that the subject matter sits within one or more fields of study, but the focus is on the internal structure of the subject matter.
Category D:	A series of concepts, issues, or procedures, which are integral to the formation of a whole with a coherent structure and meaning; with an awareness that the subject matter is structured according to one or more organising principles within a field (or fields) of study, but the focus is on the internal structure of the subject matter and the way the concepts or procedures are related.
Category E:	A coherent whole, which is supported by organising theories within one or more broad fields of study; with an awareness that the subject matter comprises themes or issues which are problematic, such as a series of debates, but the focus is on the ways in which the whole is generalised to a higher level of abstraction.

Source: Prosser, Martin, Trigwell, Ramsden, and Middleton (2008, 7-8).

APPENDIX 3
Four Qualitatively Different Conceptions of Research

Category A:	A series of projects that do not in themselves extend disciplinary knowledge, but are self-contained. They may draw on disciplinary-based knowledge and procedures in order to solve a problem. The object of study is constituted in terms of atomistic or independent parts. In this category, the act is to address problems while drawing on the field with the intention of benefiting the profession or society.
Category B:	The further development of a series of field-of-study-based concepts, issues, or procedures which are linked and integrated coherently. The focus is/may be on developing a technical mechanism or tool for analysis which already exists or whose parameters are set by others. The object of study is constituted in terms of independent parts which are related to the whole field. The act is to identify problems from the field with the intention to add to or expand the field.
Category C:	The application or development of theory within the boundaries of the field of study. It involves the use of existing technical mechanisms or analytical tools, but theory development using established theoretical constructs is its focus. The object of study is seen as a whole (field) that is composed of its constituent parts. The act is to iterate between the problem and the field with the intention of further developing the field.
Category D:	The development and change of understanding about a field; is open ended and inquiry-focused. Research creates more questions which have to be answered. It is about developing ideas broader than those contained within the field of study by bringing together ideas external to the field of study. The object of study is the whole (field) and how it is related to other wholes (fields). The act is to constitute the problem from the field with the intention of changing the field.

Source: Prosser, Martin, Trigwell, Ramsden, and Middleton (2008, 8-9).

Four propositions for fostering student engagement are elaborated: establishing high expectations; providing high impact learning experiences; emphasizing what matters; and creating rich learning environments.

8

STUDENT ENGAGEMENT AND LEARNING: EXPERIENCES THAT MATTER

Jillian Kinzie

INTRODUCTION

The reality for higher education worldwide is that more students than ever before are entering post-secondary education with increasingly diverse backgrounds. In the US, more students from historically under-represented groups are attending college and many have complex enrollment patterns with nearly 60 percent of traditional-age undergraduates attending more than one institution (Adelman 2006). Current conditions increase the pressure to develop learning environments that respond to a more diverse student body and to create higher-quality learning environments that prepare all students for the 21st-century global marketplace and a lifetime of continuous learning. At the same time, mounting concerns about the need for US institutions to be more accountable for assuring student-learning outcomes while boosting degree-completion rates make it imperative for institutions to focus on what must be done to uphold their share of the social contract and help more students succeed.

Taking Stock: Research on Teaching and Learning in Higher Education, ed. J. Christensen Hughes and J. Mighty. Montreal and Kingston: McGill-Queen's University Press, Queen's Policy Studies Series. © 2010 The School of Policy Studies, Queen's University at Kingston. All rights reserved.

One approach to improving student success in higher education that has received considerable attention in recent years is increasing "student engagement," or the extent to which students take part in educationally effective practice (Kuh 2001, 2003; Pascarella and Terenzini 2005). A substantial body of research indicates that once students start college or university, a key factor to whether they will survive and thrive is the extent to which they take part in educationally purposeful activities. Engagement is simultaneously about students' investment in educational activities and also about the intentional structuring and facilitation of students' involvement in enriching learning experiences. Quite simply, to ensure that all students graduate and make the most of their undergraduate education, universities must first ensure the learning environment provides rich and educationally meaningful opportunities, and then focus squarely on increasing student engagement. Although it is undeniable that students' background characteristics and motivation are important factors in their academic success, many post-secondary institutions in the US, Canada, and more recently Australia, are working with greater intentionality to foster optimal learning environments that increase student engagement and advance student learning and success.

This chapter introduces the value of student engagement as a way of thinking about quality in undergraduate education and as a practical approach to creating rich learning environments that promote student learning and success. Following a brief introduction to the student-engagement framework and findings associated with engagement and learning, four propositions and recommendations about teaching practices and engagement are outlined.

The Student-Engagement Framework

Student background characteristics and their pre-college experiences influence to a certain degree whether they will enroll in post-secondary education, how they will perform academically, and whether they will persist and attain their educational objectives. In fact, the best predictor of one measure of academic achievement, college grades, is the combination of an individual student's academic preparation, high-school achievement, aspirations, and motivation. However, once students start college, another key factor in their success—broadly defined—is "student engagement," or the extent to which they take part in educationally effective practices. In their landmark publication, *Principles of Good Practice for Undergraduate Education*, Chickering and Gamson (1987) underscored seven categories of effective educational practices that directly influence student learning and the quality of their educational experiences. They are: student-faculty contact, co-operation among students, active learning, prompt feedback, time on task, high expectations, and respect for diverse talents and ways of learning. Generally speaking, the more students engage in these kinds of activities, the more they learn and the more likely they are to persist and graduate from college. At institutions where faculty members use these and other effective educational practices more frequently in their classes and in co-curricular learning experiences, students are more engaged overall and gain more from college.

Student engagement represents two critical features. The first is the amount of time and effort students put into their studies and other educationally purposeful activities. The quality of students' investment in the learning process is directly related to how much students learn and their ability to persist and to complete their degree (Astin 1993). The second component of student engagement is how the institution deploys its resources and organizes the curriculum, other learning opportunities, and support services to induce students to participate in activities that lead to the experiences and desired outcomes such as persistence, satisfaction, learning, and graduation (Kuh 2001). As Pascarella and Terenzini concluded: "the impact of college is largely determined by individual effort and involvement in the academic, interpersonal, and extra-curricular offerings on a campus … it is important to focus on the ways in which an institution can shape their academic, interpersonal, and extra-curricular offerings to encourage student engagement" (2005, 602). The promise of a student-engagement framework in higher education is that it helps institutions focus on using effective educational practices to induce students to do the things that matter most to their learning and success.

The National Survey of Student Engagement (NSSE) (see www.nsse.iub. edu), a survey widely used in the US and also in Canada, was designed to help institutions focus on engagement in effective educational practice by assessing students' participation in activities associated with desired learning outcomes, persistence, and satisfaction. NSSE annually obtains information from scores of baccalaureate colleges and universities about student participation in programs and activities that institutions provide for their learning and personal development. Survey items represent empirically confirmed "good practices" in undergraduate education. The body of research on college impact and a host of studies using NSSE measures have yielded findings about the positive relationship between engagement and student learning and development, leading researchers to conclude that student engagement is an intermediate outcome and a robust proxy for student success.

Student engagement as measured by NSSE is associated with a wide array of desired college outcomes. A brief review of some of the associations indicates a positive relationship between undergraduate grade point average (GPA) and all the effective educational practices measured on NSSE (NSSE 2005). GPA is associated with time spent preparing for class, coming to class prepared, asking questions in class, tutoring other students, receiving prompt feedback from faculty, maintaining high-quality relationships with faculty, and having a favorable evaluation of overall educational experiences in college. Although the relationship is strong, the direction of the relationship—if good grades influence engagement or if engagement influences grades—is unknown. More importantly, a study of the effect of engagement on first-year college grades by pre-college ability (measured by a standardized college-board score), shows that the grades of lower-ability students were positively affected by engagement in educationally effective activities to a greater degree compared with higher-ability students (NSSE 2006). Another important finding from this same study relates to student retention, which showed a positive relationship between engagement and first- to second-year persistence. Institutions have conducted similar studies, for example, Humboldt State University identified engagement activities strongly associated with persistence to the second year (Hughes and Pace 2003). Students' satisfaction with their undergraduate education is associated with the extent to which they perceive the environment to be supportive of their learning. Although how students feel about their education does not necessarily directly affect how much they learn or what they are able to do, perceptions do directly affect how much effort students will expend on educationally purposeful activities, which consequently has direct effects on their learning and personal development.

Some of the most noteworthy research on engagement and learning outcomes is emerging from the Wabash National Study of the Liberal Arts. Findings from the first year of this longitudinal study links engagement and a handful of good teaching practices—including high-quality student-faculty interactions, rigorous levels of academic challenge, and high expectations for students, as well as diversity experiences such as attending debates or lectures on a current political/social issue during the academic year, and meaningful discussions with diverse peers—with learning outcomes such as moral reasoning, leadership, well-being, critical thinking, and intercultural effectiveness (Overview of Findings 2008). Notably, the higher students scored on each scale, the more growth they showed on the outcomes; the reverse was also true. Also, the level of growth on the outcomes was related to the frequency with which they experienced good teaching practices and supportive institutional conditions. Other promising findings, as reported in the Association of American Colleges and Universities (AAC&U) 2007 publication, *College Learning for the New Global Century*, and in the 2007 NSSE annual report, *Experiences that matter: Enhancing student learning and success,* showed that some educational activities, so-called "high-impact practices," are unusually effective at providing substantial educational benefits to students. High-impact practices such as learning communities, writing-intensive courses, undergraduate research, service-learning, and senior capstone projects appear to engage participants at levels that elevate their performance across multiple engagement and desired-outcomes measures.

On the whole, extant research on student engagement and learning suggests that the degree of student growth is connected with the frequency of student engagement in educationally effective practices. Therefore, the impact of higher-education institutions can be enhanced by helping students experience more of these good teaching practices and supportive institutional conditions.

Propositions and Recommendations for Teaching and Engagement

The discussion in this section of the paper draws from decades of studies on the impact of college and research on student engagement emanating from annual NSSE reports and related project activities, such as *Student Success in College* (Kuh, Kinzie, Schuh, Whitt and Associates 2005) and *Piecing Together the Student Success Puzzle* (Kuh et al. 2007). Four propositions and recommendations about teaching practices and engagement are outlined. First, understanding what students expect of and from their college experience is crucial for faculty members wishing to employ instructional approaches to help students become intentional learners and for institutions that intend to fashion policies and practices that effectively address students' learning needs. Second, stimulating classroom experiences and engagement in "high-impact" practices can raise student learning and impart greater benefits to all students. Third, what faculty members emphasize and think is important to learning can influence what students do. Fourth, educators must be concerned with the total learning environment—in and outside the classroom, socio-cultural aspects, and physical settings—and the implementation of strategies that help guide the student toward intended outcomes.

Proposition 1: Expectations Matter to Student Learning and Success, Particularly in the First Year of University. The establishment of high-performance expectations, inside and outside the classroom, appropriate to students' abilities and aspirations, is critical to student success. To do this, an institution must first understand who its students are, what they are prepared to do academically, and what they expect of the institution and themselves.

Setting high expectations, and then supporting and holding students accountable for reaching them, is an effective strategy for encouraging student success. High expectations for student performance characterized institutions with higher-than-predicted student engagement and graduation rates (Kuh, Gonyea, and Williams 2005). According to Blose (1999), students tend to adjust their behavior and comply with the academic expectations of the environment. Although high expectations for student success should be encouraged at all institutions, expectations should be shaped by information about who the students are and what they expect, and must be accompanied by realistic advice to students about what is necessary to succeed at their particular institution.

Students' expectations of college play an important role in determining the extent to which they actually participate in various educational activities during college. Some students have built high expectations for their post-secondary education experiences based on stories from family, friends, and teachers, while others have not. These varied expectations influence student willingness to take on and engage in various academic experiences. However, across a variety of important educational dimensions, first-year university students expect to do more during their first year than they actually do (NSSE 2005, 2007, 2008). For example, findings pairing student-level data from the Beginning College Survey of Student Engagement (BCSSE) (see www.bcsse.iub.edu) collected before students start university courses, with NSSE data collected towards the end of their first year of college, indicate that although 60 percent of entering students expected to spend more than 15 hours per week preparing for class, only 40 percent studied that much during their first year of college; although most entering students expected to participate in co-curricular activities, nearly one-third (32 percent) spent *no* time in these activities during their first year.

Moreover, expectations for engagement are related to actual engagement in educationally purposeful activities in three specific areas: the level of academic challenge they experience, and the extent to which they engage in active and collaborative learning and interact with faculty (NSSE 2008). Although more than half of entering students achieved levels of engagement that met or exceeded their expectations, some students who entered with high expectations did not achieve them. These findings expose a worrisome gap and demonstrate that information about student expectations is particularly useful when compared to what actually occurs during the first year of college.

Findings about the gap between expectations and experiences in the first year of college suggest that it is important to intentionally shape student expectations for engagement. These findings and decades of research on the need to create a coherent first-year experience (Upcraft, Gardner, and Barefoot 2005) highlight the importance of the first year in engaging students in the habits of learning. Educators need to detail the specific activities that will lead to success by clarifying institutional values and expectations early and often to prospective and matriculating students. For example, if an activity or experience is valuable, consider requiring it (e.g., students must revise an assignment with a writing tutor before submitting). Provide early, meaningful feedback to new students about their performance and tie this to multiple learning-support networks, early warning systems, and safety nets so students get the feedback and support they need to take corrective action.

Fundamental to setting high expectations and ensuring that students meet or exceed them, is the belief that every student can learn under the right conditions. This "talent development" philosophy requires that faculty embrace and address students' diverse talents and needs (Astin 1985; Chickering 2006; Chickering and Gamson 1987). A substantial number of new students may not fully understand and appreciate their role as learners. Far fewer students use campus learning and support services than say they will when starting college (NSSE 2005). To address these concerns, faculty members, advisors, and student-affairs professionals must clearly and consistently communicate to students what is expected and provide feedback as to the quality of students' performance. Turner (1998) suggests that faculty spend time teaching and modeling to students what it means to be "academic citizens." This view means being more explicit about how to approach the readings, specifying class responsibilities and holding students accountable, and adopting the stance that *all* students come to college able to do the work but with no clear sense of what they should be doing and why this is important for learning and success. This position requires that faculty members resist the view that lack of preparation is caused by defects in students, and instead accept that it is better pedagogical practice to make clear the demands of academic work and spell out what students need to do.

Given that students set in place in their first semester of university the pattern of time allocation that will serve them across their years in higher education, it is critical that educators clearly communicate their expectations for student performance before students matriculate, reinforce these expectations throughout the first year, and hold students accountable for high levels of performance.

Proposition 2: Stimulating Educational Experiences and Certain "High-Impact" Practices Raise Student Learning and Impart Greater Benefits to all Students. Stimulating educational experiences—such as active and collaborative learning, student-faculty interaction, peer interactions, and experiences with diversity—encourage students to devote more time and effort to their learning, help them develop a learning support network, and are associated with higher levels of learning for all students.

Most of the scholarship on teaching and learning indicates that the passive lecture format where faculty do most of the talking and students listen is contrary to almost every principle of an optimal learning environment (Barr and Tagg 1995; Guskin 1997; Tagg 2003). Active and collaborative learning is more effective because students learn more when they are intensely involved in their education and are asked to think about and apply what they are learning in different settings. Collaborating with others on academic work and problem solving prepares students to deal with the messy, unscripted situations they will encounter daily during and after college and substantially increases the amount of time and effort students spend learning (Guskin 1997). Variations in teaching approaches, using all forms of active learning—including games, simulations, presentations, quizzes, group learning, inquiry and problem-based learning, integrative assignments, case studies, and other forms of experiential learning—appeal to different learning styles and, more importantly, offer opportunities for students to demonstrate their diverse talents and skills.

Active learning experiences also are positively associated with increased frequency of student contacts with faculty members—probably because the nature of class activities and out-of-class assignments requires it—and more positive views of the campus environment. According to Braxton, Milem, and Sullivan (2000), these positive associations appear to be mediated by getting to know classmates better through collaborative exercises, all of which positively influence student integration and persistence.

Informal student-faculty interaction activities— talking with instructors outside of class, working on a research project with a faculty member, and serving on committees with faculty—are also positively associated with student learning and development (Astin 1993; Kuh 2003; Kuh and Hu 2001). Intentional programs to facilitate student-faculty interaction have different effects on students. For example, relationships with faculty predicted development of academic competence among new students in the first year of college (Reason, Terenzini, and Domingo 2005), and sophomore success (in terms of GPA and satisfaction) was related to high-quality student-faculty interaction (Graunke and Woosley 2005; Juillerat 2000). Even occasional contact with faculty members may be sufficient across some engagement practices. For example, most students may only need to discuss career plans or work with a faculty member outside of class on a committee or project once or maybe twice a semester, whereas working on a research project with a faculty member just once during college could be a life-altering experience. However, for other activities, such as getting prompt feedback and discussing ideas outside of class, the more frequent the contact the better.

The nature and quality of peer interactions in college or university is important to what students do in college and how they feel about their experiences, and is influential to the overall impact of college (Pascarella and Terenzini 1991, 2005). In fact, according to Astin (1993, 398), peers are "the single most potent source of influence," affecting virtually every aspect of development—cognitive, affective, psychological, and behavioral. Peer interactions that foster learning include: discussing course content with other students, working on group projects for classes, tutoring other students, peer teaching and evaluation, discussing racial or ethnic issues, socializing with someone from a different racial or ethnic group, and spending time each week socializing or in student clubs or organizations. Peer interactions are also important with regard to persistence in college because students are more likely to stay in school when they feel comfortable and connected to other students with similar interests and aspirations (Tinto 1993). However, to maximize the educative potential of peers, it is important to enrich opportunities for peer teaching, assign course responsibilities to peer mentors, use structured peer assessments and evaluations, and intentionally arrange peer-learning groups to help enable students to form supportive peer-learning networks.

Peer interactions are a major contributor to another stimulating learning activity: experiences with diversity. Diversity experiences—such as having serious conversations with students of a different race or ethnicity, or students who differ in terms of political views or religious beliefs, or students who provide diverse perspectives in class discussions or assignments—have substantial and positive effects for virtually all students and across a wide range of desirable college outcomes (Hu and Kuh 2003).

The aforementioned stimulating practices tend to engage students at high levels and also have salutary effects on other important areas of engagement and learning- and personal-development gains. In addition, they were key indicators in a study that showed the compensatory effect of engagement on the first-year grades of lower-ability students and on grades and persistence to the second year of college for students from communities that historically have been underserved in US higher education (Kuh et al. 2006). While engagement in these practices generally benefits all students, it appears to have an even greater benefit for under-represented students.

The final set of educational practices worth implementing to further student success are intentional activities—such as learning communities, first-year seminars, service-learning, senior capstone, undergraduate research, internships, and study abroad—which were recently dubbed "high-impact" practices because of the substantial learning benefits they provide to all students (AAC&U 2007). Strong positive effects have been found between participation in six of these practices and self-reported gains in three sets of learning and personal-development outcomes as well as with higher-order thinking, reflective learning, and integrative learning for first-year and senior students (NSSE 2007). These practices are unusually effective at broadly engaging students in educationally effective practices because they essentially demand students experience the stimulating educational experiences mentioned earlier, such as active learning and student-faculty interaction. High-impact practices also require that students devote time and effort to a purposeful task and provide greater opportunities for students to apply what they are learning in different settings. Such practices may prove to be particularly effective strategies in research-intensive institutions, as many model processes of inquiry and can involve students directly in the research work of faculty.

The strength of the benefits associated with high-impact practices suggests a prescription for institutions of higher education: to effectively raise students' level of learning, institutions should ensure that all students experience at least two high-impact practices during their undergraduate education.

Proposition 3: What Faculty Emphasize and Think is Important to Learning Influences What Students Do. Increasing instructors' use of engaging pedagogical practices and ensuring that more students experience these and other high-impact practices are at the core of efforts to improve student learning and success. The focus on improving learning through more effective teaching was stimulated in part by expanding research and theory on human learning (National Research Council 2000), and widely disseminated papers (Barr and Tagg 1995; Cross 1998, 1999; Hutchings 1996; Tagg 2003) which documented the value of restructuring the teaching and learning environment to shift the emphasis from faculty teaching to student learning.

In the same vein that student expectations influence engagement, faculty expectations and priorities also shape student engagement and performance. This important relationship is illustrated by combining data from the Faculty Survey of Student Engagement (FSSE) (see www.fsse.iub.edu), a measure of faculty priorities and expectations of student engagement in effective educational practices and selected classroom teaching and learning activities, with NSSE results. Results confirm that what faculty emphasize and think is important to learning influences what students do, and generally students do pretty much what their faculty expect and require of them (Kuh, Laird, and Umbach 2004). For example, at institutions where faculty think writing is important, more writing activities are assigned, more timely feedback is provided to students on their academic work, and students tend to write more and also report greater progress in developing their writing skills.

The importance faculty members place on high-impact undergraduate experiences also influences the proportion of students that participate in those experiences. The more faculty members at a given institution value an activity, the more likely it is that students do it. For example, on a campus where the average faculty member believes participating in study abroad is somewhat important, only about 4 percent of students report this experience, whereas when faculty agree that study abroad is very important, nearly 50 percent of students participated in this activity.

An even more important finding about the relationship between what faculty members emphasize and what students do is related to the synergistic effects of faculty priorities and pedagogy and student engagement. For example, at institutions where faculty report an emphasis on active and collaborative learning, students not only report being more involved in these activities, including working more frequently with peers on projects in class, making presentations, and participating in class discussions, but their engagement on this activity and all engagement measures, including diversity experiences, level of academic challenge, and gains in general education, are higher than peers at other institutions. Although the relationship between what faculty emphasize and report doing in their teaching and what students ultimately do may not be surprising or profound, it illustrates the simple fact that when faculty members emphasize certain educational practices, require students to do it, and hold them accountable, students engage in these activities to a greater extent than their peers attending other colleges and universities.

The symbiotic relationship between faculty priorities and practices, and student behaviors, also has an effect on desired learning outcomes. Students at institutions where faculty emphasize a range of effective educational practices reported making more progress since starting college on various dimensions of student learning and personal development, including gains in general education and practical competence.

Findings about the relationship between faculty practices and student behaviors are important to keep in mind whenever student deficiencies or lack of motivation are raised as explanations for low levels of engagement and poor academic performance. Faculty can and do shape student performance by what they themselves value and do. These relationships illustrate the importance of aligning faculty practice and rewards with what research shows results in high levels of student engagement. The straightforward lesson: if faculty members value and systematically use effective educational practices, students will engage in them and benefit in desired ways. Therefore, it is critical to ensure that more faculty understand the practices of engagement and use these practices more frequently with their students. These findings also underscore the enormity of the challenge in implementing many of the suggestions contained within this chapter in research-intensive institutions. To the extent that faculty do not value such activity, not only will high-impact learning opportunities be less available, but students may also be less likely to seek out those opportunities that do exist.

Proposition 4: Educators Must be Concerned with the Total Learning Environment—In and Outside the Classroom. The total learning environment—in and outside the classroom, and the physical settings in which students interact with peers, the content, educators, and others—must be organized to help guide students toward intended outcomes. Strategies for fostering student learning and success are not limited to classrooms and policies and programs, but also should address the physical environments of a campus. Every opportunity—new construction, space renovation, landscape planning, campus expansion, interior design—should be used to create spaces and settings where learning and teaching can flourish and reflect a commitment to student engagement. For example, student services should be centrally located and easy to find, and spaces for informal interaction between students and faculty or staff and among students should be plentiful and accessible. Campus space should reflect and complement an institution's commitment to student engagement and success. For example, in planning and constructing new facilities or renovating existing ones, dedicated space for "socially catalytic" interactions, areas where students and faculty can meet informally or where students can work together on projects, should be purposely included.

Effective partnerships among those who have the most contact with students—faculty and student-affairs professionals—are important to creating a campus culture that supports student success (Kezar 2003; Kuh, Kinzie, Schuh, Whitt and Associates 2005). Institutions that have established a sense of shared responsibility for student success are characterized by a high degree of respect and collaboration among community members and have made student success important to everyone. An important ingredient in fostering greater collaboration is to tighten the philosophical and operational linkages between student and academic affairs. For example, increasing the role and responsibility for student affairs is to support the institution's academic mission by involving student-affairs staff as full partners in the learning enterprise, team-teaching with faculty members, participating in campus governance, and managing enriching educational opportunities for students such as first-year seminars and learning communities. This philosophical commitment enables student and academic affairs to work together in such key areas as advising and career services as well as some curricular innovations. Several of the high-impact activities, including service-learning and internships, demand both a broader consideration of the total learning environment at an institution and also suggest opportunities for greater student and academic-affairs collaboration.

The out-of-class experience of students contributes substantially to their learning and growth. Participation in co-curricular activities is positively related to persistence and is associated with other desirable outcomes such as interpersonal skills, self-confidence, and leadership (Astin 1993; Pascarella and Terenzini 2005). Involvement in co-curricular activities helps connect students to peers and the institution and reinforces the desire to graduate. Although involvement in co-curricular activities is important to student success, more than two-fifths of students (40 percent first-year students, 47 percent seniors) at baccalaureate colleges spend *no time* on these activities (NSSE 2008). In order to maximize the educational benefits of co-curricular activities, it is not only necessary to ensure that all students have a real chance to participate, but also that these experiences are educationally meaningful. In addition, co-curricular programs should be intentionally designed to complement, and not undercut, student achievement. For example, new-student orientation should emphasize activities that set the appropriate academic tone and expectations for college life. Student-affairs policies and practices should focus on creating seamless learning environments in which the boundaries between in-class and out-of-class learning are blurry, if not invisible.

The achievement of an effective, institution-wide approach to student learning depends on the development of partnerships between academic and student affairs and developing new ways that various units of higher education can work together to enrich the student experience. In fact, it takes a whole campus to educate a student.

FOCUSING ON WHAT MATTERS

In summary, concerns about the need for institutions of higher education to be more accountable for assuring student-learning outcomes and optimzing learning for a diversity of students makes it imperative for institutions to focus on what matters to student learning and success. These pressures, combined with evidence of educationally effective practices that make a difference to learning, particularly for students who have been historically underserved in higher education, provide both the impetus and direction for faculty members and other campus educators who are committed to taking action. One approach to improving undergraduate education is to focus on enhancing student engagement. Educationally effective institutions across the US and Canada have used NSSE and lessons about student engagement to shape the way students approach higher education and what they do after they arrive.

While enhancing student engagement remains challenging, particularly in research-intensive institutions, most can do far more than they are currently doing to enhance student success. The four propositions outlined here offer practical suggestions for creating rich learning environments that foster student learning and success. Findings from a variety of sources point to the value of engaging pedagogies and practices—including high-quality student-faculty interactions, rigorous levels of academic challenge and high expectations for students, active learning, diversity experiences, and meaningful peer interactions—for improving student learning outcomes and success. Engaging pedagogies matter to student success because they involve students more intensely in their learning, increase their time on task, and harness peer influence in educationally purposeful ways. However, to achieve their full potential, these and other high-impact practices must be done well and be made available to every student. It's clear that institutions must structure supports for faculty to do these things and create clear pathways that guide students to these activities. Using promising policies and practices will increase the odds that students become engaged at high levels and experience success.

REFERENCES

Adelman, C. 2006.*The Toolbox Revisited: Paths to Degree Completion from High School through College*. Washington, DC: Office of Vocational and Adult Education, US Department of Education.

Association of American Colleges and Universities (AAC&U). 2007. *College Learning for the New Global Century*. Washington, DC: Author.

Astin, A.W. 1985. Involvement: The Cornerstone of Excellence. *Change* 17(4):35-9.

Astin, A.W. 1993. *What Matters in College? Four Critical Years Revisited*, 1st edition. San Francisco: Jossey-Bass.

Barr, R.B. and J. Tagg. 1995. From Teaching to Learning: A New Paradigm for Undergraduate Education. *Change* 27(6):12-25.

Blose, G. 1999. Modeled Retention and Graduation Rates: Calculating Expected Retention and Graduation Rates for Multicampus University Systems. *New Directions for Higher Education* 27(4):69-86.

Braxton, J.M., J.F. Milem, and A.S. Sullivan. 2000. The Influence of Active Learning on the College Student Departure Process: Toward a Revision of Tinto's Theory. *Journal of Higher Education* 71(5):569-90.

Chickering, A.W. 2006. Creating Conditions So Every Student Can Learn. *About Campus* 11(2):9-15.

Chickering, A.W. and Z.F. Gamson, eds. 1987. Seven Principles for Good Practice in Undergraduate Education. *AAHE Bulletin* (March):3-7.

Cross, K.P. 1998. Classroom Research: Implementing the Scholarship of Teaching. *New Directions for Teaching and Learning* 75:5-12.

Cross, K.P. 1999. What Do We Know About Students' Learning, and How Do We Know It? *Innovative Higher Education* 23(4):255-70.

Graunke, S.S., and S.A. Woosley. 2005. An Exploration of the Factors that Affect the Academic Success of College Sophomores. *College Student Journal* 39(2):367-77.

Guskin, A.E. 1997. Learning More, Spending Less. *About Campus* 2(3):4-9.

Hu, S. and G.D. Kuh. 2003. Diversity Experiences and College Student Learning and Personal Development. *Journal of College Student Development* 44(3):320-34.

Hughes, R. and C.R. Pace. 2003. Using NSSE to Study Student Retention and Withdrawal. *Assessment Update* 15(4):1-2.

Hutchings, P. 1996. The Peer Review of Teaching: Progress, Issues and Prospects. *Innovative Higher Education* 20(4):221-34.

Juillerat, S. 2000. Assessing the Expectations and Satisfactions of Sophomores. In *Visible Solutions for Invisible Students: Helping Sophomores Succeed*, Monograph 31, ed. L.A. Schreiner and J. Pattengale, 19-29. Columbia, SC: University of South Carolina, National Resource Center for the First-Year Experience and Students in Transition.

Kezar, A. 2003. Achieving Student Success: Strategies for Creating Partnerships Between Academic and Student Affairs. *NASPA Journal* 41:1-22.

Kuh, G.D. 2001. Assessing What Really Matters to Student Learning: Inside the National Survey of Student Engagement. *Change* 33(3):10-17.

Kuh, G.D. 2003. What We're Learning About Student Engagement from NSSE: Benchmarks for Effective Educational Practices. *Change* 35(2):24-32.

Kuh, G.D., R.M. Gonyea, and J.M. Williams. 2005. What Students Expect from College and What They Get. In *Promoting Reasonable Expectations: Aligning Student and Institutional Thinking about the College Experience*, ed. T. Miller, B. Bender,

J. Schuh & Associates, 34-64. San Francisco: Jossey-Bass/National Association of Student Personnel Administrators.

Kuh, G.D. and S. Hu. 2001. The Effects of Student-Faculty Interaction in the 1990s. *Review of Higher Education* 24(3):309-32.

Kuh, G.D., J. Kinzie, J. Buckley, B. Bridges, and J.C. Hayek. 2007. Piecing Together the Student Success Puzzle: Research, Propositions, and Recommendations. *ASHE Higher Education Report* 32(5). San Francisco: Jossey-Bass.

Kuh, G.D., J. Kinzie, T. Cruce, R. Shoup, and R.M. Gonyea. 2006. *Connecting the Dots: Multi-Faceted Analyses of the Relationships Between Student Engagement Results from the NSSE, and the Institutional Practices and Conditions That Foster Student Success: Final Report Prepared for Lumina Foundation for Education.* Bloomington, IN: Indiana University, Center for Postsecondary Research.

Kuh, G.D., J. Kinzie, J.H. Schuh, E.J. Whitt and Associates. 2005. *Student Success in College: Creating Conditions that Matter.* San Francisco: Jossey-Bass.

Kuh, G.D., T.F.N. Laird, and P.D. Umbach. 2004. Aligning Faculty and Student Behavior: Realizing the Promise of Greater Expectations. *Liberal Education* 90(4):24-31.

National Research Council. 2000. *How People Learn: Brain, Mind, Experience, and School.* Washington, DC: National Academy Press.

National Survey of Student Engagement (NSSE). 2005. *Student Engagement: Exploring Different Dimensions of Student Engagement.* Bloomington, IN: Indiana University Center for Postsecondary Research.

NSSE. 2006. *Engaged Learning: Fostering Success for All Students.* Bloomington, IN: Indiana University Center for Postsecondary Research.

NSSE. 2007. *Experiences That Matter: Enhancing Student Learning and Success.* Bloomington, IN: Indiana University Center for Postsecondary Research.

NSSE. 2008. *Promoting Engagement for All Students: The Imperative to Look Within.* Bloomington, IN: Indiana University Center for Postsecondary Research.

Overview of Findings from the First Year of the Wabash National Study of Liberal Arts Education. 2008. Wabash National Study of Liberal Arts Education. Center of Inquiry in the Liberal Arts at Wabash College. Accessed 15 September 2008 at www.Liberalarts.Wabash.Edu/Studyresearch

Pascarella, E. T. and P.T. Terenzini. 1991. *How College Affects Students: Findings and Insights from Twenty-Years of Research* (1st Ed.). San Francisco: Jossey-Bass Publishers.

Pascarella, E.T. and P.T. Terenzini. 2005. *How College Affects Students: A Third Decade of Research.* San Francisco: Jossey-Bass.

Reason, R.D., P.T. Terenzini, and R.J. Domingo. 2005. *First Things First: Developing Academic Competence in the First Year of College.* Paper Presented at the Annual Meeting for the Association for Institutional Research, San Diego, CA (May).

Tagg, J. 2003. *The Learning Paradigm College.* Bolton, MA: Anker Publishing Company.

Tinto, V. 1993. *Leaving College: Rethinking the Causes and Cures of Student Attrition* (2nd Ed.). Chicago: University of Chicago Press.

Turner, R.C. 1998. Adapting to a New Generation of College Students. *Thought and Action, The NEA Journal of Higher Education* 33-41. Accessed 17 December 2009 at http://www.nea.org/assets/img/PubThoughtAndAction/TAA_99Fal_06.pdf

Upcraft, M.L., J.L. Gardner, and B.O. Barefoot. 2005. *Challenging and Supporting the First-Year Student: A Handbook for Improving the First Year of College.* San Francisco: Jossey-Bass.

Missing knowledge and implementation dilemmas in the exploration of the relationships between faculty research and teaching, and student approaches to learning

9

MIND THE GAP: ALIGNING RESEARCH AND PRACTICE IN TEACHING, LEARNING, AND EDUCATIONAL DEVELOPMENT

W. Alan Wright

INTRODUCTION

The chapters in this section of the book have successfully presented an overview of the research regarding the relationship between various approaches to teaching and approaches to learning, how instructor experiences of research and understanding of subject matter factor in the mix, and how massive survey data reinforce the research showing that *engagement* stands as a valid proxy for student learning and success in assessing the institutional pulse of teaching and learning effectiveness. The authors of these chapters, international leaders in the field of tertiary education, present an accurate picture of what we know about the relationship between teaching and learning from the research, yet their contributions lead us to questions about missing knowledge and implementation dilemmas. Just as we pay heed to lessons from these authors, we also must "mind the gap" between our current knowledge and several unresolved research and application questions, some of which I will raise here.

Taking Stock: Research on Teaching and Learning in Higher Education, ed. J. Christensen Hughes and J. Mighty. Montreal and Kingston: McGill-Queen's University Press, Queen's Policy Studies Series. © 2010 The School of Policy Studies, Queen's University at Kingston. All rights reserved.

The questions include the applicability of the relational model to a wide variety of university teachers, especially award-winning teachers, who have not necessarily articulated their conceptualization of teaching in self-reports. The issues include the central importance of fostering greater learning autonomy among undergraduate students and the need to identify and promote operational strategies to this end, distinguishing learner priorities from teacher priorities where applicable. The chapters in this section do not focus in any depth on the research dealing with student background and characteristics as a factor in the teaching and learning environment: what is the place of that research in lending perspective to what we know about effective teaching and learning?

To complete the treatment of what we know about the teaching and learning nexus we must also consider the teaching profile as a dynamic rather than a static entity, identifying patterns and strategies for development. The notion of the professional development of faculty, or educational development, must be more closely examined as a collective activity: what do we know about what works at the level of mass movement towards enhanced teaching and learning? Finally, many studies concentrate efforts on measuring teaching effectiveness at the individual level, and some zero in on the teacher as superhero, the pedagogical prodigy. Although the exercise of identifying the enlightened teacher is useful, hope for change beyond the prospect of cloning the best instructors lies in part with stimulating and recognizing collegial action in the academic arena. What are our best leads, our best options and obligations in that regard? By raising some of these questions, I hope to place the excellent work of our contributing authors in a broader context, to suggest links to other proven avenues of research, and to propose work mindful of the gap between our current research and practices and a more satisfying future picture in that regard.

The Best of the Best

In his very successful monograph, *What the Best College Teachers Do*, Bain (2004) intrigues the reader with glimpses into the pedagogical hearts and minds of nearly 70 of the best university teachers in the US. Bain's study represents a very different kind of research process than most of those described in the three chapters in this section. He spent a great deal of time and energy seeking out a generous sampling of the country's most effective teachers, conducting interviews, and gathering evidence of excellence from several standpoints. Bain is concerned that "teaching is one of those human endeavors that seldom benefits from its past," lamenting that, in the case of great teachers, "their insights die with them" (3). He sets out "to capture the collective scholarship" of his cohort of outstanding teachers, "to record not just what they do but also how they think, and most of all, to begin to conceptualize their practice" (4). Great teachers have in common, according to Bain's work, the ability to help students learn in ways that had a "sustained, substantial, and positive influence on how those students think, act, and feel" (5).

Bain's research has its place in this volume because it represents a brand of research that is potentially very influential among practitioners; the findings—derived from decades of observation, data collection, and interviews—are packaged in a monograph that appeals to a wide audience. His work also provides a point of comparison for local studies, such as the one I recently conducted. In a class offered by a teacher with awards at the institutional, regional, and national levels to his credit, I asked the nearly 400 students to answer a very simple, open-ended question: "What do you like about this class?" They listed many of the qualities captured in several chapters in this book: passion, enthusiasm, energy, optimism, careful planning, organization, clarity, stimulation, interactivity, and engagement.

Teaching Improvement, Teaching Change

In chapter six, Keith Trigwell describes the most effective university teachers as adopting "student-focused strategies" either "aimed at students developing their conceptions" or "aimed at students changing their conceptions." He also acknowledges in reference to Ramsden et al. (1995) that "good teachers are also good learners.... Good teaching is therefore dynamic, reflective, and constantly evolving." Dr. Trigwell concludes: "Teachers' approaches to teaching can be changed."

The challenge of the professional development of faculty is not fully explored in this section of the volume, and the scope of this chapter does not permit a full treatment of this dimension. Yet it is not without importance, for it is one thing to determine whether a university professor is teacher-focused as opposed to student-focused in his or her approach, and quite another to recognize that the choice of approach is in fact a choice, and therefore not fixed. Research into the most effective models for fostering teaching change is essential if we are to go beyond a simple discovery, a snapshot in time, identifying differences in approaches to teaching.

Weimer's *Improving College Teaching: Strategies for Developing Instructional Effectiveness* (1990) is an excellent early example of published work based on the notion that, as "works in progress," professors can systematically address their approaches to teaching through her recommended "instructional improvement process" (34).

Student Self-Directed Learning

Effective teaching, as noted earlier by Keith Trigwell, "encourages self-directed learning." The chapters by Michael Prosser and Jillian Kinzie also suggest that the growth of learning autonomy, the goal of creating conditions in which students take increasing responsibility for their own learning, is paramount in higher education. The promising early literature on the subject of self-directed or autonomous learning (Boud 1988a, 1988b; Brockett and Hiemstra 1991; Candy 1988, 1991; Cornwall 1988; Danis and Tremblay 1985; Guglielmino 1977; Higgs 1988; Knowles 1975) has to an extent been overlooked in post-secondary education's decade of attempts to make the "paradigm shift" from the teaching perspective to the learning perspective (Barr and Tagg 1995). How can teachers adopt strategies fostering learning autonomy, the ultimate goal of our tertiary education system in the eyes of many educators? Boud (1988a) delineated several practices in his published work during the 1980s, yet there has been relatively little systematic effort to study and to implement many of the specific strategies he identified.

In ongoing research based on Boud's identified strategies for fostering learning autonomy, I have surveyed almost 300 teaching faculty from Canada and the US during professional workshops and in classroom settings over the last several years, asking them to choose the most promising of strategies to encourage students to take more responsibility for their own learning. The top-ranked five of the 14 strategies listed were: providing students with the opportunity to reflect on their own learning; opportunities for students to work collaboratively; encouraging students to use instructors as guides and counsellors; asking students to engage in self-assessment; and asking students to find resources needed for learning (see Appendix 1).

How do teacher priorities compare with undergraduate student priorities drawn from the same list? Over 1,000 students from a variety of disciplines were asked to identify the strategies that they thought would benefit their own ability to take greater responsibility for their own learning. Some of the student responses correspond to teacher priorities and others do not. Working collaboratively with other students, and using teachers as guides and counsellors, were among the favoured choices for students surveyed as they were for faculty (collaboration ranked second among the professors and third among the students, while using teachers as guides ranked third for professors and fourth for students).

Where do student and faculty views of priority strategies for student autonomy differ? In our survey, faculty singled out the importance of reflecting on one's learning process as essential for their students by ranking it number one, while the students surveyed ranked it seventh of the 14 items listed. Faculty also emphasized the importance of student engagement in self-assessment as a developmental activity for students, while the student survey ranked that strategy eighth.

What, finally, do our student respondents favour as avenues to promote their own development as learners? They rank setting goals at the top of their list and identifying learning needs as their second priority. Faculty respondents, on the other hand, rank goal-setting as only moderately important (seventh of 14) and student identification of learning needs as slightly more important at sixth place.

In conclusion, then, our surveys show: (a) faculty and students together recognize the value of student collaborative work and the role of faculty as guides, (b) faculty emphasize both student reflection and self-evaluation, and (c) students emphasize the importance of participating in goal setting and identification of their own learning needs. While these observations do not provide, and are not intended to provide, a set formula for introducing strategies fostering learning autonomy in a given environment, they point to the need for academic communities to open sophisticated dialogues involving students regarding the various elements of engagement in the learning process. These observations suggest that it is time to give thoughtful consideration to how, precisely, to move learning autonomy along from noble concept to active reality at the proverbial chalk face, class by class. This process should, according to my reading of the research on the dynamics of teaching and learning, involve deliberate dialogue between students and instructors in a spirit of increasing attention to and participation in the intentional alignment of all phases of the teaching and learning process, from goal-setting and planning to formative and summative evaluation.

Student Background and Characteristics

Jillian Kinzie, in the introduction to her chapter on engagement, writes: "Although it is undeniable that student background characteristics are factors in success, institutions … are focusing their efforts on increasing student engagement to improve student learning and success." In his introduction to teaching-learning relations, Keith Trigwell explains that "students' approaches to learning are seen to be more a relation between student and context than characteristics of the student." Dr. Trigwell does include, however, "characteristics of the student" in his Model of Student Learning. Both authors make an excellent case for the research perspectives they review in this volume. But post-secondary researchers and practitioners concerned about student access and success should not dismiss the work on teaching and learning in higher education which factors in student characteristics and student background when seeking theoretical models and practical solutions to the prominent recruitment and retention issues in today's tertiary environment.

The authors of *Institutional Strategy and Practice: Increasing the Odds of Access and Success at the Post-Secondary Level for Under-Represented Students* (Wright et al. 2008) underline the importance of considering the factors associated with dropping out of tertiary studies for students from under-represented populations such as First Nations communities, lower-income families, and first-generation students of higher education (see Appendix 2). Educational solutions must take into account the risk factors many members of the under-represented groups bring with them to their new settings. These include issues around well-being, finances, social and family support, academic preparation and results, motivation, and self-esteem (Wright et al. 2008).

The many programs, policies, and practices cited in this monograph reflect current research addressing the particular needs of under-represented groups. In evaluating the educational solutions and practices that have arisen from teaching and learning research, educators must be careful not to assume that "one size fits all." Diverse student characteristics and backgrounds may play an important role in a given setting or case.

An Emphasis on Leadership and Community

Keith Trigwell's chapter gives some attention to research on teaching effectiveness, as measured by successful learning strategies resulting from collective actions of academic staff. Jillian Kinzie's chapter emphasizes student engagement, as the concept has appeared in many high-profile research studies as well as in the vast survey data arising from the fine work of the National Survey of Student Engagement (NSSE), as a credible proxy for successful student learning. The above notwithstanding, one aspect of research on teaching and learning as well as one aspect of educational development that remains relatively unrefined and under-represented in the literature is the precise role of departments and departmental leadership, as well as collaborative initiatives among faculty, in establishing values, practices, and habits of mind that are key to effective teaching within communities of pedagogues.

Let us take a brief look at this question, emphasizing the place of departmental teaching excellence under outstanding leadership and innovative faculty collaborations both in confirming what we know about the relationship between effective teaching and authentic student learning and as an important avenue for transferring research knowledge into practice.

Teaching Excellence through Departmental Leadership. In 1995, a volume on *Teaching Improvement Practices: Successful Strategies for Higher Education* (Wright and Associates) presented the results of a study involving respondents from institutional centres for teaching and learning in over 330 universities worldwide (see Appendix 3). A survey required educational developers to evaluate the potential of 36 practices designed to enhance the quality of teaching in the academy. The researchers grouped the 36 practices into nine categories of four questions, which were rank-ordered on the basis of mean scores. The categories gaining the most support of the developers in terms of perceived potential for improving teaching across campus were: demonstrated leadership on teaching matters by deans and academic department heads; and recognition and emphasis on teaching in employment policies and practices in personnel decisions (such as hiring and tenure/promotion, see 6-21). These two groupings led the way in terms of perceived potential for positive impacts on teaching, with categories such as the leadership of senior academic administration, summative measures of teaching, and even developmental and training activities trailing behind in terms of their perceived importance in enhancing teaching across campus (11). In short, hundreds of respondents in the business of supporting teaching enhancement from several countries perceived that leadership for teaching effectiveness begins at the department-head level and that it must be supported by tangible decisions that recognize the importance of teaching effectiveness in the area of career development.

Although the results of the survey research described above were compelling and provided an interesting point of departure to launch or to adjust an educational development plan on a given campus, more study was required to examine and describe the precise role of the department head in fostering excellence in teaching. To this end, Gibbs, Knapper, and Piccinin (2007) reported on a unique international study of the leadership of department heads in excellent teaching departments in 11 renowned universities in several different countries. Their findings described the successes of department heads in building communities of practice, recognizing and rewarding teaching-development efforts as well as teaching excellence, and setting high teaching expectations (2). Department heads also engaged students in the process of change, involved them in the decision-making process about teaching, and in the implementation of innovations. Significant and recent research therefore indicates that the nature and quality of academic leadership is a central lever in the dynamics of departments noted for teaching excellence.

Teaching Excellence through Innovative Collaboration. The Alan Blizzard Award, created by the Society for Teaching and Learning in Higher Education (STLHE), is a program intended to stimulate and reward collaborative efforts to enhance the effectiveness of university teaching and learning and, through the published papers exploring these collaborative projects, to disseminate a scholarship of effective collaborative practice as well (see Appendix 4). Since 1998, the monographs written by award-winning teams from universities across Canada have provided a number of significant insights into the value of and typical patterns connected with innovative collaborative practice.[1] These projects build on and go beyond, in many ways, findings from research on effective teaching and learning, which is frequently based on measures of success in the courses of an instructor working essentially alone.

The papers published by the winning groups recount in considerable detail the process of observation, reflection, negotiation, data collection, further reflection, and renegotiation that are fundamental to collaborative teaching practice. While all of the writers indicated that this process is extremely time intensive, its benefits for the individuals involved, and for the students, are very clear. These include:

- interdisciplinary negotiation and the construction of new knowledge;
- the development of an observable model of inter-departmental collaboration;
- the development of collegial teams involving faculty, graduate assistants, and support staff;
- a commitment to reflective practice and materials review that becomes visible on a broader scale;
- a broader impact campus-wide than the excellent teaching practices of individuals;
- national and international visibility of award-winning projects leading to presentations nationally and overseas;
- renewal of project team members, which helps to initiate new professors into effective practices and encourages new ideas and energies;
- commitment to the idea that teachers can develop their abilities and effectiveness over time through professional contact with colleagues.

The Blizzard Papers suggest that collaboration among academics and support staff to develop team-taught curriculum initiatives, when successful, can lead to learning environments that display many of the characteristics which, according to the research, are favourable to evolved teaching and deep, sustained learning of lasting value.

CONCLUSION

The chapters in this section are in perfect harmony with one of the main objectives of this volume as they illustrate many of the recent advances in our knowledge about the relationships between teaching and learning. The contributing authors deal with essential questions regarding the characteristics of a pedagogical environment required to engage students and to stimulate deep and authentic learning. Many of these characteristics have been carefully described. I do believe, however, that we must *mind the gap* between our acquired knowledge and the many pieces of the puzzle yet to be put into place. In particular, researchers must pursue work on those teaching profiles and behaviours which best correspond to student acquisition of intended learning outcomes, explore further the specific avenues to student-learning autonomy, delve more deeply into the issue of engagement as it plays out for at-risk students in the context of access and success questions, and measure the far-reaching impacts of collective excellence in tertiary pedagogy. The dynamics of professional development of post-secondary faculty as they evolve towards more sophisticated pedagogies must be studied, as should broad-based educational development programs, policies, and practices. What we now know from the research about the nature of teaching and learning in higher education must be linked to the realm of educational development to provide the vital bridge between sound theory and broad-based practice.

NOTES

I am grateful to Bev Hamilton, assistant to the vice-provost, teaching and learning, for her research contributions in preparing this article, as well as to Jessica Raffoul of the Centre for Teaching Learning for her help with style and format.

[1] This compilation of processes and benefits is based on a review of the Alan Blizzard Award Winning Papers (see Appendix 4; also Ostafichuk et al. 2008; McCahan et al. 2007; Zundel et al. 2006; Harnish et al. 2005; Caswell et al. 2004; Heyes et al. 2003; Lechowicz et al. 2002; Justice et al. 2001; Alisharan et al. 2001).

REFERENCES

Alisharan, S., A. Boardman, B. Cox, P. Frost, D. Jennings, N. Langton, T. McCormick, P. Nemetz, W. Norman, and R. Pollay. 2001. *Team Teaching and Team Learning in UBC's MBA Core.* The Alan Blizzard Award Paper: Special Publication of the Society for Teaching and Learning in Higher Education and McGraw-Hill Ryerson, Windsor. Accessed at http://www.mcmaster.ca/stlhe/awards/previous.recipients.html

Bain, K. 2004. *What the Best College Teachers Do.* Cambridge: Harvard University Press.

Barr, R.B. and J. Tagg. 1995. From Teaching to Learning: A New Paradigm for Undergraduate Education. *Change Magazine* (November/December):12-25.

Boud, D.J., ed. 1988a. *Developing Autonomy in Learning,* 2nd edition. London: Kogan Page.

Boud, D.J. 1988b. Moving Towards Autonomy. In *Developing Autonomy in Learning,* 2nd edition, ed. D.J. Boud. London: Kogan Page.

Brockett, R.G. and R. Hiemstra. 1991. *Self-Direction in Adult Learning: Perspectives on Theory, Research, and Practice.* London: Routledge.

Candy, P. 1988. On the Attainment of Subject-Matter Autonomy. In *Developing Autonomy in Learning,* 2nd edition, ed. D.J. Boud. London: Kogan Page.

Candy, P. 1991. *Self-Direction for Lifelong Learning: A Comprehensive Guide to Theory and Practice.* San Francisco: Jossey-Bass Publishers.

Caswell, D., D. Douglas, M. Eggermont, D. Howard, C. Johnston, R. Day, and P. Deacon. 2004. *Fostering Creative Problem-Solving in a Multi-Disciplinary Environment.* The Alan Blizzard Award Paper: Special Publication of the Society for Teaching and Learning in Higher Education and McGraw-Hill Ryerson. Accessed at http://www.mcmaster.ca/stlhe/awards/previous.recipients.html

Cornwall, M. 1988. Independent Learning in a Traditional Institution. In *Developing Autonomy in Learning,* 2nd edition, ed. D.J. Boud. London: Kogan Page.

Danis, C. and N. Tremblay. 1985. The Self-Directed Learning Experience: Major Recurrent Tasks to Deal With. Paper presented at the Fourth Annual Conference of the Canadian Association for the Study of Adult Education, Montreal, QC.

Gibbs, G., C. Knapper, and S. Piccinin. 2007. The Role of Departmental Leadership in Fostering Excellent Teaching. *In Practice* 13:1-4.

Guglielmino, L.M. 1977. Development of the Self-Directed Learning Readiness Scale. PhD dissertation, University of Georgia.

Harnish, D., S. Barrett, J. Butler, E. Cates, C. deLottinville, M. Jordana, E. Kustra, J. Landicho, A. Lee, A. McLellan, J. McKinnell, S. Nastos, D. Nifakis, S. Park, S. Ritz, M. Secord, H. Szechtman, and K. Trim. 2005. *Skill Development with Students and Explicit Integration Across Four Years of the Curriculum.* The Alan Blizzard Award Paper: Special Publication of the Society for Teaching and Learning in Higher Education and McGraw-Hill Ryerson. Accessed at http://www.mcmaster.ca/stlhe/awards/previous.recipients.html

Heyes, C., P. Beach, C. Berccea, J. Hodgson, D. Kahane, L. Kretz, B. Leachy, C. Lepock, C. McTavish, E. Panasiuk, J. Runke, J. Simpson, L. A. Spencer, and J. Welchman. 2003. *"Always Ask Why?" Teaching Philosophy 101: The "Supersection" Experience at the University of Alberta.* The Alan Blizzard Award Paper: Special Publication of the Society for Teaching and Learning in Higher Education and McGraw-Hill Ryerson. Accessed at http://www.mcmaster.ca/stlhe/awards/previous.recipients.html

Higgs, J. 1988. Planning Learning Experiences to Promote Autonomous Learning. In *Developing Autonomy in Learning*, 2nd edition, ed. D.J. Boud. London: Kogan Page.

Justice, C., C. Cuneo, S. Inglis, S. Miller, J. Rice, S.Sammon, and W. Warry. 2001. *A Grammar for Inquiry: Linking Goals and Methods in a Collaboratively Taught Social Sciences Inquiry Course.* The Alan Blizzard Award Paper: Special Publication of the Society for Teaching and Learning in Higher Education and McGraw-Hill Ryerson, Windsor. Accessed at http://www.mcmaster.ca/stlhe/awards/previous.recipients.html

Knowles, M.S. 1975. *Self-Directed Learning: A Guide for Learners and Teachers.* New York: Association Press.

Lechowicz, M.J., D. Baker, M. Lapointe, J. Paquette, W. Pollard, M. Waterway, and T. Wheller. 2002. *Developing Critical Thinking Skills in a Multidisciplinary Context: Meeting the Challenges of Collaborative Teaching in the McGill School of Environment.* The Alan Blizzard Award Paper: Special Publication of the Society for Teaching and Learning in Higher Education and McGraw-Hill Ryerson. Accessed at http://www.mcmaster.ca/stlhe/awards/previous.recipients.html

McCahan, S., P. Anderson, R. Andrews, M. Kortschot, S. Romas, K. Woodhouse, and P. Weiss. 2007. *Engineering Strategies and Practice: Team Teaching a Service Learning Course for a Large Class.* The Alan Blizzard Award Paper: Special Publication of the Society for Teaching and Learning in Higher Education and McGraw-Hill Ryerson. Accessed at http://www.mcmaster.ca/stlhe/awards/previous.recipients.html

Ostafichuk, P., E. Croft, M. Davy, M. Fengler, S. Green, A. Hodgson, P. Loewen, W. Poole, S. Rogak, G. Schajer, M. Schoen, T. Teslenko, B. Wetton, and J. Yan. 2008. *Mech 2: A Collaboratively Designed and Delivered Program for Second-Year Mechanical Engineering.* The Alan Blizzard Award Paper: Special Publication of the Society for Teaching and Learning in Higher Education and McGraw-Hill

Ryerson. Accessed at http://www.mcmaster.ca/stlhe/awards/previous. recipients.html

Ramsden, P., D. Martgetson, E. Martin, and S. Clarke. 1995. *Recognising and Rewarding Good Teaching*. Canberra: Australian Government Printing Services.

Weimer, M. 1990. *Improving College Teaching*. San Francisco: Jossey-Bass Publishers.

Wright, A. and Associates. 1995. *Teaching Improvement Practices: Successful Strategies for Higher Education*. Bolton: Anker Publishing Company, Inc.

Wright, A., M. Frenay, M. Monette, B. Tomen, L. Sauvé, C. Smith, N. Gold, D. Houston, J. Robinson, and N. Rowen. 2008. *Institutional Strategy and Practice: Increasing the Odds of Access and Success at the Post-Secondary Level for Under-Represented Students*. Montreal: The Canadian Millennium Scholarship Foundation.

Zundel, P., M. Bishop, M. Carr, G. Clarke, J. Colford, K. Fong, J. Foster, R. Hutchins, V.Joyce, N. Long, E. Lynch, T. Mengel, V. Reeves, C. Roderick, J. Pazienza, A. Sharp, R. Sapcek, and J. Valk. 2006. *Outcomes-Based Learning at a Whole Program Level*. The Alan Blizzard Award Paper: Special Publication of the Society for Teaching and Learning in Higher Education and McGraw-Hill Ryerson. Accessed at http://www.mcmaster.ca/stlhe/awards/previous.recipients.html

APPENDIX 1
Development of Learning Autonomy Survey Results (January 2009)

The main characteristic of autonomy as an approach to learning is that students take significant responsibility for their own learning, over and above responding to instruction. Each respondent selected five approaches to learning autonomy s/he judged appropriate in his or her educational environment. This tabulation represents the results of the compiled responses from undergraduate classes at two universities (University of Windsor and Université du Québec (Lévis). The table order is based on a compilation of responses from 297 Canadian and US university professors shown in descending order of response frequency.

Approach to learning autonomy ordered by faculty ranking	Total faculty (n=297)	Undergraduate student ranking	Total undergraduate students (n=1,088)
1. Reflecting on one's learning processes	185	7	368
2. Working collaboratively with others	182	3	478
3. Using teachers as guides and counsellors rather than instructors	148	4	463
4. Engaging in self-assessment	137	8	361
5. Finding resources needed for learning	132	6	410
6. Identifying learning needs	113	2	529
8. Setting goals	107	1	624
7. Selecting learning projects	93	10	330
9. Creating problems to tackle	82	12	269
10. Learning beyond the educational institution (museums, archives, etc.)	81	9	345
11. Determining criteria to apply to one's work	73	11	309
12. Planning learning activities	55	13	250
13. Choosing when and where to learn	19	5	411
14. Deciding when learning is complete	17	14	186

Source: Author's compilation.

APPENDIX 2
Factors Associated with Dropping Out of Post-Secondary Studies

	Well-being	Finances	Social/family/ friends' support	Academic preparation and results	Motivation	Self-esteem
Aboriginal students	• Isolation • Stress • Racist attitudes on campus	• Need for financial aid	• Far from home community • Lack of awareness of cultural realities on campus	• Choice of studies • Engagement • Academic history	• Value of education • Intention to persist	• Poor opinion of one's own ability
Low-income students	• Isolation • Stress	• Need for financial aid	• Parents lack PSE credentials	• Choice of studies • Engagement • Academic history	• Value of education • Intention to persist	• Poor opinion of one's own ability
First-generation students	• Isolation • Stress	• Need for financial aid for some	• Parents lack PSE credentials	• Choice of studies • Engagement • Academic history	• Value of education • Intention to persist	• Poor opinion of one's own ability

Source: Wright et al. (2008, 7).

APPENDIX 3
Teaching Improvement Practices, Categories by Rank

Category	All respondents		
	Rank	Mean	S.D.
Leadership: deans & heads	1	29.25	6.41
Employment policies & practices	2	28.26	6.13
Development opportunities & grants	3	27.15	5.75
Formative evaluation of instruction	4	26.05	5.49
Structure and organization	5	25.65	5.46
Leadership: senior administration	6	25.55	7.28
Educational events	7	25.46	5.59
Developmental resources	8	24.42	4.92
Summative evaluation of instruction	9	22.25	6.17

Source: Wright and Associates (1995, 11).

APPENDIX 4
Excerpts from the Alan Blizzard Award Papers

- Interdisciplinary negotiation and the construction of new knowledge; repositioning experts as learners as well. "We are convinced that our own learning at the interfaces among our disciplinary specialties has led to the creation of an unusually effective teaching and learning environment" (Lechowicz et al. 2002, 2).

- A model of rotating speakers that students experience as fragmented evolves towards a model based on close collaboration and/or interdisciplinarity (Lechowicz et al. 2002; Heyes et al. 2003). The process of establishing how to collaborate is often very explicit and results in a model that enables practice to be visible and observed. "[E]ach member of the teaching team has his or her area of responsibility ... a significant amount of communication and consultation ensures coordination between various course elements" (McCahan et al. 2007, 16).

- Multiple layers of the teaching team working together as colleagues, including professors and graduate assistants. "[I]n a traditionally solitary and hierarchical discipline, we are more optimistic and informed about the possibilities for genuinely collaborative relationships among faculty and graduate students" (Heyes et al. 2003, 2).

- The explicit reflection processes such as materials review are enhanced by a group process and ongoing commitment (McCahan et al. 2007, 16). "The ... supersection remains a work in progress" (Heyes et al. 2003, 15). At McMaster University, the team held weekly meetings for more than four years to discuss course and student learning.

- Reflective practice of teachers becomes visible in a collective. "We had bonded as a team in the working group and had learned so much from our interactions that we wanted to keep the spirit alive in the course and communicate our growing insights to the students" (Lechowicz et al. 2002, 8).

- Visibility of these major projects has greater campus influence than actions of the individual. "Your efforts have been central to our success in obtaining the additional funds we have received to enhance undergraduate learning experiences" (Heyes et al. 2003, 34; Zundel et al. 2006). The visibility also extends to the national and international level (e.g., McMaster University invited to consult with the University of Calgary, the University of Mexico, the University of Ottawa, the University of Ontario Institute of Technology, and Lund University, Sweden).

- Communicates clearly that teachers are made, not born. The McGill team, for example, described the importance of developing methods to integrate new staff into the teaching team and of providing time for them to "catch the spirit of the enterprise" (Lechowicz et al. 2002, 9). New faculty in this program reviewed PowerPoint slides from the previous year's presentations, and sat in on and participated in many lectures before taking on a teaching role in order to develop the necessary ethos and skills.

- Transfer of skills, attitudes, and practices from within collaborative projects to courses and programs beyond the project. "Being cross-appointed ... has been an invaluable experience for me, in terms of my own professional development, my professional well-being and my teaching abilities. Collaborating with them is proving to be much more valuable than deciding what to do with the introductory courses on my own" (Zundel et al. 2006, 14).

- Renewal and academic staff turnover on teams leads to a further exchange of pedagogical expertise. "[I]t is essential to develop methods to integrate new staff into the teaching team.... These newcomers can also bring "a fresh insight ... the course ... will often be improved by the infusion of new ideas and energy" (Lechowicz et al. 2002, 9).

- Learning ethos of teams: "As an integrated team we are learning more ourselves than any of us ever imagined we would, and this learning among the professors is revealing new ways to teach the students" (Lechowicz et al. 2002, 12).

Source: Author's compilation.

SECTION IV

WHAT WE KNOW ABOUT EXEMPLARY TEACHING PRACTICES

SECTION COMMENTARY

Thomas Carey

This section of the book introduces complementary perspectives about how advances in our understanding of teaching and learning, as described in the previous chapters, can be translated into the identification of exemplary practices in post-secondary education. The authors have each made significant contributions to our understanding of how students learn, as well as how we can apply such knowledge and evidence to enhance the learning experience and success of our students.

Carl Wieman has received the highest honors in science for discovery research (Nobel Prize in Physics, 2001), teaching (University Professor of the Year in the US, 2004), and the scholarship of teaching and learning (American Association of Physics Teachers Oersted Medal, 2007). Drawing on the work of Shulman (1986), Dr. Wieman argues in his chapter that enhancing teaching practice requires much more than just mastery of the topic—it requires *pedagogical content knowledge*[1] and a commitment to employing learning activities that ensure students think about and actively process important ideas.

Jan H.F. Meyer has been a distinguished academic and leader in academic development on three continents. He is well-known for his pioneering work in *threshold concepts*. This and other aspects of his research, including metalearning and models of student learning that are sensitive to disciplinary contexts and individual differences, are skillfully presented in his chapter.

The focus of this section of the book on "exemplary practices" may initially have caused readers some concern; indeed, there was considerable discussion at the research symposium (that led to this book) on the feasibility or desirability of identifying particular teaching practices as being more or less effective than others (without ample qualification regarding context and circumstances). Similarly, in his chapter, Dr. Meyer warns against premature determination of what will work best in a given situation *before the course even commences or the students are known.* However, the "exemplary practices" outlined in these chapters are more about the teacher's process of conceptualizing and creating instruction than about the instructional process itself. Dr. Meyer uses as illustration a particular program for newer teachers at his institution; Dr. Wieman complements this example with a focus on encouraging scientific researchers to mobilize knowledge and methods from research on learning. Taken together, these two chapters demonstrate how instructors can apply the knowledge and evidence about teaching in their subject areas in ways that acknowledge the variations in context and in student capabilities and needs.

In the final chapter, which concludes this section, I provide some personal reflections as a practitioner/researcher in mobilizing knowledge and evidence for exemplary teaching. The focal point for these reflections is another form of variation: diversity in the nature of the knowledge and evidence which can contribute to exemplary teaching, and implications for teachers and those who support their development as educators.

NOTE

[1] "[T]he ways of representing and formulating the subject that make it comprehensible to others" (Shulman 2008).

REFERENCES

Shulman, L.S. 1986. Those Who Understand: Knowledge Growth in Teaching. *Educational Researcher* (February):4-14. (AERA Presidential Address).

Shulman, L. 2008. *Pedagogical Content Knowledge*, article in The Work of Dr. Lee Shulman. Accessed 12 January 2010 at http://www.leeshulman.net/domains-pedagogical-content-knowledge.html

> *Taking a more scholarly approach to education—that is, utilizing research on how the brain learns, carrying out careful research on what students are learning, and adjusting our instructional practices accordingly—has great promise to not only help us better teach students, but also to transform how they think about science.*

10

WHY NOT TRY A SCIENTIFIC APPROACH TO SCIENCE EDUCATION?

Carl Wieman

The purpose of science education is no longer simply to train that tiny fraction of the population who will become the next generation of scientists. We need a more scientifically literate populace to address the global challenges that humanity now faces and that only science can explain and possibly mitigate, such as global warming, as well as to make wise decisions, informed by scientific understanding, about issues such as genetic modification. Moreover, the modern economy is largely based on science and technology, and for that economy to thrive and for individuals within

Reprinted with permission. This article was previously published as Wieman, C. 2007. Why Not Try a Scientific Approach to Science Education? *Change: The Magazine of Higher Learning* (September/October). Free version available online at http://www.changemag.org/Archives/Back%20Issues/September-October%202007/full-scientific-approach.html (accessed 7 May 2009). Subscription version hosted at Ebscohost http://web.ebscohost.com/ehost/pdf?vid=4&hid=104&sid=16fac5d3-f233-4e53-8f75-48f7b25f623b%40sessionmgr111

it to be successful, we need technically literate citizens with complex problem-solving skills.

In short, we now need to make science education effective and relevant for a large and necessarily more diverse fraction of the population.

What do I mean by an effective education in science? I believe a successful science education transforms how students think, so that they can understand and use science like scientists do (see Figure 1). But is this kind of transformation really possible for a large fraction of the total population?

FIGURE 1
Transporting Student Thinking from Novice to Expert

Source: Author's compilation.

The hypothesis that I and others have advanced is that it is possible, but only if we approach the teaching of science like a science. That means applying to science teaching the practices that are essential components of scientific research and that explain why science has progressed at such a remarkable pace in the modern world.

The most important of these components are:

- Practices and conclusions based on objective data rather than—as is frequently the case in education—anecdote or tradition. This includes using the results of prior research, such as work on how people learn.
- Disseminating results in a scholarly manner and copying and building upon what works. Too often in education, particularly at the post-secondary level, everything is reinvented, often in a highly flawed form, every time a different instructor teaches a course. (I call this problem "reinventing the square wheel.").

- Fully utilizing modern technology. Just as we are always looking for ways to use technology to advance scientific research, we need to do the same in education.

These three essential components of all experimental scientific research (and, not incidentally, of the scholarship of teaching and learning) can be equally valuable in science education. Applied to the teaching of science, they have the capability to dramatically improve both the effectiveness and the efficiency of our educational system.

The Learning Puzzle

When I first taught physics as a young assistant professor, I used the approach that is all too common when someone is called upon to teach something. First, I thought very hard about the topic and got it clear in my own mind. Then I explained it to my students so that they would understand it with the same clarity I had.

At least that was the theory. But I am a devout believer in the experimental method, so I always measure results (see Figure 2). And whenever I made any serious attempt to determine what my students were learning, it was clear that this approach just didn't work. An occasional student here and there might have understood my beautifully clear and clever explanations, but the vast majority of students weren't getting them at all.

FIGURE 2
Student Reaction to My Brilliantly Clear Explanations

Source: Author's compilation.

For many years, this failure of students to learn from my explanations remained a frustrating puzzle to me, as I think it is for many diligent faculty members. What eventually led me to understand it was that I was encountering the even bigger puzzle of my graduate students.

I have conducted an extensive research program in atomic physics over many years that has involved many graduate students, on whose professional development I have spent a lot of time and thought. And over the years I became aware of a consistent pattern. New graduate students would come to work in my laboratory after 17 years of extraordinary success in classes, but when they were given research projects to work on, they were clueless about how to proceed. Or worse, often it seemed that they didn't even really understand what physics was.

But then an amazing thing happened: after just a few years of working in my research lab, interacting with me and the other students, they were transformed. I would suddenly realize they were now expert physicists, genuine colleagues. If this had happened only once or twice it would have just seemed an oddity, but I realized it was a consistent pattern. So I decided to figure it out.

One hypothesis that occurred to me, as it has to many other research advisors who have observed similar transformations, is that the human brain has to go through a 17-year "caterpillar" stage before it is suddenly transformed into a physicist "butterfly" (see Figure 3). But I wasn't satisfied with that explanation, so I tackled it like a science problem. I started studying the research on how people learn, particularly how they learn science, to see if it could provide a more satisfactory explanation of the pattern. Sure enough, the research did have another explanation to offer that also solved the earlier puzzle of why my classroom teaching was ineffective.

FIGURE 3
Brain-Development Possibility: 17 Years as Intellectual Caterpillar before Transformation into Physicist Butterfly?

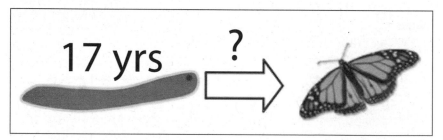

Source: Author's compilation.

Research on Learning

In a traditional science class, the teacher stands at the front of the class lecturing to a largely passive group of students. Those students then go off and do back-of-the-chapter homework problems from the textbook and take exams that are similar to those exercises.

The research has several things to say about this pedagogical strategy, but I'll focus on three findings—the first about the retention of information from lecture, the second about understanding basic concepts, and the third about general beliefs regarding science and scientific problem-solving.

The data I discuss were mostly gathered in introductory college physics courses, but these results are consistent with those of similar studies done in other scientific disciplines and at other grade levels. This is understandable, because they are consistent with what we know about cognition.

Retaining Information. Lectures were created as a means of transferring information from one person to many, so an obvious topic for research is the retention of the information by the many. The results of three studies—which can be replicated by any faculty member with a strong enough stomach—are instructive. The first is by Redish (2003), a highly regarded physics professor at the University of Maryland. Even though the students thought his lectures were wonderful, Joe wondered how much they were actually learning. So he hired a graduate student to grab students at random as they filed out of class at the end of the lecture and ask, "What was the lecture you just heard about?" It turned out that the students could respond with only with the vaguest of generalities.

Hrepic, Zollman, and Rebello (2007) at Kansas State University carried out a much more structured study. They asked 18 students from an introductory physics class to attempt to answer six questions on the physics of sound and then, primed by that experience, to get the answers to those questions by listening to a 14-minute, highly polished commercial videotaped lecture given by someone who is supposed to be the world's most accomplished physics lecturer. On most of the six questions, no more than one student was able to answer correctly.

In a final example, a number of times Perkins et al. (2005) and I have presented some non-obvious fact in a lecture along with an illustration, and then quizzed the students 15 minutes later on the fact. About ten percent usually remember it by then. To see whether we simply had mentally deficient students, I once repeated this experiment when I was giving a departmental colloquium at one of the leading physics departments in the US. The audience was made up of physics faculty members and graduate students, but the result was about the same—around ten percent.

Given that there are thousands of traditional science lectures being given every day, these results are quite disturbing. Do these findings make sense? Could this meagre transfer of information in lectures be a generic problem? (Table 1)

These results do indeed make a lot of sense and probably are generic, based on one of the most well-established—yet widely ignored—results of cognitive science: the extremely limited capacity of the short-term working memory. The research tells us that the human brain can hold a maximum of about seven different items in its short-term working memory and can process no more than about four ideas at once. Exactly what an "item" means when translated from the cognitive science lab into the classroom is a bit fuzzy. But the number of new items that students are expected to remember and process in the typical hour-long science lecture is vastly

TABLE 1
Comparison of Learning Results from Traditionally Taught Courses and Courses Using Research-Based Pedagogy

Traditional Instruction	Research-Based Instruction
Retention of information from lecture: 10% after 15 minutes	Retention of information from lecture: More than 90% after 2 days
Gain in conceptual understanding: 25%	Gain in conceputal understanding: 50-70%
Beliefs about physics and problem-solving: significant drop	A small improvement

Source: Author's compilation.

greater. So we should not be surprised to find that students are able to take away only a small fraction of what is presented to them in that format.

Understanding Basic Concepts. We physicists believe that one of the great strengths of physics is that it has a few fundamental concepts that can be applied very widely. This has inspired physics-education researchers to study how well students are actually learning the basic concepts in their physics courses, particularly at the introductory level.

These researchers have created some good assessment tools for measuring conceptual understanding. Probably the oldest and most widely used of these is the Force Concepts Inventory (FCI) by Hestenes, Wells, and Swackhamer (1992). This instrument tests students' mastery of the basic concepts of force and motion, which are covered in every first-semester post-secondary physics course. The FCI is composed of carefully developed and tested questions that usually require students to apply the concepts of force and motion in a real-world context, such as explaining what happens when a car runs into a truck. The FCI—now administered in hundreds of courses annually—normally is given at the beginning and end of the semester to see how much students have learned during the course.

Hake (1998) compiled the FCI results from 14 different traditional courses and found that in the traditional lecture course, students master no more than 30 percent of the key concepts that they didn't already know at the start of the course (see Figure 4). Similar sub-30-percent gains are seen in many other unpublished studies and are largely independent of lecturer quality, class size, and institution. The consistency of those results clearly demonstrates that the problem is in the basic pedagogical approach: the traditional lecture is simply not successful in helping most students achieve mastery of fundamental concepts. Pedagogical approaches involving more interactive engagement of students show consistently higher gains on the FCI and similar tests.

FIGURE 4
Fractional Improvement in FCI Score

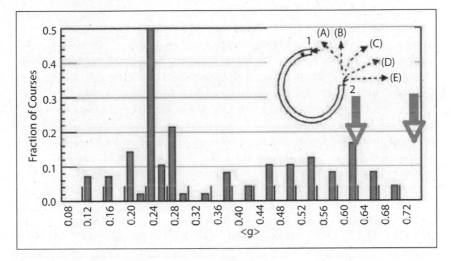

Note: FCI = Force Concepts Inventory.
Source: Plot from Hake (1998).

Affecting Beliefs. Students believe certain things about what physics is and how one goes about learning the discipline, as well as how one solves problems in physics. If you interview a lot of people, you find that their beliefs lay on a spectrum that ranges from "novice" to "expert." My research group and others have developed survey instruments that can measure where on this scale a person's beliefs lay.

What do we mean by a "novice" in this context? Adapting the characterization developed by Hammer (1997), novices see the content of physics instruction as isolated pieces of information—handed down by an authority and disconnected from the world around them—that they can only learn by memorization. To the novice, scientific problem-solving is just matching the pattern of the problem to certain memorized recipes.

Experts—i.e., physicists—see physics as a coherent structure of concepts that describe nature and that have been established by experiment. Expert problem solving involves employing systematic, concept-based, and widely applicable strategies. Since this includes being applicable in completely new situations, this strategy is much more useful than the novice problem-solving approach.

Once you develop the tools to measure where people's beliefs lay on this expert-to-novice scale, you can see how students' beliefs change as a result of their courses. What you would expect, or at least hope, is that students would begin their college physics course somewhere on the novice side of the scale and that, after completing the course, they would have become more expert-like in their beliefs.

What the data say is just the opposite. On average, students have more novice-like beliefs after they have completed an introductory physics course than they had when they started; this was found for nearly every introductory course measured. More recently, my group started looking at beliefs about chemistry. If anything, the effect of taking an introductory college chemistry course is even worse than for taking physics.

So we are faced with another puzzle about traditional science instruction. This instruction is explicitly built around teaching concepts and is being provided by instructors who, at least at the college level, are unquestionably experts in the subject. And yet their students are not learning concepts, and they are acquiring novice beliefs about the subject. How can this be?

Research on learning once again provides answers. Cognitive scientists have spent a lot of time studying what constitutes expert competence in any discipline, and they have found a few basic components. The first is that experts have lots of factual knowledge about their subject, which is hardly a surprise. Second, experts have a mental organizational structure that facilitates the retrieval and effective application of their knowledge. Third, experts have an ability to monitor their own thinking ("meta-cognition"), at least in their discipline of expertise. They are able to ask themselves: "Do I understand this? How can I check my understanding?"

A traditional science instructor concentrates on teaching factual knowledge, with the implicit assumption that expert-like ways of thinking about the subject come along for free or are already present. But that is not what cognitive science tells us. It tells us instead that students need to develop these different ways of thinking by means of extended, focused mental effort. Also, new ways of thinking are always built on the prior thinking of the individual, so if the educational process is to be successful, it is essential to take that prior thinking into account.

This is basic biology. Everything that constitutes "understanding" science and "thinking scientifically" resides in the long-term memory, which is developed via the construction and assembly of component proteins. So a person who does not go through this extended mental construction process simply cannot achieve mastery of a subject.

When you understand what makes up expert competence and how it is developed, you can see how cognitive science accounts for the classroom results that I presented earlier. Students are not learning the scientific concepts that enable experts to organize and apply the information of the discipline, nor are they being helped to develop either the mental organizational structure that facilitates the retrieval and application of that knowledge or a capacity for metacognition. So it makes perfect sense that they are not learning to think like experts, even though they are passing science courses by memorizing facts and problem-solving recipes.

Improved Teaching and Learning. If we now return to the puzzle of my graduate students—why their first 17 years of education seemed so ineffective, while a few years of doing research turned graduate students into expert physicists—we see that the first part of the mystery is solved: those traditional science courses did little to develop expert-like thinking about physics. But why is working in a research lab so different?

A lot of educational and cognitive research can be reduced to this basic principle: people learn by creating their own understanding. But that does not mean they must or even can do it without assistance. Effective teaching facilitates that creation by getting students engaged in thinking deeply about the subject at an appropriate level and then monitoring that thinking and guiding it to be more expert-like.

When you put it in those terms, you realize that this is exactly what all my graduate students are doing 18 or 20 hours a day, seven days a week. (Or at least that is what they claim ... the reality is a bit less.) They are focused intently on solving real physics problems, and I regularly probe how they're thinking and give them guidance to make it more expert-like. After a few years in that environment, they turn into experts, not because there is something magic in the air in the research lab but because they are engaged in exactly the cognitive processes that are required for developing expert competence.

Once I realized this, I started to think how these ideas could be used to improve the teaching of undergraduate science. Of course it would be very effective to put every student into a research lab to work one-on-one with a faculty member rather than taking classes. While that would probably work very well and is not so different from my own education, obviously it is not practical as a widespread solution. So if the economic realities dictate that we have to use courses and classrooms, how can we use these ideas to improve classroom teaching? The key is to get these desirable cognitive activities, as revealed by research, into normal course activities.

I am not alone in coming to this conclusion. There is a significant community of science-education researchers, particularly in physics, who are taking this approach to the development and testing of new pedagogical approaches. This is paying off in clear demonstrations of improved learning. Indeed, some innovative pedagogical strategies are sufficiently mature that they are being routinely replicated by other instructors with similar results.

So what are a few examples of these strategies, and how do they reflect our increasing understanding of cognition?

Reducing Cognitive Load. The first way in which one can use research on learning to create better classroom practices addresses the limited capacity of the short-term working memory. Anything one can do to reduce cognitive load improves learning. The effective teacher recognizes that giving the students material to master is the mental equivalent of giving them packages to carry (see Figure 5). With only one package, they can make a lot of progress in a hurry. If they are loaded down with many, they stagger around, have a lot more trouble, and can't get as far. And when they experience the mental equivalent of many packages dumped on them at once, they are squashed flat and can't learn anything.

So anything the teacher can do to reduce that cognitive load while presenting the material will help. Some ways to do so are obvious, such as slowing down. Others include providing a clear, logical, explicit organization to the class (including making connections between different ideas presented and connections to things the students already know),

FIGURE 5
Result of Loading Student Up with Low, Medium, and High Cognitive Loads

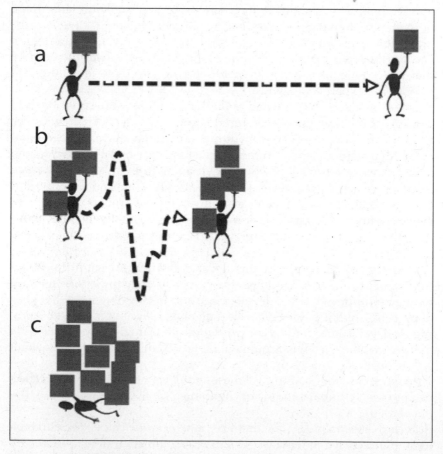

Note: a = low, b = medium, and c = high.
Source: Author's compilation.

using figures where appropriate rather than relying only on verbal descriptions, and minimizing the use of technical jargon. All these things reduce unnecessary cognitive demands and result in more learning.

Addressing Beliefs. A second way teachers can improve instruction is by recognizing the importance of student beliefs about science. This is an area my own group studies. We see that the novice/expert-like beliefs are important in a variety of ways, for example, they correlate with content learning and choice of major. However, our particular interest is how teaching practices affect student beliefs. Although this is a new area of research, we find that with rather minimal interventions, a teacher can avoid the regression mentioned above.

The particular intervention we have tried addresses student beliefs by explicitly discussing, for each topic covered, why this topic is worth learning, how it operates in the real world, why it makes sense, and how it connects to things the student already knows. Doing little more than this eliminates the usual significant decline and sometimes results in small improvements, as measured by our surveys. This intervention also improves student interest, because the beliefs measured are closely linked to that interest.

Stimulating and Guiding Thinking. My third example of how teaching and learning can be improved is by implementing the principle that effective teaching consists of engaging students, monitoring their thinking, and providing feedback. Given the reality that student-faculty interaction at most colleges and universities is going to be dominated by time together in the classroom, this means the teacher must make this happen first and foremost in the classroom.

To do this effectively, teachers must first know where the students are starting from in their thinking, so they can build on that foundation. Then they must find activities that ensure that the students actively think about and process the important ideas of the discipline. Finally, instructors must have mechanisms by which they can probe and then guide that thinking on an ongoing basis. This takes much more than just mastery of the topic; it requires, in the memorable words of Shulman (1987), "pedagogical content knowledge."

Getting students engaged and guiding their thinking in the classroom is just the beginning of true learning, however. This classroom experience has to be followed up with extended "effortful study," where the student spends considerably more time than is possible in the classroom developing expert-like thinking and skills.

Even the most thoughtful, dedicated teachers spend enormously more time worrying about their lectures than they do about their homework assignments, which I think is a mistake. Extended, highly focused mental processing is required to build those little proteins that make up the long-term memory. No matter what happens in the relatively brief period students spend in the classroom, there is not enough time to develop the long-term memory structures required for subject mastery.

To ensure that the necessary extended effort is made, and that it is productive, requires carefully designed homework assignments, grading policies, and feedback. As a practical matter, in a university environment with large classes, the most effective way for students to get the feedback that will make their study time more productive and develop their meta-cognitive skills is through peer collaboration.

Using Technology. I believe that most reasonably good teachers could engage students and guide their thinking if they had only two or three students in the class. But the reality of the modern university is that we must find a way to accomplish this with a class of 200 students. There are a number of new technologies that, when used properly, can be quite effective at extending instructors' capabilities so that they can engage and guide far more students at once.

A caveat: far too often, the technology drives instruction and student thinking rather than educational purposes driving the development and use of the technology. A second caveat: there is far too little careful testing of various technologies' effectiveness in increasing the learning of real students. However, here are three demonstrably effective uses of technology.

"Just-in-time teaching" was introduced by Novack et al. (1999). The technique uses the Web to ask students questions concerning the material to be covered, questions that they must answer just before class. The students thus start the class already engaged, and the instructor, who has looked at the students' answers, already knows a reasonable amount about their difficulties with the topic to be covered.

A second technology that I have worked with extensively is personal-response systems or "clickers." Each student has a clicker with which to answer questions posed during class. A computer records each student's answer and can display a histogram of those responses. The clicker efficiently and quickly gets an answer from each student for which that student is accountable but which is anonymous to their peers.

I have found that these clickers can have a profound impact on the educational experience of students. The most productive use of clickers in my experience is to enhance the Peer Instruction (PI) technique developed by Mazur (1997), particularly for less active or assertive students.

I assign students to groups the first day of class (typically three to four students in adjacent seats) and design each lecture around a series of seven to ten clicker questions that cover the key learning goals for that day. The groups are told they must come to a consensus answer (entered with their clickers) and be prepared to offer reasons for their choice. It is in these peer discussions that most students do the primary processing of the new ideas and problem-solving approaches. The process of critiquing each other's ideas in order to arrive at a consensus also enormously improves both their ability to carry on scientific discourse and to test their own understanding.

Clickers also give valuable (albeit often painful) feedback to the instructor when they reveal, for example, that only ten percent of the students understood what was just explained. But they also provide feedback in less obvious ways. By circulating through the classroom and listening in on the consensus-group discussions, I quickly learn which aspects of the topic confuse students and can then target those points in the follow-up discussion. Perhaps even more important is the feedback provided to the students through the histograms and their own discussions. They become much more invested in their own learning. When using clickers and consensus groups, I have dramatically more substantive questions per class period—more students ask questions, and the students represent a much broader distribution by ethnicity and gender—than when using the peer-instruction approach without clickers.

A third powerful educational technology is the sophisticated online interactive simulation. This technique can be highly effective and takes less time to incorporate into instruction than more traditional materials. My group has created and tested over 60 such simulations and made them available for free (www.phet.colorado.edu). We have explored their use in lecture and homework problems and as replacements for, or enhancements of, laboratories.

The "circuit construction kit" is a typical example of a simulation (see Figure 6). It allows one to build arbitrary circuits involving realistic-looking resistors, light bulbs (which light up), wires, batteries, and switches and get a correct rendition of voltages and currents. There are realistic volt and ammeters to measure circuit parameters. The simulation also shows cartoon-like electrons moving around the circuit in appropriate paths, with velocities proportional to current. We've found this simulation to be a dramatic help to students in understanding the basic concepts of electric current and voltage, when substituted for an equivalent lab with real components.

As with all good educational technology, the effectiveness of good simulations comes from the fact that their design is governed by research on how people learn, and the simulations are carefully tested to ensure they achieve the desired learning. They can enhance the ability of a good instructor to portray how experts think when they see a real-life situation and provide an environment in which a student can learn by observing and exploring. The power of a simulation is that these explorations can be carefully constrained, and what the student sees can be suitably enhanced to facilitate the desired learning. Using these various effective pedagogical strategies, my group and many others have seen dramatic improvements in learning.

FIGURE 6
Circuit Constructions Kit Interactive Simulation

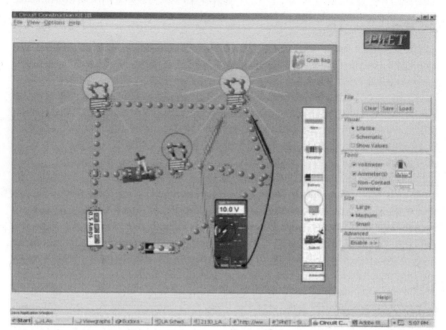

Source: Physics Education Technology Project, University of Colorado (2009).

Institutional Change

We now have good data showing that traditional approaches to teaching science are not successful for a large proportion of our students, and we have a few research-based approaches that achieve much better learning. The scientific approach to science teaching works, but how do we make this the norm for every teacher in every classroom, rather than just a set of experimental projects? This has been my primary focus for the past several years.

A necessary condition for changing college education is changing the teaching of science at the major research universities, because they set the norms that pervade the education system regarding how science is taught and what it means to "learn" science. These departments produce most of the college teachers who then go on to teach science to the majority of college students, including future school teachers. So we must start by changing the practices of those departments.

There are several major challenges to modifying how they educate their students. First, in universities there is generally no connection between incentives in the system and student learning. A lot of people would say that this is because research universities and their faculty don't care about teaching or student learning. I don't think that's true—many instructors care a great deal. The real problem is that we have almost no authentic assessments of what students actually learn, so it is impossible to broadly measure that learning and then connect it to resources and incentives. We do have student evaluations of instructors, but these are primarily popularity contests and not measures of learning.

The second challenge is that while we know how to develop the necessary tools for assessing student learning in a practical, widespread way at the university level, carrying this out would require a significant investment. Introducing effective research-based teaching in all college science courses—by, for instance, developing and testing pedagogically effective materials, supporting technology, and providing for faculty development—would also require resources. But the budget for R&D and the implementation of improved educational methods at most universities is essentially zero. More generally, there is no political will on campus to take the steps required to bring about cultural change in organizations like science departments.

Our society faces both a demand for improved science education and exciting opportunities for meeting those demands. Taking a more scholarly approach to education—that is, utilizing research on how the brain learns, carrying out careful research on what students are learning, and adjusting our instructional practices accordingly—has great promise. Research clearly shows the failures of traditional methods and the superiority of some new approaches for most students. However, it remains a challenge to insert into every college and university classroom these pedagogical approaches as well as a mindset that teaching should be pursued with the same rigorous standards of scholarship as scientific research.

CONCLUSION

Although I am reluctant to offer simple solutions for such a complex problem, perhaps the most effective first step will be to provide sufficient carrots and sticks to convince the faculty members within each department or program to come to a consensus as to their desired learning outcomes at each level (course, program, etc.) and to create rigorous means to measure the actual outcomes. These learning outcomes cannot be vague generalities but rather should be the specific things they want students to be able to do that demonstrate the desired capabilities and mastery and hence can be measured in a relatively straightforward fashion. The methods and instruments for assessing the outcomes must meet certain objective standards of rigor and also be collectively agreed upon and used in a consistent manner, as is done in scientific research.

REFERENCES

Hake, R. 1998. Interactive-Engagement Versus Traditional Methods: A Six-Thousand-Student Survey of Mechanics Test Data for Introductory Physics Courses. *The American Journal of Physics* 66:64-74.

Hammer, D. 1997. Discovery Learning and Discovery Teaching. *Cognition and Instruction* 15(4):485-529.

Hestenes, D., M. Wells, and G. Swackhamer. 1992. Force concept inventory. *The Physics Teacher* 30(March):141-58.

Hrepic, Z., D.A. Zollman, and N.S. Rebello. 2007. Comparing Students' and Experts' Understanding of the Content of a Lecture. *Journal of Science Education and Technology* 16(3):213-24. Accessed 18 December 2009 at http://www.springerlink.com/content/fv08012346146467/fulltext.pdf

Mazur, E. 1997. *Peer Instructions: A User's Manual*. Upper Saddle River, NJ: Prentice Hall.

Novak,G., E. Patterson, A.Gavrin, and W. Christian. 1999. *Just-in-Time Teaching: Blending Active Learning with Web Technology*. Upper Saddle River, NJ: Prentice Hall.

Perkins, K.K., M.M. Gratny, W.K. Adams, N.D. Finkelstein, and C.E. Wieman. 2005. In *Towards Characterizing the Relationship between Students' Self-Reported Interest in and their Surveyed Beliefs about Physics. Proceedings of the 2004 Physics Education Research Conference*, ed. J. Marx, P. Heron, and S. Franklin. Melville, NY: American Institute of Physics. Accessed 14 September 2009 at http://www.colorado.edu/physics/EducationIssues/PERC2005Formatted_submitted.pdf

Physics Education Technology Project (PhET). 2009. Free online physics, chemistry, biology, earth science, and math simulations. Accessed 22 December 2009 on the University of Colorado website at http://phet.colorado.edu/index.php

Redish, E. 2003. *Teaching Physics with the Physics Suite*. Hoboken, NJ: Wiley.

Shulman, L. 1987. Knowledge and Teaching: Foundations of the New Reform *Harvard Educational Review* 57:1-22.

> *Supporting students through responding to variation in students' disciplinary learning, developing metalearning capacity, and focusing on the effective teaching and learning of threshold concepts—concepts that transform student understanding.*

11

HELPING OUR STUDENTS: LEARNING, METALEARNING, AND THRESHOLD CONCEPTS

Jan H.F. Meyer

INTRODUCTION

There is much that can be said about student learning (and, more precisely, *variation* in student learning) and the relevance to teaching practice of a knowledge of these matters in a generic sense. Indeed, one advocated "exemplary" form of pedagogy—that of "student-centred teaching"—assumes that teachers have some knowledge of how *their own* students engage learning. The acquisition of such knowledge leads for many teachers to a reconceptualisation of practice, and the desire to be responsive to patterns of variation in their students' learning in a reflexive manner. It does not require a great deal of effort for university teachers (in whatever discipline) to solicit, interpret, and understand the likely consequences of some of the more common and classic generic patterns of variation. And, in grasping these opportunities, there is variation that can be captured in an empirical learning and teaching "model of engagement" which will be presented further on.

Taking Stock: Research on Teaching and Learning in Higher Education, ed. J. Christensen Hughes and J. Mighty. Montreal and Kingston: McGill-Queen's University Press, Queen's Policy Studies Series. © 2010 The School of Policy Studies, Queen's University at Kingston. All rights reserved.

It is something of a benchmark for teachers to move beyond the comfortable generic metaphors of learning and to actively solicit, and respond to, variation in their students' disciplinary learning. This is a big step forward in terms of reflexive teaching practice. And for teachers to take the next step and help their students become aware of, and take control over, their own learning is an even bigger step because it extends the locus of teaching practice in a most empowering sense for students.

An integrative emphasis on *variation in learning* and developing *metalearning capacity* invites a central rather than a peripheral focus: a conceptual "object of learning." In developing this focus, the analytical framework of *threshold concepts* is introduced as a means to identify transformative "waypoints" in student-learning journeys; a lens that focuses on the learning of concepts that really matter, involving both cognitive and ontological shift.

A Personal Reflection on Student-Learning Research

This chapter is set against more than three decades of research that tells us much about the student experience of learning in higher education. I have chosen 1976 as the starting point of this reflective, and admittedly subjective, account because it was in that year that Marton and Säljö published their seminal paper on student learning that provided a fresh perspective for thinking about student learning. Unlike preceding work that was grounded in various psychological theories and constructs and their accompanying discourses, this new perspective offered a formalised view of learning as experienced and narrated by students themselves. What Marton and Säljö disturbingly demonstrated was that students differed from one another in their learning intentions in the "reading" of an academic text—a basic learning activity that we assume students can carry out in accordance with our expectations—and that these differences could be conceptually accommodated in terms of the now ubiquitous "deep/surface" metaphor, reflecting a categorisation not of students themselves but rather of the *variability in what they do and why they do it* in terms of learning process and underlying intention.

Simply put, students varied in their understanding of the requirement "to read" in a given expectational context of being prepared to "answer questions" on what they had read. Some focused on extracting meaning from the text while others focused on the features of the text. And these differences mattered, as Marton and Säljö (1976) clearly demonstrated, in terms of an empirical association between the quality of the process, and the quality of the outcome *of reading*. Arguing the case for the conceptually posited directionality of this association in more generic terms was one thing. Empirically determining this directionality in terms of statistical modelling was quite another matter that presented (and still presents) its own methodological challenges. The intractable problem is that one cannot infer causality from a correlation coefficient. Nevertheless, 30 years on, Richardson (2006)—using a sophisticated path analysis (quantitative) methodology—has plausibly demonstrated "causal efficacy," whereby variation in various learning processes has a direct effect on marks obtained in assessment. And so we progress in our understanding of the student-learning experience.

The "deep/surface" distinction captured the imagination of many researchers and, given that this distinction was originally discerned in terms of a qualitative analysis of student-interview transcripts, there was an immediate impetus to contemporaneous work already being carried out circa 1976, notably by Biggs and Entwistle. The theoretical contributions of Biggs and Entwistle are reflected elsewhere in this book and it is not the purpose here to summarise, in particular, the subsequent psychometric development of research instruments (student-learning inventories) that sought to both operationalise and extend the originally posited "deep/surface" domain. Richardson (2000) provides a detailed account of this prodigious and evolving work, covering an intervening period of some 25 years that saw a sustained and increasing interest in developing what is now often referred to as the empirically grounded "student experience of learning" (SEL) framework.

Reductionism can be dangerous, but it is worth reflecting on the fact that post-1976 it dawned on many qualitative and quantitative researchers (and their research students) that a new era of educational research had been ushered in by asking students a simple and straightforward set of questions about how they went about learning: what they did, how they did it, why they did it, and so on. In the case of Marton and Säljö, student responses to questions such as these were framed in the context of reading an academic text. Resultant interview data were subjected to an emerging qualitative analytical process—that of phenomenography—that, in the ensuing decades, captivated the minds of hundreds of researchers eager to explore its capacity for revealing, in particular, *qualitative differences* in students' experiences of learning.

Phenomenography presented a new and relatively simple distinctive analytical "methodology," with an accompanying terminology and discourse that had an immediate appeal and that was immediately accessible to both researchers and teachers across the disciplines. Virtually anybody could begin researching all manner of student-learning phenomena and, although the transcription and phenomenographic analysis of interview data was time consuming, the start-up costs were modest given the relatively small numbers of students typically involved. Phenomenography did something very special for research into student learning. It provided a compelling and enduring *authenticity* for primary evidence about how students varied in their engagement with learning, and it prompted categorisations *not of students* but of the patterns of variation in how they went about learning, the likely consequences of which were arguably the concern of *every* teacher.

In a complementary fashion, both qualitative and quantitative studies of student learning reconstituted the simple "deep/surface" metaphor in all manner of contexts and, in terms of accumulating quantitative studies, additionally so in terms of patterns (of variation) of increased multivariate complexity. The net result, which forms the backdrop of this chapter, is that a remarkably consistent body of evidence emanating from a broad landscape of scholarly endeavour began to systematically hammer home a simple truth: that students *varied* in their engagement of learning and that this variation had *explanatory and diagnostic power*.

Teachers who were concerned about the learning well-being of their students began to take this evidence seriously, as did their professional colleagues within the academic-development community. The research base and its application became more embracing and more focused. Teachers started asking questions: If there is evidence of "variation" in general ("deep/surface"+ extended) terms of how students engage both the context and the content of learning, what does this evidence represent in practical and ethical terms *for me*? How transferable and amenable to reconstitution in *my* subject or discipline is this "deep/surface" meta-phor in terms of specificity and explanatory power? And what are the implications for *my* teaching practice? The point here is that if we know something about how students go about learning in general, how does this help the teachers of particular subjects? And again there are chapters in this book that address these issues.

To reiterate: much is known about how students *vary* in their engage-ment of learning. It is not difficult to solicit this variation from students; that is, externalise it in a manner amenable to observation and estimation for modelling purposes. We also know how to analytically determine and conceptually interpret the dimensionality of this variation. Increasingly we also have a deeper understanding of the association between the dimensionality of this variation and learning outcomes.

But there are those who continue to ask what the point is of all this re-search on student learning. Well, for a start, it opens up opportunities for *all* teachers to actively address the learning well-being of their students. If reflexive teaching is something to be valued, then here is the means to give expression to that value through actionable theory informed by a knowledge of individual differences in how students conceive, and en-gage the process of, learning. And since we know so much about student learning, in so many disciplinary contexts, and across a range of institu-tional and cultural settings, it seems self-evident that we can *and should* use this knowledge to improve the learning and teaching experiences of students. And, as an aside, it can be argued that if the knowledge and the efficient means exist to do this then it is unethical to deny students these opportunities.

The knowledge referred to is actionable in the most fundamental sense. It can inform teaching at a number of levels, one of which has already been alluded to: What do students understand by our expectations of them "to read?" What exactly does "to read" mean for a student in, say, the context of law, mathematics, programming, or history? Better still, what does *close reading* mean in the analysis of literary text? One generic aspect of actionable theory tells us that the requirement of a learning task, more subtly students' (often distorted) *perceptions* of what is required of them, influences their *response* to the learning task. In the simplest case we might explicitly "model," as a teaching strategy, what we require of students in terms of the requirement "to read" a text, or "to write" an essay. Another generic aspect of actionable theory tells us that students' *conceptions of learning* in a given context has a consequential effect on the learning process(es) they apply to the task. This effect arises precisely because students' conceptions of learning are couched *in process terms*. And, in general, conceptions of learning are influenced by perceptions of the learning context, and especially of the assessment protocols embedded in it. A third aspect of generic actionable theory tells us that learning processes are controlled by regulation strategies as influenced, for example, by the conception(s) of learning and perceptions of the learning context.

So, as an illustration, we might posit thus: based on a reading of the assessment cues (in lectures) and the "ticky box" multiple-choice test at the end, a student forms a temporal "cram and dump" conception of "learning" that is essentially accumulative. The idea is to get as much factual information into your head so that you can tick the boxes and get the marks. The learning process in this case is essentially a form of mechanical memorising under a strategic form of self-regulation. How do we know this likelihood? This is what students tell us!

I'm more focused on achieving a high mark than I am in gaining more knowledge. If I were to shift more focus towards placing value on the learning in itself, high marks might come as an added benefit…. I harbour some resentment towards students who consistently memorise information without understanding it, write it down on an exam without really thinking, and then forget it all afterwards, but I am also guilty of the same practice. (Student D10)[1]

The above scenario invites *in situ* evidence-based teaching responses to *individual differences* in learning. Insofar as such differences are amenable to categorisation and interpretation *beyond* the now limiting "deep/surface" metaphor, we are challenged (in respect of each such category) to consider appropriate teaching responses. The locus of what constitutes "teaching" now expands to a locus of "*learning* and teaching." It is at this level that the "one size fits all" advocacy of managerialist "good practice" becomes less tenable. But it is the case that reconstituting actionable theory based on individual differences remains an indulgent activity for many teachers in higher education. And not everybody is up for it, as we will soon see.

A Model of Engagement with Variation in Student Learning

A strategy for engaging teachers with the often alien concept of "variation" in student learning is now presented. The context is a graduate-certificate programme that articulates with probationary requirements at a research-intensive UK university. One important and summatively assessed learning outcome of this programme also articulates with an external accreditation requirement: that of demonstrating a theoretically and empirically based interpretive understanding of "how students learn, both generally and in the subject."

It has already been emphasized that much is known about how students vary in their engagement of learning. This knowledge exists at various levels of conceptual sophistication, and the discursive aspects of some of them are admittedly alien and inaccessible to many university teachers (in science and engineering, for example) who do not have a disciplinary background in higher education and a knowledge of its theoretical perspectives. There is a challenge here to unpack and demystify the required knowledge in a form that is accessible to *all* university teachers, and there are many exemplary examples of how to do this in the standard texts that are used to support graduate-certificate programmes for university teachers, certainly in the UK and Australian contexts with which I am most familiar.

But there is a big gap between reading about, being taught about, reflecting on, and discussing this knowledge of how students learn *in general*, and how they learn *in the subject or discipline*. Part of the problem is that, within the voluminous research literature on student learning, there are relatively few studies that focus on learning within a subject or disciplinary context. Evidence about how learning is engaged in general, as reflected in generic patterns of variation, is dismissed by many teachers as being of little use. This reaction is understandable because they are less interested in reading about how students in general may exhibit a "deep" or "surface" learning engagement and more interested in how, within *their own* subject or discipline, these categorisations may be reconstituted by *their own* students in ways that are of immediate relevance and perhaps quite different from the stereotypes.

The general literature does not, for example, provide any obvious detail about how "deep" or "surface" learning might—and perhaps uniquely so—be characterised in, say, accounting, economics, music, or mathematics. However, studies in these same disciplinary contexts such as those respectively reported by Lucas and Meyer (2005), Meyer and Shanahan (2001), Reid (2001), and Eley and Meyer (2004) do provide empirical insights that might at least convince teachers in these disciplines that there is something worth exploring here in terms of their own students.

However, teachers themselves also vary in the learning task of soliciting and interpreting variation in their own students' learning. This teacher variation has been captured in an empirical model developed by Meyer (2005) in the context of a graduate-certificate programme on learning and teaching in higher education that articulates with *probationary requirements* for newly appointed university teachers. Participants are required, as part of a summatively assessed assignment, to interview their own students about their learning via a carefully managed and ethically approved protocol. For participants meeting the probationary requirement this is most definitely not an indulgent activity. And there are always those who voluntarily choose to participate outside this requirement.

Resultant interview data then have to be analysed and theoretically interpreted against the research literature, and the findings have to be reflected upon in terms of their implications for the real business of personal rather than hypothetical practice, especially in terms of reflexive teaching and assessment.

> Theories are never more convincing for a researcher than when previously abstract ideas manifest themselves as immediate and concrete evidence. [The assignment] provided compelling, and at times alarming, evidence of what had been up to then, for this learner-teacher at least, the largely theoretical notion of "variation in student learning." In many cases the transcripts illustrated the research-literature examples exactly. For me, this produced a sudden and clear understanding of the literature I had read, and I returned enthusiastically to articles I had previously struggled to assimilate. It was quite rewarding to see that many of the conclusions that I have drawn from these interviews were actually backed by research in the field. The student-learning assignment brought home to me a fundamental truth of student learning; that all students learn differently.

The above quotations, and those that appear further on in this section, are literal extracts from participants' written assessed work or evaluative comments, but are composite (multiple voices present in each set) to protect the anonymity of the sources. The focus here is on the variation exhibited by participants in carrying out this assignment, and this variation is presented below in an adaptation of the model described in Meyer (2005, 363-65):

1. *No initial engagement*: discourse is alien and troublesome.
   I found this assignment difficult to do, because I did not feel that I had any real command of the concepts. All the theory was boring and irrelevant. Theory is a lot of wind.

2. *Descriptive*: there is semantic infiltration, use of extended discourse.·
    The approach to studying is a major explaining factor among the
    multivariate factors causing variation in the learning outcomes. I found
    evidence of the "paradox of the Chinese learner" during my interviews.
    The influence of context and locus on student learning is very import-
    ant. I can pick out the precise moment at which my own approach
    changed from that of a diligent "surface" learner to that of a "deep" and
    "transformative" learner ... as my understanding deepened, I was able
    to put the material together in a different way. It could be categorized
    [on SOLO] as a shift to "relational" and "extended abstract" levels of
    understanding.

3. *Interpretive*: student-learning constructs and discourse are used for
    interpretive purposes.
    My teaching practice has been considerably enriched as a direct result
    of this assignment, in that it convinced me of the value of "repetition as
    a means of encouraging understanding." I now have a clear sense of the
    rationale behind certain traditional language-teaching methods. How
    the students learned was the key to understanding what they learned.

4. *Evaluative*: discourse informs judgments in context, the first stage of
    reflective practice.
    As a result of these interviews, I radically rethought my teaching. At the
    most fundamental level, this exercise has awakened an awareness of
    the variety of ways in which students learn. My experiences ... brought
    home very clearly what was evident from the literature; different stu-
    dents learn differently. It was evident ... that at least two of the students
    fell into the classical categories of deep ... and surface ... learners with
    associated different conceptions of learning. I initially began to reflect
    without even knowing I was doing it. It is clear ... that superficially
    similar students possess very different conceptions of learning which
    relate to their motivations, methods, and intentions.... I now find that I
    question traditional teaching methods, often, and sometimes unthink-
    ingly, adopted by me in the past. [This exercise] has provided me with
    an invaluable opportunity to reflect on my teaching: to consider how I
    teach, why I teach that way, why it works, and how my teaching could
    be improved.

5. *Actionable*: there is informed decision making *in situ*, there is actionable
    theory underpinning a mental model of *learning* and teaching.
    This exercise has drastically altered my conception of teaching. I have
    been required to view teaching and learning from the student perspec-
    tive. This course ... offered information on how to encourage students
    to adopt an approach that leads to understanding ... allowed me to see
    how students experienced and perceived my teaching ... adopting the

students' perspective [it is now] much easier to see how I must change my teaching. I have found evidence that suggests that the modifying strategic element employed by deep learners does not always lead to successful learning outcomes. This reinforces the conclusion ... that the way a student approaches a task depends on the perceived rather than actual learning environment. In my consideration, one response would be to attempt to ascertain the students' conceptions of their learning context as the course progresses. My belief was that by making the assessment process more transparent, and allowing the students space to self-assess their learning requirements, their control over the learning situation would increase. I think it [the assignment] will turn out to be a useful tool in diagnosing how Ph.D. students think, why students may be failing or, more generally, why their experience or performance may be unsatisfactory.

What this model demonstrates is that, in varying degrees, it is possible to engage teachers with a learning task focused on the ways in which their own students learn—a task that is generally experienced as a positive and energising experience because the resultant variation in student learning, correctly interpreted, constitutes a manifestation of *personal actionable theory*. There is an immediate foundation on which to reflect and act:

This [assignment] confirmed to me that the distinction between surface and deep approaches to learning is a useful one, and that it might prove to be quite fertile to know the factors that can be employed to encourage a more active and explorative approach in students. My own learning from this exercise is that I now have access to a conceptual framework which I did not have before. I can apply this in lesson designs, and will be less disposed to adopt a "deficit model" of student-learning needs. These interviews showed some factors that were within my immediate power to change ... allowed me to see how students experienced and perceived my teaching. By adopting the students' perspective it became now much easier to see how I must change my teaching. [The students] seemed to scrutinise and adjust their perceptions of learning during the interview itself, and to regard it as an opportunity to learn. I could profitably engage more frequently, and in greater depth, with my students on an individual basis so as to be able to assess and learn from what and how *they* are learning as individuals.

Metalearning Capacity

Given that a manifestation of variation in student learning can form a foundation of personal actionable theory for teachers invites a further question: Can a knowledge of their own learning also help students to independently form a reflective foundation on which to develop their learning expertise? Yet another generic aspect of actionable theory tells us that students can vary in their learning engagement of different topics within the same subject, and it is this intra-individual variability that is of interest here. How might students themselves be exposed to this variability and its possible consequences? A theoretical basis for such exposure appeals to the concept of *metalearning capacity* after the work of Biggs (1985)—the capacity of a student to be aware of, and in control of, his or her own learning in some given context. Metalearning embeds a number of constructs; in particular the crucial process aspects of learning and, implicitly, a set of "regulation" constructs that represent the overlapping domains of attribution theory, locus of control theory and, most importantly for present purposes, self-regulation theory after the work of Vermunt (1998). Developing metalearning capacity transcends subject boundaries and represents a fundamental aspect of self-regulation (of learning processes) that is theoretically and empirically linked to the achievement of personal understanding. It is fundamental to any commitment to student-centred teaching, and student learning and well-being. Looked at another way, metalearning capacity also represents a form of personal actionable theory *for students.*

A problem lays in the fact that most entering university students are not likely to have had an opportunity to talk to their teachers (or anybody else) at school about *how* they typically went about learning *in process terms.* For the most part, students have never really thought about themselves in this way and, if asked, they generally experience difficulty, beyond habitual or preferential activities, in describing what *they know about themselves as learners.* They also generally vary in possessing a precise vocabulary to differentiate between contrasting aspects of what they do as learners, as well as a conceptual framework within which to organise and reflect on such contrasts. For some the *repertoire* of learning activities that can be orchestrated in response to learning-task requirements is narrow and difficult to expand. There is a persistency about doing things in certain limiting ways. For others the repertoire is wide, known to self, expandable in light of experience, and allows choice in terms of flexible responses to learning tasks.

For students to become *aware* of their learning in a metalearning sense, there has to be a recognition of self in relation to "learning" in some context and a consideration of what, in their own minds, they actually do when they are "learning" in that context. This recognition or initial "knowledge of self" may be well-developed for some students who have reflected upon, and feel comfortable with, themselves as learners. But for the rest, a stimulus is required—something to prompt an empowering initial realisation of self as learner in process terms, the emphasis being on "what am I doing?" rather than "who am I?" This distinction is crucial because empowerment for students begins with the realisation that their learning processes can vary, precisely because they are sensitive to the perceived context in which they are being orchestrated. Indeed, the processes involved might be a conscious (and perhaps inappropriate, even dissonant) response to the perceptions formed about that context and its learning requirements. The responses can therefore change, under internal self-control preferably, in strategically appropriate ways and across different (subject) response contexts. And, as already mentioned, similarly so *within* a subject context.

There are surprisingly few studies on developing students' metalearning capacity in terms of the Biggs formalisation. Earlier studies by Meyer and Shanahan (2004), and Meyer et al. (2006), have reported on the conceptual architecture of a mechanism—in this case a Web-based interface—that students can log onto in order to generate a *learning profile* of themselves. There is thus an immediate basis for reflection, a representation of self that has in fact been self-constructed and that can literally be gazed upon. This representation of self *should* therefore be recognisable as such, and be further amenable to self-interpretation given suitable guidance.

> I feel the learning profile is an accurate snapshot of my approach to learning. (Student D18)

This self-interpretation may in turn be further reflected on, either as a reassuring image of self, or in terms of an opportunity to work on issues *identified by self* as requiring change. Students are quite capable of committing these reflective accounts to paper, via a short essay, for example, that can then form a basis for discussion as part of further teaching support. And it is in the variability of these reflective accounts that one can discern (or not) the second, being *"in control of"* aspect of metalearning capacity.

This metalearning exercise can furthermore be repeated, thus providing evidence, in particular, of the dynamics of change. There is a powerful example of how these dynamics may be captured and interpreted in an empirical (quantitative and qualitative) study by Meyer, Ward, and Latreille (2009). This study also demonstrates quite clearly that a majority of students generally benefit from their metalearning experiences.

The Learning Profile and its Constructs. The profile is generated from quantitative response data to a set of statements about learning that traverse the domain of the Reflections on Learning Inventory (RoLI), an instrument grounded in students' self-reported learning experiences that captures variation in students' learning engagement, in particular, in process terms. The detail of the development of the RoLI and its domain can be found in Meyer (2004) and is not presented here. What needs to be conceptualised here is that it is firstly possible to generate, for each student, a set of subscale scores (the subscales embedded in the RoLI that define its internal structure) and, secondly, that this set of scores can be rank ordered and presented visually as a bar chart in which contrasting aspects of learning are pre-colour-coded for interpretive purposes. So, for example, one RoLI subscale captures variation in terms of the construct of "knowing about learning" and a high score would be interpreted here as an indicator (colour coded green in the bar chart) of knowing something that is likely to support learning. Conversely, a high score on another subscale such as "memorising as rehearsal" (mechanical rehearsal), likely to inhibit learning, would be colour coded red.

> I can also see that the red bar for memory as a rehearsal is quite high and I know that this is a big part of my learning and revising style. This may have been inhibiting my learning process so I need to try to stop learning in this way. (Student D20)

The "traffic light" analogy given to students is that they are on a journey by road and are trying to reach a destination (a personal, intended-learning outcome). This (learning) journey may encounter various forms of delays and obstacles along the way, possibly even stuck places (more of this later). Green (go) and red (stop) colours signify elements of learning engagement that are respectively interpreted as supporting or inhibiting progress (in learning) *in the particular response context*, while amber (caution) signifies an aspect of learning that might be delaying, or not, depending on its context-sensitive interpretation.

> Overall I need to be aware of what ways of learning are "go" signals, and which are "red" and therefore potentially inhibiting; with this in mind I should be able to have a more distinct graph result and a better outcome to my learning. I need to be able to explain what I know, and know it before I learn it. (Student D5)

Thus conveyed is a spectrum of patterning depending on the "mix" of colours and the degree of conceptual consonance reflected therein. Basically the cleaner the separation between the "greens" and "reds" (with the "greens" scored relatively higher than the "reds"), the better. In contrast, a journey that starts off problematically (relatively high scores on "reds" compared to "greens") may in fact lead to stuck places.

The profile is intended to engage students in the *first step* of developing metalearning capacity; namely, an *awareness* of their self-reported learning engagement in a particular response context.

> I believe that my profile has illustrated both positive and negative features that contribute to my learning…. Learning techniques that I use which have been brought to my attention as negative qualities are "knowledge discrete and factual" and "learning is fact based." These highlighted areas show that I place certain reliance on learning facts and mistake this as learning. (Student D21)

And some "mixed" patterns of colours can signify a conceptually *dissonant* form of learning (which may be transitional) that may also be generally troublesome in trying to reach the destination.

> Mixed patterns of colours (green, amber, and red) tend to show possible troubles when trying to learn and solve problems. This may show my inability to adjust sufficiently quickly to the rapidly changing learning environment that is university. On the other hand, am I particularly concerned? The answer is no. The concept of learning about learning provides the opportunity to sort out any problems. (Student D6)

This basic self-portrait of themselves as learners may be supported in the *second step* in the form of a non-judgemental *guide* on how to interpret their profiles followed by additional activities: a consideration of likely consequences in terms of the quality of personally intended learning outcomes, and whether this is what they comfortably had in mind, and by *learning conversations* conducted by tutors or teachers who have developed an understanding of the underlying conceptual model of (qualitative variation in) student learning that the domain of the RoLI represents. Other forms of support include seminars on student learning in which, as a group, students are presented with a contrasting range of stereotypical examples of learning profiles (together with theoretical interpretations) and invited to thus provisionally "locate" themselves. Discussions and examples of how students can self-initiate change in their own learning are clearly crucial here. And, in many cases, there is also a need for self-initiated private counselling and supportive learning-change management.

Thus emphasized is how a knowledge of student-learning engagement can be used to help students *to help themselves* develop their metalearning capacity. There really is no excuse for not doing this. The means lie within the grasp of every teacher. In fact, it is possible for universities to create opportunities on a large scale for students to engage in this empowering activity as an *integral* part of the institutional learning and teaching environment. The strategic importance and competitive advantage of creating such opportunities is obvious, particularly at the crucial interface between school and university learning. A further consideration is whether metalearning constructs, in turn, have any role to play in learning and teaching strategies; whether they can be integrated into the learning experiences of students as part of course design and delivery. An example of how this integration may be achieved is provided in the study by Shanahan and Meyer (2003).

Introducing Threshold Concepts

This section looks afresh at the foregoing discussion on student learning and metalearning, and positions it within the developing theoretical framework of *threshold concepts*. If there is some excitement and commitment in capitalising, for the benefits of our students, on what is known about student learning and metalearning, and if our energies are going to be accordingly directed, then we might as well focus our attention on the "objects of learning" that really matter. There is much to celebrate here.

> "Student learning engagement" is a broad term, and the variation within it can be generally formalised in terms of empirical (or conceptual) "models" of differing multivariate complexity ... [however,] generic models [of learning] are only useful, and indeed "actionable," up to a rapidly reached point at which they become inadequate proxies for the dynamics of student learning within discipline-specific courses. It is here, at this interface of reached uselessness, that the existence of threshold concepts provides immediate and compelling signposting for avenues along which to solicit variation in student learning and understanding (and misunderstanding) in a far more critical sense. The responsiveness to variation is no longer in the general sense (how are you going about learning?), or even the discipline sense (how are you going about learning subject x?), but is now operating at a critical microperspective level within the epistemology of the discipline itself and its discourse. (Meyer and Land 2005, 380-81)

Thus re-emphasized is that soliciting variation in how students learn in general is of limited value; there is little explanatory power in the response variation. The same is true in respect of metalearning. When the variation reflects a disciplinary or subject-response context, the picture sharpens; there is a finer-grained discernment, and increased explanatory and diagnostic power in the variation for both teacher and student to capitalise on. The former is interested in the reconstitution and extension to practice of generic theory interpretable within a disciplinary discourse, and the latter with insights that can empower self-regulated *expertise in learning*. But there is still, even at this level, a lack of specificity in terms of actionable theory. An even finer-grained view of variation opens up new opportunities here because it can encapsulate those objects of learning represented by threshold concepts which, when successfully internalised, occasion the cognitive and ontological shifts that are the outcomes of transformational learning.

Distinguishing Threshold Concepts. We begin with a visual-spatial metaphor that is transportable across subject boundaries:

> A threshold concept can be considered as akin to a portal, opening up a new and previously inaccessible way of thinking about something. It represents a transformed way of understanding, or interpreting, or viewing something without which the learner cannot progress. As a consequence of comprehending a threshold concept, there may thus be a transformed internal view

of subject matter, subject landscape, or even world view. This transformation may be sudden or it may be protracted over a considerable period, with the transition to understanding proving troublesome. Such a transformed view or landscape may represent how people "think" in a particular discipline, or how they perceive, apprehend, or experience particular phenomena within that discipline (or more generally). (Meyer and Land 2006, 3)

A frequently asked question is what distinguishes threshold concepts from, say, "fundamental," "core," or "key" concepts? This is not a helpful start because many teachers use terms like "core," "fundamental," and "key" interchangeably. It is also not helpful to ask what the definition of a threshold concept is. Threshold concepts cannot be described as an essentialist, definitive list of characteristics. The classificatory pursuit of threshold concepts in any scientific sense is a pointless one. It is nevertheless the case that some teachers encountering the notion of threshold concepts for the first time are initially inclined to identify, think, and get excited about them in terms of certain "qualities," such as "troublesomeness," that may be foregrounded more than others.

For some, this initial apprehension may be sharper than for others. An indelible recollection springs to mind, that of Phil, an *electrical* engineering colleague, who enthusiastically put up his hand in one of my seminars on threshold concepts and exclaimed: "We've got one of those!" On subsequent reflection another one came to mind—that of *reactive power*, *imaginary* power, *wattless* power—without which *real* power cannot be transmitted down a transmission line. And, as Phil later explained to me, when you understand reactive power, "the world looks different."

An animated conversation in another setting with Michael,[2] an *electronic* engineer from another university, sparked a realisation on his part of an immediate parallel between "reactive power" and the threshold concept of "characteristic impedance." The latter is fundamental in understanding the complex process of how to transmit information without any reflections. Failure to do so has some simple examples in the everyday phenomena of the "ghosting" of a television picture or "ringing" in an audio system. To appreciate the trouble that lays ahead, keep in mind at this point that a first-year student's appreciation of "impedance" is very much that of *resistance* (an intuitively easy concept to grasp) as taught at school. Resistance is caused by a conducting material "impeding" the flow of electrons through it. Viewed as such, it's a basically simple idea. Enough resistance in the element (electrical conductor) of a domestic plug-in kettle causes heat sufficient to quickly boil water. And for a cable (such as a copper transmission line connecting a power source to a load) resistance *increases proportionately with length.*

Characteristic impedance (like reactive power) is an equally troublesome threshold concept for engineers looking at the transmission of *information* such as a television signal (rather than power) down a different kind of transmission line, typically in the form of a coaxial cable. But unlike resistance, characteristic impedance is counter-intuitively *independent of the length of the transmission line* (the coaxial cable) even though its units of measurement are the same, in ohms. (Equally counter-intuitive is that a *vacuum* also has a finite characteristic impedance of 376.7 ohms, in fact.)

However, the two very different transmission lines described above do share a common *equivalent circuit;* that is, an abstraction in which the actual physical systems are represented by a circuit diagram consisting of the simplest possible arrangement of the three key electrical components—the resistor, the capacitor, and the inductor. And now there is more trouble because the resultant abstraction in this particular case *bears little or no physical resemblance* to the actual systems in terms of the appearance, and the clearly defined function, of these components as found by students in their laboratory store room. So, there is plenty of trouble here for students.

But if, on the other hand, reactive power and characteristic impedance thus reflect variation in a commonly shared *critical feature* of transmission-line theory *that is occluded* in the equivalent circuit, then some really provocative teaching questions and opportunities arise. This particular story continues to unfold (Flanagan, Taylor, and Meyer 2010).

Another "quality" of threshold concepts that may vary in its fore-grounding is that of *integration*:

> We turn now to the question of how to operationalise "integration" and "transformation" in ways that distinguish conceptual change in threshold concepts from conceptual change in other traditions. Practice in these trad-itions has examined different conceptions of the same phenomenon and the conditions—including those that arise from the learner's intentions and emotions—in which it is more likely that they will shift from a less complex to a more complex conception of the phenomenon. This focus on conceptions of one particular phenomenon is different from that suggested by "threshold concepts." Threshold concepts have been suggested as ways of thinking about a wide range of phenomena that fall within the scope of a particular discipline or mode of thought. The transformation that is sug-gested as an outcome of understanding a threshold concept should be seen in changes in conception of several (perhaps many) phenomena and this way of thinking about conceptual change is different from that suggested by other traditions. (Davies 2010)

In similar vein a new transformational understanding, in the process of being acquired, and once acquired (cognitively or ontologically) will also be *discursive* (exhibiting modes of reasoning and explanation, and how people "think" within a particular discipline):

> It is hard to imagine any shift in perspective that is not simultaneously ac-companied by (or occasioned through) an extension of the students' use of

language. Through this elaboration of discourse new thinking is brought into being, expressed, reflected upon and communicated. The extension of language might be acquired, for example, from that in use within a specific discipline, language community or community of practice, or it might, of course, be self-generated. It might involve natural language, formal language or symbolic language. (Meyer and Land 2005, 374)

This is enough to get us started. A comprehensive discussion on these and other "features," as well as their theoretical underpinning can be found in Timmermans (2010).

The Threshold Concepts Framework. There is now an established and expanding literature on the theoretical framework of *threshold concepts and troublesome knowledge* as an Internet search on this term will reveal. A summary of the genesis, and subsequent development and application, of this framework within various disciplines lies beyond the scope of this chapter. The curious reader is simply referred to one version of the seminal paper by Meyer and Land (2003) that can be accessed online. A cross section of the subsequent progression of the seminal ideas contained therein (within various disciplinary perspectives) is compactly reflected in Land, Meyer, and Smith (2008). Another compact collection of more advanced applications, some of which directly address issues of teaching and assessment, can be found in Meyer, Land, and Baillie (2010).

There are many disciplinary perspectives reflected in the edited volumes referred to above, notably in accounting, biology, computer science, cultural studies, history, earth sciences, economics, engineering, law, music, philosophy, and theology. These perspectives provide an accessible entry to the more advanced, peer-reviewed discourses that have been published in specialist journals. Contextualising threshold concepts within interdisciplinary learning environments is also part of the focus of attention (Land and Meyer 2010).

The framework has also been embraced by some within the professional-development community. It has found a place within the formal provision of graduate-certificate programmes in the UK and in Australia.

A word of caution: the threshold-concepts framework is also subversive. It rattles the cage of the managerially efficient "outcomes-based education," a conveyor-belt model of course design and delivery—a model so deterministic that it requires of teachers in some UK universities the setting of the final-examination paper before the course even commences or the students are known. So let's forget about individual differences in learning. And let's give Mager (1975) some credit here for what this model is attuned to. He came up with his version of what is now the fashionable mantra of "intended learning outcomes" (circa 1962).

Learning within a managerialist perspective might be likened to that of students as eggs travelling along the same conveyer belt, being subjected to various forms of scrutiny, and possible rejection, before reaching the final quality-control check of the graded learning outcomes. (Meyer and Land 2007, 14)

So if an employer needs, say, half a dozen (in UK parlance) "upper second" new accounting graduates, well, there they are ready to go in the egg box! Is this really what "higher" education should be about?

But what if an employer, inspired by *Historical Thinking and Other Unnatural Acts* (Wineburg 2001), seeks a graduate who can "think" like an historian?

Unlike the linear or industrialised model described above, this [threshold-concepts] approach views learning as a form of journey, during which the student not only gains insights great and small, but is also changed as an individual by new knowledge. (Meyer and Land 2007, 14)

What, if anything, might an "upper second" signify in this ontological dimension of variation of transformed learner status and identity and how would it be determined?

Threshold Concepts and Other Perspectives. The threshold-concepts framework invites engagement with other perspectives. There is an immediate critical engagement, for example, as Meyer, Land, and Davies (2008) have argued, with pedagogical "theories of variation." This engagement is a productive one, despite specific reservations expressed about some of the generalisations made in respect of the application of *variation theory* as developed in the phenomenographic tradition.

The threshold-concepts framework presents challenges for assessment that "conveyor-belt" thinking cannot respond to. To begin with, how can one "bring into view" for students a transformative portal that lies *beyond* their ontological horizon? There is no neat taxonomy of objectives in the ontological domain to help us fine tune the outcomes here. One way forward, suggested by the work of Pang and Meyer (2010), rests on the conjecture that students, in varying degrees, may possess some tacit and as yet non-formalised understanding of what a particular portal represents long before it "comes into view" within the technical discourse of the discipline. This study demonstrates that the use of proxy economic scenarios in which school pupils—in this case with no prior formal knowledge of economics or economic language—can locate themselves in interview settings does solicit variation in what has been referred to by Perkins (2006) as an "episteme," a "way of knowing," a tacit feel for what the "underlying game" is.

In the absence of economic terminology, a few pupils in Pang and Meyer's study demonstrated a relatively sophisticated tacit grasp of what was for them the unknown threshold concept of "opportunity cost."

Furthermore, in talking about how choices may be exercised in what for them was an increasingly abstract sequence of proxy economic scenarios, there was also evidence that some of the pupils *were learning something new* about the concept of "choice" in terms of sacrifice of, rather than selection from, alternatives.[3]

It is worth reflecting on another "bringing into view" example that draws in, integrates, and provides transferable theoretical underpinning for what might otherwise be viewed as an isolated example of an enquiry-based teaching strategy. Consider an example from mathematics. Easdown (2007) below sets the scene in arguing the case for "proof" as a threshold concept in mathematics:

> It is common for new students to say that they "like mathematics" but "hate proofs." For many proof technique is a difficult hurdle to overcome and has all of the hallmarks of a *threshold concept*, in the sense of Meyer and Land (2003, 2005). The ability to understand and construct proofs is *transformative*, both in perceiving old ideas and making new and exciting discoveries. It is *irreversible* and often accompanied by a "road to Damascus" effect, not unlike a religious conversion or drug addiction. The most inspiring mathematical proofs are *integrative* and almost always expose some hidden *counter-intuitive* interrelations. And of course they are *troublesome*: it can take a long time, even years, for students to learn to appreciate proofs and to develop sufficient technique to write their own proofs with confidence. (28)

How might the construction of a proof be "brought into view" for students? Sandefur (2005) summarized failed attempts to teach students how to construct a proof, concluding that "… one of the most important reasons that we failed is that none of us really knew how students learn to solve problems" (2). In turning his attention to remedying this situation, he describes how, as a pure mathematician, he observed over a period of several years how students varied in their attempts to construct a proof and how this knowledge has been used to develop a learning and teaching strategy that effectively models this process. One of the keys used to unlock the variation involved is what he refers to as videoed "think alouds"—recorded observations of students verbalising what they are thinking in attempting to construct a proof. There are two interesting things about his account: the use of variation, and the fact that he provides no apparent theoretical underpinning for his methodology. What he perhaps unknowingly describes is a powerful example of the application of *self-explanation theory* after the work of Chi et al. (1994) and earlier work by Chi and colleagues that, according to Meyer and Land (2010), should be capable of generating explanations of the variation reflected in reaching an understanding (or not) of threshold concepts. The final point here is that Sandefur's work, like that of Pang and Meyer, and that of Flanagan, Taylor, and Meyer mentioned earlier, signals the means to identify, *from the student-learning perspective,* variation in the "critical features" of threshold concepts. There is much that can be done with a knowledge of this variation. It has been demonstrated:

> ... that it is possible to derive pedagogical principles from the idea of threshold concepts and that activities that are devised on the basis of these principles are distinctive when compared to other approaches to teaching and learning which at first sight are quite similar. (Davies and Mangan 2008, 48)

Taking Stock

What has been discussed in this chapter is a celebration of progress. It is exciting to explore new ideas and practices that progress our understanding of how our students vary in their learning engagement, and how we might reflexively respond to that variation as teachers. For example, it is clear from the work of Meyer, Ward, and Latreille (2009) that variation in student learning, and developing students' metalearning capacity, can *simultaneously* be focused on at the level of discrete threshold concepts— the very concepts that for many students represent the troublesome stuck places in their learning journeys. It is also clear from this study that it is possible to statistically model changed or changing metalearning capacity in the learning of a threshold concept. And what this modelling also reveals are the dimensions of the dynamics of change so crucial to our understanding of the critical learning episodes that really matter.

We need to let go of some old, tired, and worn-out formulaic ideas about teaching practice. Conveyor-belt thinking is not going to help our students internalise threshold concepts or our capacity to assess the dynamics of their transformational learning journeys. We need to move on and develop, and respond to "... a coherent analysis of the problems facing learners" (Davies and Mangan 2008, 48). What is being advocated here is *not* a tired restatement of the general position that, insofar as variation in learning can be neatly categorised, we should look for an appropriate teaching response to each category (assuming such a theoretically justified response exists). The threshold-concepts framework generates *new sources* of variation in the cognitive and ontological shifts in students' learning journeys, and within different uncharted modes of liminality. And what is becoming clear is that the patterns of variation emanating from these new sources are not amenable to "categorisation" in terms of the old metaphors. We need to take our eyes off the rear-view mirror and look ahead.

This chapter began with a reflective account of some of the classic ideas that have helped us to better understand our students' learning, and it ends with the observation that *integrated* thinking about variation in student learning, metalearning, and threshold concepts opens up a new landscape for us as teachers. There is a powerful triangulation synergy of ideas here to help *us* to help our students, and for students to *help themselves*.

NOTES

[1] Note that this quotation, and following quotations attributed to students with D-numbers, are anonymised verbatim extracts from reflective essays written by students about their learning as part of a study by Meyer, Ward, and Latreille (2009).

[2] Michael Flanagan has since gone on to develop a definitive website on the status of some threshold concepts that are relevant to his own disciplinary interests (electronic engineering and computing), including links to mathematics, physics, and statistics as supporting disciplines. His website is being expanded in 2010 to cover other disciplinary contexts and is well worth visiting (at http://www.ee.ucl.ac.uk/~mflanaga/thresholds.html).

[3] The contrast here is between the "cost" of a choice as seen in terms of the cost of what has been sacrificed, rather than the cost of what has been selected. The definition of "opportunity cost" does not emphasize the sacrifice of alternatives (plural) but of the *best* alternative foregone.

> This is one of the most fundamental concepts in economics. It is a *threshold concept:* once you have seen its importance, it affects the way you look at economic problems. When you use the concept of opportunity cost, you are *thinking like an economist*. And this may be different from thinking like an accountant or from the way you thought before. (Sloman 2006, 8)

It is remarkable that some of the school pupils interviewed in the Pang and Meyer (2010) study were able to demonstrate a tacit inclination to in fact *begin* "thinking like an economist." The significance of this observation lies in the conjecture that, were these same pupils to choose to study economics in the future, they would do so *having already made* a preliminary ontological shift such that when they encounter the formalization of "opportunity cost" they might say "OK , I think like this anyway but now it has a name" rather than getting stuck trying to comprehend a definitional way of analytical thinking that is alien and counter-intuitive.

REFERENCES

Biggs, J.B. 1985. The Role of Metalearning in Study Processes. *British Journal of Educational Psychology* 55(3):185-212.

Chi, M.T.H., N. de Leeuw, M.-H. Chiu, and C. LaVancher. 1994. Eliciting Self-Explanations Improves Understanding. *Cognitive Science* 18(3):439-77.

Davies, P.I. 2010. Transforming Knowledge Structures: A Procedure for Developing Students' Understanding of Threshold Concepts. Paper to be presented at the 3rd Biennial Threshold Concepts Symposium, University of New South Wales, 1-2 July.

Davies, P. and J. Mangan 2008. Embedding Threshold Concepts: From Theory to Pedagogical Principles to Learning Activities. In *Threshold Concepts within the Disciplines*, ed. R. Land, J.H.F. Meyer, and J. Smith, 37-50. Rotterdam and Taipei: Sense Publishers.

Easdown, D. 2007. The Role of Proof in Mathematics Teaching and *The Plateau Principle*. UniServe Science Symposium proceedings. Science Teaching and Learning Research including Threshold Concepts. The University of Sydney, 27-28 September.

Eley, M.G. and J.H.F. Meyer. 2004. Modelling the Influences on Learning Outcomes of Study Processes in University Mathematics. *Higher Education* 47(4):437-54.

Flanagan, M.T., P. Taylor, and J.H.F. Meyer. 2010. Compounded Thresholds in Electrical Engineering. In *Threshold Concepts and Transformational Learning*, ed. J.H.F. Meyer, R. Land, and C. Baillie. Rotterdam: Sense Publishers. In press.

Land, R. and J.H.F. Meyer. 2010. Threshold Concepts and Troublesome Knowledge (6): Issues of Interdisciplinarity. Paper to be presented at the 3rd Biennial Threshold Concepts Symposium, University of New South Wales, 1-2 July.

Land, R., J.H.F. Meyer, and J. Smith. ed. 2008. *Threshold Concepts within the Disciplines*. Rotterdam and Taipei: Sense Publishers.

Lucas, U. and J.H.F. Meyer. 2005. "Towards a Mapping the Student World": The Identification of Variation in Students' Conceptions of, and Motivations to Learn, Introductory Accounting. *The British Accounting Review* 37(2):177-204.

Mager, R.F. 1975. *Preparing Instructional Objectives*, 2nd edition. Belmont: Fearon Publishers.

Marton, F. and R. Säljö. 1976. On Qualitative Differences in Learning. II – Outcome as a Function of the Learner's Conception of the Task. *British Journal of Educational Psychology* 46(2):115-27.

Meyer, J.H.F. 2004. An Introduction to the RoLI. *Innovations in Education and Teaching International* 41(4):491-97.

Meyer, J.H.F. 2005. Closing the Gap between Educational Research and Educational Development: A Model of Engagement. In *Improving Student Learning 12 – Diversity and Inclusivity*, ed. C. Rust, 360-76. Oxford: Oxford Brookes University.

Meyer, J.H.F. and R. Land. 2003. Threshold Concepts and Troublesome Knowledge: Linkages to Ways of Thinking and Practising within the Disciplines. In *Improving Student Learning. Improving Student Learning Theory and Practice – 10 Years On*, ed. C. Rust, 412-24. Oxford: Oxford Brookes University. Also separately published earlier as accessed 5 January 2010 at http://www.tla.ed.ac.uk/etl/docs/ETLreport4.pdf

Meyer, J.H.F. and R. Land. 2005. Threshold Concepts and Troublesome Knowledge (2): Epistemological Considerations and a Conceptual Framework for Teaching and Learning. *Higher Education* 49(3):373-88.

Meyer, J.H.F. and R. Land, eds. 2006. *Overcoming Barriers to Student Understanding: Threshold Concepts and Troublesome Knowledge*. London and New York: Routledge.

Meyer, J. and R. Land. 2007. Stop the Conveyor Belt, I Want to Get Off. *Times Higher Education* 17(August):14.

Meyer, J.H.F. and R. Land. 2010. Threshold Concepts and Troublesome Knowledge (5): Dynamics of Assessment. In *Threshold Concepts and Transformational Learning*, ed. J.H.F. Meyer, R. Land, and C. Baillie. Rotterdam: Sense Publishers. In press.

Meyer, J.H.F., R. Land, and C. Baillie, eds. 2010. *Threshold Concepts and Transformational Learning*. Rotterdam: Sense Publishers. In press.

Meyer, J.H.F., R. Land, and P. Davies. 2008. Threshold Concepts and Troublesome Knowledge (4): Issues of Variation and Variability. In *Threshold Concepts within the Disciplines*, ed. R. Land, J.H.F. Meyer, and J. Smith, 59-74. Rotterdam and Taipei: Sense Publishers.

Meyer, J.H.F. and M.P. Shanahan. 2001. A Triangulated Approach to the Modelling of Learning Outcomes in First-Year Economics. *Higher Education Research and Development* 20(2):127-45.

Meyer, J.H.F. and M.P. Shanahan. 2004. Developing Metalearning Capacity in Students – Actionable Theory and Practical Lessons Learned in First-Year Economics. *Innovations in Education and Teaching International* 41(4):443-58.

Meyer, J.H.F., M. Shanahan, L.S. Norton, D. Walters, S. Ward, and H. Hewertson. 2006. Developing Students' Metalearning Capacity: A Grounded Assessment Framework. In *Improving Student Learning 13 – Improving Student Learning Through Assessment*, ed. C. Rust, 248-66. Oxford: Oxford Brookes University.

Meyer, J.H.F., S.C. Ward, and P. Latreille. 2009. Threshold Concepts and Metalearning Capacity. *International Review of Economics Education* 8(1):132-54.

Pang, M. and J.H.F. Meyer. 2010. Modes of Variation in Pupils' Apprehension of a Threshold Concept in Economics. In *Threshold Concepts and Transformational Learning*, ed. J.H.F. Meyer, R. Land, and C. Baillie. Rotterdam: Sense Publishers. In press.

Perkins, D. 2006. Constructivism and Troublesome Knowledge. In *Overcoming Barriers to Student Understanding: Threshold Concepts and Troublesome Knowledge*, ed. J.H.F. Meyer and R. Land, 33-47. London and New York: Routledge.

Reid, A. 2001. Variation in the Ways that Instrumental and Vocal Students Experience Learning Music. *Music Education Research* 3(1):26-40.

Richardson, J.T.E. 2000. *Researching Student Learning: Approaches to Studying in Campus-Based and Distance Education*. Buckingham: Open University Press.

Richardson, J.T.E. 2006. Investigating the Relationship between Variations in Students' Perceptions of their Academic Environment and Variations in Study Behaviour in Distance Education. *British Journal of Educational Psychology* 76(4):867-93.

Sandefur, J. 2005. Problem Solving: What I Have Learned from My Students. A paper presented at the Kaist International Math Education Conference. Accessed 28 January 2009 at http://www9.georgetown.edu/faculty/sandefur/ProofPaper.pdf

Shanahan, M. and J.H.F. Meyer. 2003. Measuring and Responding to Variation in Aspects of Students' Economic Conceptions and Learning Engagement in Economics. *International Review of Economics Education* 1(1):9-35.

Sloman, J. 2006. *Economics*, 6th edition. Harlow: Pearson Education Limited.

Timmermans, J. 2010. Changing Our Minds: The Developmental Potential of Threshold Concepts. In *Threshold Concepts and Transformational Learning*, ed. J.H.F. Meyer, R. Land, and C. Baillie. Rotterdam: Sense Publishers. In press.

Vermunt, J.D. 1998. The Regulation of Constructive Learning Processes. *British Journal of Educational Psychology* 68(2):149-71.

Wineburg, S. 2001. *Historical Thinking and Other Unnatural Acts: Charting the Future of Teaching the Past*. Philadelphia: Temple University Press.

> *An approach to exemplary teaching practice that integrates craft, professional, and scientific knowledge in support of student learning.*

12

Three Perspectives on Teaching Knowledge: Craft, Professional, and Scientific

Thomas Carey

Introduction

The previous chapters in this section outline significant advances in our understanding of how students learn, as well as how we can apply such knowledge and evidence to enhance the learning experience and student success. The analyses and examples highlight how instructors can apply the evidence about learning, and knowledge about teaching, in their subject areas in ways that acknowledge variations in context and in student capabilities and needs. The two chapters present complementary perspectives: both are situated in specific settings and both are presented by the authors as "works in progress." The authors continue to extend their work into new subject areas where pedagogical-content knowledge is not as well advanced.

In this closing section, I explore one particular thread that emerges in both chapters concerning how we can advance the practice of teaching in post-secondary education. I agree with both Jan H.F. Meyer's emphasis on a professional "reconceptualisation of the practice of teaching ... [to include] knowledge of how students learn *in general*, and how they learn

Taking Stock: Research on Teaching and Learning in Higher Education, ed. J. Christensen Hughes and J. Mighty, Montreal and Kingston: McGill-Queen's University Press, Queen's Policy Studies Series. © 2010 The School of Policy Studies, Queen's University at Kingston. All rights reserved.

in the subject or discipline," and Carl Wieman's emphasis on "disseminating results in a scholarly manner and copying and building upon what works." Where I would like to push the boundaries of the discussion is in thinking about the nature of the body of knowledge with which we want our teachers to engage, and the resulting implications for actions that educational developers might take in identifying and promoting exemplary practices.

These are personal reflections on the role of practitioner/researcher, based on the evidence of several past and ongoing educational development projects across a range of contexts in post-secondary educational institutions and systems. These experiences have led me to value the contributions regarding exemplary practice which can be made by teachers without formal knowledge or training in pedagogical content knowledge, extending to them the graceful comments Jan H.F. Meyer makes about the tacit understanding of students, who "in varying degrees may possess some ... as yet non-formalised understanding of what a particular concept represents long before it comes into [explicit] view." I also would question the universality of Carl Wieman's recommendation that "teaching should be pursued with the same rigourous standards of scholarship as scientific research."

My central hypothesis is that we can move forward most effectively with an approach to exemplary practices which values and integrates craft knowledge, professional knowledge, and scientific knowledge from our most effective teachers and scholars.

Teaching Knowledge as Craft Knowledge

A craft is the skilled practice of an occupation. We don't often use the word "craft" in higher education, except for work in the creative arts and some specialized academic studies such as "stagecraft." Yet most teachers would identify with the idea that their practice involves skill, and that the skills of an effective teacher share attributes with other craft knowledge, e.g., that the skills are acquired more by apprenticeship than formal study, or "over the years in the school of hard knocks" (Barth 2004).[1] Our most effective teachers have a wealth of craft knowledge, "knowledge gained by experience which teachers use everyday in their classrooms but which is rarely articulated in any conscious manner" (Day 2005, 21)

Because this knowledge is rarely articulated explicitly, learning from craft knowledge tends to rely on direct experience with a mentor or master teacher, and is therefore difficult to "scale up" as an institutional initiative—but this challenge need not prevent us from seeking more effective and more efficient ways to leverage craft knowledge in order to advance teaching practice. Educational developers often use methods like *group classroom visitations* as one way to increase the exchange of craft knowledge.[2] Another option is a collection of exemplary resources which illustrate effective practices in areas like explaining academic integrity to students (Bringelson et al. 2006). I believe much more could be done to identify and promote exemplary teaching practice through sharing amongst our teaching faculty.

Barth has written eloquently on the local conditions which promote exchange of craft knowledge about teaching. He lists some signs indicating that educators have the kind of collegiality required, which he characterizes as "playing well together."

- Educators talking with one another about practice;
- Educators sharing their craft knowledge;
- Educators observing one another while they are engaged in practice;
- Educators rooting for one another's success.[3]

Teaching Knowledge as Professional Knowledge

We now commonly talk about "professional development" for teachers in post-secondary education, and various qualification schemes like the one discussed by Jan H.F. Meyer assume there is a professional body of knowledge to be studied. Treating knowledge about teaching in post-secondary education as professional knowledge recognizes that teaching, like other learned professions, requires "mastery of a specialized body of knowledge that is applied with wisdom and ethical concern"[4] and followed as our lifework.

A key distinction between *professional knowledge* and *craft knowledge* is explicit representation and organization as a body of knowledge, including the following attributes:

> Professional knowledge must be storable and shareable.... It must be created with the intent of public examination, open for discussion, verification, refutation, and modification.... When we consider sharing teachers' professional knowledge, a rationale should be included explaining why a lesson was created. This rationale should also indicate:
>
> - Why was this instructional activity created to support this kind of learning?
>
> - In what way was students' thinking expected to change over the course of the lesson?
>
> - Why did such change occur (or not occur)?[5]

New formats are emerging to represent and share professional knowledge about teaching in higher education, including adaptations of "Lesson Study,"[6] discipline-specific websites of instructional practices,[7]

reflective case studies,[8] the qualifications frameworks and programs referenced by Dr. Meyer, and the collections of educational research referenced
by Dr. Wieman. The community engaged in physics education research
is leading the way in producing resources for professional teaching that
will aid in mobilizing the body of knowledge from exemplary practice
and research[9] into context-sensitive practices which acknowledge the
differing needs and resources across institutions, instructors, and student
populations (e.g., Loverude 2004).

An ongoing challenge for faculty and educational developers is the lack
of respect for professional teaching in many parts of our institutions. We
use phrases like Dr. Wieman's about "dissemination of results in a scholarly manner" or speak of "scholarly teaching" (Martin 2007) to describe
activities regarded in other domains as normal professional work. This
may reflect in part the awareness that our institutions are more likely to
value these activities if they can appear under the "scholarship" column
of an annual faculty evaluation rather than the "teaching" column. As
part of the larger exploration of the scholarship of teaching and learning,
this emphasis on the scholarly aspects of teaching has greatly advanced
understanding and practice of teaching in higher education, both within
Canada and in many other countries. However, I believe our response to
the challenge of professionalism in teaching must be multi-dimensional;
emphasizing only scholarly teaching may prove to be counter-productive,
as it can promote confusion about the value of both our professionalism
and our scholarship.

Similar challenges have been addressed in other areas of education,
where integrations of different types of knowledge—craft expertise, professional practice, and research insights—are evolving to enhance teaching
and learning, with appropriate respect for their complementary roles.
Consider the following description of recent work to integrate teacher's
expertise with research on school success, which will serve as a bridge
to the last topic theme of this chapter, the role of scholarship in teaching:

> The traditional model, based on separate and distinct research and practice
> communities, with the former possessing knowledge that will inform the lat-
> ter, is no longer valid. The road between research and practice as a two-way
> street needs to be considered, where both are valid sources of knowledge
> about teaching. To be sure, teachers need to study and conduct research on
> learning and cognition and to incorporate up-to-date findings of research
> into their practice. At the same time, they can also gain important knowledge
> about teaching through their own and one another's experience. Researchers,
> for their part, need to carefully examine the knowledge that teachers and
> school leaders have acquired. Only by recognizing and using both sources
> of knowledge can educators truly transform schools and turn teaching into
> a true profession. Combined with research knowledge that is informed by

practice, craft knowledge—codified, tested, and shared—can build a new foundation for the teaching profession. (Burney 2004, 526)

Teaching Knowledge as Scholarship

Let me illustrate this blurring of boundaries between research and practice with a personal anecdote. I recently worked with a team of instructors from several Ontario colleges who were collaborating on the redesign of introductory courses in mathematics. There were dual goals for this program:

- The primary goal of the team was to enhance the student-learning experience and student success in their own courses;
- A secondary goal was to analyze the lessons learned from these re-design experiences—in particular, to share with one another results from the course redesigns, and jointly evaluate the local versus general nature of the factors contributing to (or limiting) success;
- A third subsidiary goal or outcome from the project was to synthe-size the team's explorations, discussions, and results into knowledge products which could be used by other instructors to accelerate their adaptation of exemplary practices and research insights for other courses.

These results raised a practical question: Did we need to seek ap-proval for our course-redesign work from our institutional research ethics boards? None of these instructors considered themselves to be engaged in a research study, and few had any experience in preparation and submission of an application to approval of a study involving "human subjects." The team members did not view their activity as fitting under the definition of research used in their institutional policies: "systematic investigation to establish ... principles or generalizable knowledge." In the language used by their Research Ethics Board (REB), they were carrying out:

> ... studies related directly to assessing the performance of an organization or its employees or students, within the mandate of the organization, or ac-cording to the terms and conditions of employment or training.[10]

Such studies are deemed by institutional policy to be exempt from REB review, i.e., part of normal professional work to improve quality continually. Team members were expected to evaluate what worked and did not work in their pilot-course offerings. Doing this would not involve collecting any data from human subjects beyond what they would collect to achieve the normal organizational assessment referred to in the policy. However, we *were* asking them to work with us to build understanding of what local versus generalizable factors contributed to their results (successful or not), partly to inform practice elsewhere but also to help transfer exemplary practice to other instructors within their own departments. This deeper analysis may have required some sharing within the team of the assessment data beyond what would be required if they were focused solely on their own institutional needs, unless we were to define the boundary of the organization referred to in the policy as the system of colleges rather than a single institution.

Of course, we didn't waste much time trying to parse institutional policies in any further depth: one of our supporting educational developers worked with team members to apply for exempt status from their REBs to ensure they had fulfilled their responsibilities. But the experience of trying to tease apart the activities of a professional from the activities of a scholar illustrated for us that the boundary will be often blurred and sometimes in flux.

This anecdote illustrates the challenge of formulating a firm boundary between teaching as professional work and as scholarly work. With this understanding of the dynamic relationship between knowledge from practice and knowledge from research, Dr. Wieman's earlier phrase about "disseminating results in a scholarly manner and copying and building upon what works" might be expanded (and reversed) as follows:

- Descriptions of promising practices: "I tried this in my context and got the following positive results."
- Descriptions of exemplary practices: "We tried this in our different contexts, and began to sort out where and how it produced desirable results."
- Prescriptive bodies of understanding with contingent statements of causality about what factors have produced the outcomes of interest.[11]

This last kind of result (i.e., contingent statements of causality), while ideal, is seldom achieved in practice. It is ideal because "teachers and administrators need to know reliably what will happen if they implement a policy in their specific situations, not what will happen on average" (Christensen et al. 2008, 177). However, the feasibility of achieving the ideal is increasingly being called into question by leading educational researchers who are directly involved in improving practice. They are using language about the integration of multiple types of evidence in a "continuum of studies" (Roschelle et al. 2008), asking for a better balance between "scientific" and "critical" research (Carr and Kemmis 1986), and invoking strong language about recognizing the difficulties of "moving a model of research that works in one domain (drug trials) into the forced service of another intellectual domain (education)" (Sloane 2008).

The next section of this book deals with various ways we might move toward a more *evidence-based* practice of teaching. We should understand this direction as involving knowledge-based, perhaps even knowledge-intensive, practice in teaching, with "evidence" being interpreted broadly as a progression wherein each stage represents the best knowledge available at any given time to guide practice.

CONCLUDING THOUGHTS

It would take more space than this chapter allows, but somewhere in this ongoing discussion we need to think more about how we can move beyond identifying and promoting exemplary teaching practices to developing faculty as *expert teachers*. Kreber has made the important distinction between "excellent teachers" and "expert teachers" (Kreber 2002):[12]

> "Excellence in teaching" is usually identified on the basis of a judgment made about *performance* ... it is deemed far more pertinent that the *performance* was perceived as successful or effective by those who had the experience (i.e., present and former students, peers, and the instructors themselves).... Awards for teaching excellence, for example, are ordinarily not adjudicated on the basis of how much someone *knows* about teaching.... Over time, most faculty develop a repertoire of approaches and strategies that tend to work well. Nonetheless, some teachers continue to engage in reflective thinking about what works and what does not, and ask themselves why it worked or did not work.

> The expertise literature (Bereiter and Scardamalia 1993) suggests that faculty who continuously engage in self-regulating their learning about teaching develop into "expert teachers".... The difference is that ... people pursuing "expert careers" continually reinvest their mental resources ... which, in turn, leads them to develop more sophisticated skills and knowledge ... experts continuously seek out new opportunities to further their understanding of problems. It is precisely by identifying, analyzing, and solving problems that experts, over time, develop problem-solving strategies that are *even more effective*. This desire to be *even more effective* underlies the motivation of experts. (12-13)

Finally, we need not infer a contradiction between Dr. Meyer's wariness about overly prescribed approaches to curriculum and course design, e.g., his conveyor-belt analogy, and Dr. Wieman's emphasis on replicable results from studies of teaching and learning, including tools like the "Force Concept Inventory." I like the phrase used by one of the participants in our collaborative course-redesign teams:

You can give us a recipe for combining instructional ingredients into an intellectually nutritious meal, but each of us as teachers adds our own "secret sauce" to give it a special taste.

Notes

[1] See the chapter on "Craft Knowledge."

[2] Open Classroom program, http://www.cte.uwaterloo.ca/faculty_programs/open_classroom.html.

[3] Barth (2004), as summarized by Stephanie Sandifer in her *Change Agency* weblog, 26 February 2007. Accessed 9 April 2009 at http://www.ed421.com/?p=232.

[4] Sharon Strom, *The Knowledge Base for Teaching*, ERIC Digest, Report No. ED330677 (ERIC Document Reproduction Service No. ED330677). Retrieved from ERIC database.

[5] Christopher D. Sessums, *A Knowledge Base for the Teaching Profession: Initial Thoughts*, posted in his personal weblog, 3 February 2009. Accessed 9 April 2009 at http://eduspaces.net/csessums/weblog/570770.html. Sessums is adapting ideas from Hiebert, Gallimore, and Stigler (2002).

[6] College Lesson Study Project, University of Wisconsin – La Crosse and UW System Office of Professional & Instructional Development. Accessed 22 December 2009 at http://www.uwlax.edu/sotl/lsp/

[7] E.g., Teach the Earth, http://serc.carleton.edu.

[8] E.g., the ELIXR program, http://elixr.merlot.org.

[9] E.g., *Reviews in Physics Education Research*, http://www.compadre.org/per/per_reviews/.

[10] *Tri-Council Policy Statement: Ethical Conduct for Research Involving Humans*, 1st edition, 1998. Article 1.1. Accessed 9 April 2009 at http://www.pre.ethics.gc.ca/eng/policy-politique/tcps-eptc/section1-chapitre1/#1p1.

[11] This language is adapted from Chapter 7 of Christensen, Johnson, and Horn (2008).

[12] We can also make a useful distinction between "excellent teachers," whose performance exceeds that of their peers but may not be easily replicated, and "exemplary teachers," whose teaching processes can be disseminated so that their performance can be replicated by others who follow those processes as a model for effective teaching.

References

Barth, R.S. 2004. *Learning by Heart*. San Francisco: Jossey-Bass.

Bereiter, C. and M. Scardamalia. 1993. *Surpassing Ourselves*. Chicago and La Salle: Open Court Press.

Bringelson, L., D. Bean, D. Buzza, P. Marks, A. Kirker, M. Jack, and J. Willwerth. 2006. UW-ACE Instructional Repository: A System for Supporting Evidence Based Instructional Design. MERLOT International Conference, Ottawa.

Burney, D. 2004. Craft Knowledge: The Road to Transforming Schools. *Phi Delta Kappan* 85(7):526-31.

Carr, W. and S. Kemmis. 1986. *Becoming Critical: Education, Knowledge, and Action Research*. London: Routledge.

Christensen, C., C.W. Johnson, and M.B. Horn. 2008. *Disrupting Class: How Disruptive Innovation Will Change the Way the World Learns*. New York, NY: McGraw-Hill.

Day, T. 2005. Teachers' Craft Knowledge: A Constant in Times of Change? *Irish Educational Studies* 24(1):21-30.

Hiebert, J., R. Gallimore, and J.W. Stigler. 2002. A Knowledge Base for the Teaching Profession: What Would It Look Like and How Can We Get One? *Educational Researcher* 31(5):3-15.

Kreber, C. 2002. Teaching Excellence, Teaching Expertise, and the Scholarship of Teaching. *Innovative Higher Education* 27(1):5-23.

Loverude, M. 2004. Measuring the Effectiveness of Research-Based Curriculum at a University Serving a Diverse Student Population. 2003 Physics Education Research Conference - AIP Conference Proceedings, 9 September, Vol. 720:7-10.

Martin, L. 2007. Defining the Scholarship of Teaching and Scholarly Teaching. *Teaching and Learning in Higher Education* 46(Spring):1, 3. Hamilton, ON: Society for Teaching and Learning in Higher Education.

Roschelle, J., C. Singleton, N. Sabelli, R. Pea, and J. Bransford. 2008. Mathematics Worth Knowing, Resources Worth Growing, Research Worth Noting: A Response to the National Mathematics Advisory Panel Report. *Educational Researcher* 37(9):610-17.

Sloane, F.C. 2008. Randomized Trials in Mathematics Education: Recalibrating the Proposed High Watermark. *Educational Researcher* 37(9):624-30.

SECTION V

TOWARDS EVIDENCE-BASED PRACTICE

SECTION COMMENTARY

Julia Christensen Hughes and Joy Mighty

This final section presents chapters by Christopher Knapper, Alastair J. S. Summerlee and Julia Christensen Hughes, and our closing chapter for the book. The focus of this section is a "call to action." Other chapters to this point have taken stock of the research and convincingly made the case that there is a relationship between how faculty teach and how students learn in higher education and, further, that change is needed in both. In this section, we explore other forces for change and, from a variety of perspectives, what we might do in support of deep approaches to student learning.

In Chapter 13, Christopher Knapper begins by citing several large-scale, seminal research projects and concludes that "there is increasing empirical evidence from a variety of international settings that prevailing teaching practices in higher education do not encourage the sort of learning that contemporary society demands." He then identifies what steps we might take in addressing this issue, drawing on the findings of a research study he recently carried out in collaboration with Gibbs and Piccinin (Gibbs, Knapper, and Piccinin 2009). This project, referred to as the "Oxford Study," investigated the practices of 22 departments in 11 research-intensive universities known for their commitment to effective teaching and learning. Knapper and his collaborators observed that good teaching almost always involved change at three levels (teaching methods, the organization of curricula, and learning outcomes). Catalysts for these changes were identified as including a felt crisis or opportunity, a close link to practitioners and accrediting bodies, strong and distributed leadership, a clear and shared vision, extensive consultation, a climate of recognition and celebration, and adequate support and resources. Conversely, faculty-research commitments were perceived as a barrier to pedagogical innovation. In the final section of the chapter, Dr. Knapper makes the case for the professionalization of university teaching and "structural changes that can only be brought about by academic leaders."

In Chapter 14, Alastair J. S. Summerlee and Julia Christensen Hughes also make the case for change. Drawing on the literature and their experiences as a university president and dean, respectively, they identify many of the pressures confronting universities today, including underfunding and increased demand, the Internet and the ubiquity of information, employer demands for skilled graduates, pressures for greater accessibility, and changing student demographics and expectations, including attitudes of entitlement. In recommending the way forward, Drs. Summerlee and Christensen Hughes advocate for a renaissance in higher education in which our core purpose is clarified and a recommitment is made to helping resolve the complex issues facing the world today, in large part through facilitating the intellectual development and inquiry skills of our students. Further, they argue that concepts of student self-efficacy and motivation, and the reallocation of institutional resources, are seminal to this purpose. They conclude by providing examples of steps being taken at the University of Guelph in support of student learning.

Finally, in Chapter 15, Julia Christensen Hughes and Joy Mighty—drawing on all of the previous chapters in "Taking Stock"—summarize what the evidence tells us about teaching and learning in higher education and why, on the basis of what is known, we need to change. The chapter concludes with suggestions for what needs to happen in support of evidence-based practice and student learning in higher education.

REFERENCE

Gibbs, G., C. Knapper, and S. Piccinin. 2009. *Departmental Leadership of Teaching in Research-Intensive Environments*. Final Report. London: The Leadership Foundation for Higher Education.

Empirical research has clearly established that change is needed in teaching and learning practices in higher education. Bringing about such changes requires effective leadership and more attention to the scholarship of teaching and learning.

13

CHANGING TEACHING PRACTICE: BARRIERS AND STRATEGIES

Christopher Knapper

INTRODUCTION

There is now a considerable amount of empirical research on teaching and learning in higher education that provides a guide to effective teaching practice. In particular, there is an impressive body of evidence on how teaching methods and curriculum design affect deep, autonomous, and reflective learning. Yet most faculty are largely ignorant of this scholarship, and instructional practices and curriculum planning are dominated by tradition rather than research evidence. As a result, teaching remains largely didactic, assessment of student work is often trivial, and curricula are more likely to emphasize content coverage than acquisition of lifelong and life-wide learning skills. This chapter presents the findings of a recent study of excellent teaching departments in 11 research-intensive universities worldwide. The results show how good teaching can be encouraged and led, despite formidable barriers to embedding change.

Taking Stock: Research on Teaching and Learning in Higher Education, ed. J. Christensen Hughes and J. Mighty. Montreal and Kingston: McGill-Queen's University Press, Queen's Policy Studies Series. © 2010 The School of Policy Studies, Queen's University at Kingston. All rights reserved.

Faculty Conceptions of Teaching and Learning

University professors who are critical of efforts to improve teaching often challenge educational developers by asking what information and techniques we can offer that might have a tangible effect on the quality of instruction. Assuming every university teacher *did* receive some training, would it really make any difference? After all, despite years of mandatory training for elementary and high-school teachers, there is still widespread criticism of the quality of Canadian schools. This raises an intriguing question. If you as a faculty developer or educational researcher had the attention of *all* the teachers in your institution for, say, half a day, just what would you tell them? For me the answer is quite simple: I would try to raise the issue of how students learn, beginning by having faculty consider what they know intuitively from half a lifetime of learning themselves, and ending by encouraging them to become familiar with some of the seminal research from the past 30 years that helps explain how the way we teach affects the quality and effectiveness of student learning.

The act of teaching is of course meaningless without a corresponding act of learning. Yet a great irony of much university teaching is that, although professors have themselves excelled as learners, the insights gleaned from this experience are often abandoned as soon as the instructor ascends the classroom podium. Instead of reflecting on their own experience, supplemented by relevant research about effective practices, many faculty base their approach to teaching upon an uncritical adoption of the model that comes most readily to hand—their own professors.

Consequently, it is not surprising that teaching methods have remained largely unchanged since medieval times when lectures predominated largely because of a scarcity of printed books. In addition to being the most popular method among faculty, the lecture is also preferred by a great many students (see Knapper and Cropley 2000, for a review of relevant research). This is despite the fact that the higher-education literature has for some time stressed the importance of student-centred learning (see Barr and Tagg 1995), and there is increasing empirical evidence from a variety of international settings that prevailing teaching practices in higher education do not encourage the sort of learning that contemporary society demands, and indeed that most university professors claim they would like to see. What does the research on learning in university suggest about good teaching practice? Why is there such a disparity between the evidence for good practice and teachers' classroom behaviour? And is there any hope that these disparities might be corrected?

Evidence-Based Teaching

It is increasingly accepted by educational developers that effective teaching—meaning, *teaching for effective learning*—has to be based on sound empirical evidence about the sort of teaching methods and approaches that produce particular learning outcomes. Unfortunately, one conse- quence of the fact that few faculty members receive any explicit training in teaching is that we tend to approach the task in a rather amateur fash- ion, in both the good and bad sense of that term. Indeed, most faculty and university administrators are unaware that there is a considerable body of research on effective teaching practice, much of it specific to the special context of higher education. The most interesting and influential line of research over the past 25 years has focused on factors that pro- mote cognitive development in students—not simply the acquisition of information that is generally measured by traditional examinations and tests, but more generic skills, such as problem solving, critical thinking, and what the researchers have termed "deep" learning. We now know a good deal about what promotes effective learning in undergraduates and, furthermore, this substantial body of research offers many pointers to the way we might best organise teaching to promote deeper and more independent learning.

The emphasis here is not so much on *how much* students learn, but on *changes in learning processes* and how these are affected by instructional interventions (teaching) and departmental (or institutional) learning climates. Investigators have identified different learning approaches, measured changes in learning approaches over time, and tried to discover the determinants of such change. This research derives from a number of individuals working in different countries, but relying greatly on a cross- fertilisation of findings and methods of inquiry. The work is associated with the names of scholars such as Marton and Säljö in Sweden, Entwistle and Ramsden in England, and Biggs, Kember, Trigwell, and Watkins in Australia and Hong Kong.

These researchers have identified and described different learning ap- proaches, beginning with the classic papers by Marton and Säljö (1976a, 1976b), who first used the terms "deep" and "surface" approaches to learning, later renamed by Entwistle and Ramsden (1983) as "meaning orientation" and "reproducing orientation." Deep learning refers to an approach that emphasizes the pursuit of meaning and understanding for its own sake, and deep learners appear to be intrinsically motivated. For them the act of learning is its own reward, and the major goal of such learners is to integrate new learning and ideas with their existing under- standing. Surface learners, on the other hand, are primarily motivated to meet minimum-task requirements (e.g., to get through the course and pass the exam), and they see learning as mainly a matter of reproducing information without any particular interest in its meaning.

Of course, all of us frequently engage in surface learning just to get through the many tasks we face in our everyday lives, and surface learn- ing may indeed be appropriate for many routine matters. But to meet the challenges of change and complexity in modern society, university students inevitably need to use learning approaches that stress depth—in the sense of conceptual understanding and integration of new knowledge with existing ideas in order to solve complex and often novel or unanticipated problems.

What sorts of learning approaches are used by university students, and how are they affected by characteristics of the department or institution, especially by teaching methods? An early study at the Australian National University by Watkins and Hattie (1981) reached some pessimistic conclusions. It involved an ambitious longitudinal investigation of 540 students as they proceeded through their undergraduate programs, with approaches to study measured by both questionnaires and personal interviews. The research revealed that students' learning orientations, in fact, became progressively more surface over the three years of their university studies, and Watkins and Hattie attributed their results primarily to the examination system which, they concluded, discouraged adoption of deeper learning approaches.

More optimistic conclusions can be drawn from an investigation by Ramsden and Entwistle (1981), who studied over 2,000 British university students enrolled in 66 different academic departments in the humanities, social sciences, sciences, and engineering. There was no universal pattern of change in learning orientation over time, but some departments, across all the disciplines studied, did foster adoption of deeper learning approaches by their students. Such departments were characterised by "good teaching," "greater freedom in learning," and "avoidance of overloading." Good teachers were defined by Ramsden and Entwistle as instructors who tried to understand student difficulties, were ready to give help and advice on study methods, and took care to pitch material at an appropriate level. The authors defined "freedom in learning" as allowing students a choice of tasks to complete course requirements, and a choice of learning methods to accomplish these tasks. Other characteristics that appeared to promote deeper learning included setting clear goals and standards for academic work, vocational relevance (perceived links between what was being studied and students' later lives and careers), social climate (good relations between students and teachers), and less emphasis on formal teaching (attending classes) compared to individual study.

Several years later, Bertrand and Knapper (1991) did a partial replication of the Entwistle and Ramsden study in three academic departments at the University of Waterloo, using questionnaires adapted from the 1981 research. Student-learning approaches in the three departments differed markedly in the predicted directions, and persisted over time. They were also associated with aspects of teaching and academic climate identified by Ramsden and Entwistle (Knapper 1995). In other words, the association between student-learning approaches and departmental learning climate found among British undergraduates seems to operate in a very similar manner in a group of North American students.

Kember has also shown links between the orientation of individual teachers and a change in their students towards deeper learning approaches. Kember developed a scale to measure teaching values and beliefs, and distinguished, as did Barr and Tagg (1995), between "subject orientation" at one end of a continuum and "student or learning orientation" at the other. Teachers holding more learning-centred orientations, and who encourage more active learning and interaction with students, appear to promote deeper learning than teachers who hold more subject-centred values (Kember and Gow 1994).

Although the work cited above has been done mainly with student populations in Europe, Australia, and Asia, the findings about links between teaching methods and learning outcomes receive some support from American research that has adopted quite different methodologies. For example, Astin (1993)—in a massive project that involved 20,000 students, 25,000 academic staff, and 200 institutions in the US—showed that the characteristics and behaviour of teaching staff had major implications for student development. In particular, opportunities for student-faculty interaction had "positive correlations with every self-reported area of intellectual and personal growth" (383), and there were similar positive effects associated with opportunities for interactions among students themselves. In contrast, the sheer number of hours devoted to teaching was unrelated to cognitive development, suggesting it is the *quality* of teacher-student contact, not the quantity, that is of critical importance.

Pascarella and Terenzini (1991) analysed the results of over 2,600 empirical studies dealing with the impact of higher education on student learning and development. They concluded that student learning is "unambiguously linked to effective teaching, and we know much about what effective teachers do and how they behave in the classroom" (619). Such behaviours include the instructor's ability to establish rapport with students, interpersonal accessibility, feedback to students, active learning strategies, opportunities for students to interact with their peers, and "a curricular experience in which students are required to integrate learning from separate courses around a central theme" (619). Writing about the implications of their research for policy and practice, Pascarella and Terenzini conclude that academic departments should strive to "create environments that attract and engage students in both intellectual and interpersonal learning" (653).

This research is largely unknown to most academics outside of educational development centres. Nonetheless, the concept of deep learning is intuitively appealing to most teachers as a sensible goal for undergraduate education. At the same time, many instructional practices and curriculum-planning processes work against achieving a move to deeper learning. Elsewhere (Knapper 2004), I have attempted to provide a simple overview of research relevant to teaching and learning in higher education and suggested a set of guidelines for good practice.

Leading University Teaching: The Oxford Study

In 2005–2007, Gibbs, Piccinin and I were involved in a research project at the University of Oxford Learning Institute that focussed on what we termed "leadership of teaching" in 11 research-intensive universities in Europe, North America, and Australia, including such prestigious institutions as MIT, Stanford, the University of Edinburgh, and the University of Sydney.[1] Each participating university nominated two academic departments that had a demonstrated record of excellent teaching, using criteria that included results of student evaluations and graduate exit polls, data from departmental reviews or quality audits, number of faculty members with teaching awards, and whatever other indicators might be available—which varied according to the institution and national system concerned. Although we focussed on major research universities for our case studies, we believe that the findings summarised below are broadly applicable to a wide range of universities.

We visited the 22 departments in 2005 and 2006, and prepared a series of case studies based upon an extensive review of relevant documentation, and interviews with the department head and other key faculty members, students, and in some cases, other stakeholders. The cases embraced a wide range of disciplines and professional programs. In each case, our focus was not just upon teaching and learning in the department, but on the *drivers* of good teaching: which people were involved, and which strategies they used to encourage an emphasis on quality teaching. This is what was meant by the term "leadership of teaching."

Here are some of our key conclusions (Gibbs, Knapper, and Piccinin 2008):

- *Teaching approaches.* Teaching in research universities is often quite traditional and (paradoxically) unsupported by research evidence of good practice, in part because major time constraints imposed by faculty-research commitments seem to discourage innovation and change in teaching approaches. However, there are some outstanding counter-examples of innovative and effective teaching and curricula.
- *Teaching and change.* Good teaching almost always seems to involve change in teaching methods, in organisation of curricula, and in learning outcomes.
- *Crisis-driven change.* Change is often the result of a crisis or opportunity, in many cases driven by external pressures.
- *Professional programs.* Innovative teaching and changes in teaching are more common in professional programs where there are close links to practitioners and accreditation bodies, and hence greater emphasis on learning generic skills that transfer from university to the workplace.

- *Leadership of teaching.* Good teaching and changed practice does not happen accidentally, but requires leadership. Leadership of teaching may not always come from the nominal head of the unit, though support from the head is usually crucial.
- *Distributed leadership.* In most examples of successful innovation, leadership is distributed among several, sometimes all, members of a department.
- *Models of leadership.* There is no single model for leading good teaching practice: leadership can be manifested and distributed in many different ways, both formal and informal, though effective leaders of teaching do have some characteristics and behaviours in common. These include: establishing credibility and trust, building a community of good teaching practice, supporting change and innovation, articulating a rationale for change, identifying teaching problems and turning them into opportunities for change, dispersing leadership among colleagues, involving students, ensuring that good teaching and educational development efforts are recognized and rewarded, and marketing the department as a teaching success.
- *Consultation.* Most examples of changed practice involve extensive consultation with multiple stakeholders, including faculty and non-academic staff, students, and employers.
- *Vision, communication, and decision making.* Effective change in teaching and curricula requires articulation and acceptance of a clear vision for learning (often in the form of agreed, broadly stated, learning outcomes that include skills and values as well as traditional disciplinary knowledge), shared goals, open and frequent communication with all stakeholders, though not complete unanimity in decision making.
- *Recognition and rewards.* For teaching to change, and good practice to take hold, there must be a climate of recognition and celebration of teaching efforts and successes, both within the department and usually beyond.
- *Sustainability and resources.* To bring about and sustain changed practice there must be adequate support, including provision of time and resources (space, money), and leaders often play a major role in obtaining such support.
- *Evidence-based teaching.* The outstanding examples of change to good teaching practice were all evidence driven. This implies teaching approaches consistent with the research literature on effective practice as well as ongoing efforts to gather data about teaching effectiveness and learning outcomes.
- *Recidivism.* Even when changed practice has been shown to be effective, there is a slippery slope of recidivism to the traditional in teaching. Sustaining innovation and good teaching practice requires careful advance planning and constant vigilance.

The Oxford study shows that, despite the obstacles and constraints (e.g., time pressures, lack of pedagogical expertise, and a reward system that emphasizes research accomplishments), quality of learning and teaching is valued in some of the world's most prestigious research-intensive universities. But it is also true that there is a constant battle to sustain even those instructional innovations that have proved effective, let alone convince most of our colleagues that we could do better by studying the implications of student-learning research for the way we teach and plan curricula.

Developing a Scholarship of Teaching

The idea that there is a respectable body of research that could inform good instructional practice has resulted in calls for university teaching to become more professional. University teaching is one of the very few professions where practitioners receive almost no formal preparation for their work, where there is no process for the accreditation of minimum competence, and where involvement in continuing professional education is uncommon—although the growth of educational development centres has begun to change this to some extent, and in many parts of the world (e.g., Australasia and Scandinavia), the professionalisation of university teaching is well underway. Boyer and Rice (Boyer 1990) use the term "scholarship of teaching" to describe the process of undertaking research on instructional practice and using teaching methods that reflect the insights from such scholarship. Over the past 15 years, many academics have embraced the notion of teaching scholarship as a means of encouraging a more systematic approach to university teaching. But there is a danger that the term will be used simply as a slogan, and that any scholarship of teaching will always be second best to the "scholarship of discovery" or empirical, discipline-based research.

If we are to base a scholarship of teaching on established scholarly traditions, then this would have some of the following implications.

- Teaching should be *informed and evidence-based*;
- Teaching activities and achievements should be *documented*;
- Teaching approaches should in general be *replicable* by others, in the sense that someone should be able to understand enough of a teacher's approach to try it for themselves;
- Teaching should have some *conceptual underpinnings*, in the sense that there should be a reason why we do what we do as teachers;
- Teaching should involve some *assessment of process and outcomes* so that we can tell whether our teaching approaches are effective, particularly in promoting particular types of learning;
- Teaching should involve some sort of *reflection* that might lead to change and improvement;

- Teaching should build on such reflection to effect *change* (hence the idea that scholarly teaching is dynamic and even creative).

Interestingly, these characteristics were present in almost all the successful examples of good practice we observed in the Oxford case studies.

At one level, making teaching more scholarly might simply mean becoming informed about teaching in higher education through reading, discussion with colleagues, attending workshops, etc. (what most other professions do as a matter of course). But we also have to gather evidence about our teaching, for example, from students and alumni (through questionnaires, classroom-assessment techniques), by measuring learning outcomes, identifying the products of good teaching (e.g., exemplary student projects), through action research, and sometimes with controlled experiments.

While there is increasing support among educational developers for the notion that teaching should become a more scholarly activity, most of the discussion has focussed on the need for evidence-based teaching *methods*, and the important matter of deciding just *what* should be taught (curriculum content) has often been seen as "off limits" for developers. Hubball and Gold (2007) have called for a "scholarship of curriculum practice" that would help make the planning of academic programs a more rational and systematic process and help "integrate curriculum and pedagogical research in the disciplinary context of a field of study" (9).

How Research Might Produce Better Learning: What Needs to Change

I have spent most of this paper examining one aspect of the teaching-research interface: the issue of how empirical research on teaching should inform and change educational practice. Despite the difficulties of undertaking scholarship in this area (because of problems of controlling all the relevant variables in a complex environment), there is now an impressive and convincing body of research that shows how the way we organise teaching affects student-learning processes and outcomes. We know that how students are taught, what learning tasks and experiences they encounter, and how instruction and curricula are organised all have a profound effect on generic learning approaches. But has this in fact produced any real changes in educational practice?

Teaching Approaches. In my view there is little doubt that teaching has changed considerably since I began my academic career in the early 1960s, and started work as a full-time educational developer in 1976. That is to the good, since the teaching methods of 45 years ago would be inadequate to deal with the students and educational pressures of the early 21st century. The range of teaching and learning methods now in use is much broader, there is much greater awareness of ethical and diversity issues in dealing with students, and teaching is regularly documented and evaluated at both the individual and institutional level. Perhaps more importantly, there is more conversation and reflection about teaching, more concern about teaching practices and effects on learning, in part due to the establishment of educational development centres, which have acted as catalysts for discussion and innovation.

At the same time, there is a great deal about university teaching that remains problematic, and which stubbornly resists the precepts about good practice that developers have been preaching for several decades. Specifically:

- Teaching remains overwhelmingly didactic and reliant on traditional lectures, and assessment methods are often trivial and inauthentic;
- Curriculum development relies far too much on disciplinary tradition and faculty interests, rather than on student and societal needs;
- There is still a "tyranny of the academic disciplines" which mitigates against integration of knowledge and insights from different fields;
- Evaluation of teaching effectiveness and learning outcomes is often superficial.

Moreover, there are factors that suggest things may get worse before they get better. For example, in 2008, classes are generally much larger and teaching is more depersonalised than it was 20 or even ten years ago. And because students spend an increasing amount of their disposable time in formal classes, compared to the past, listening instead of processing and reflecting, there is often little time or incentive for them to engage in the independent learning that the modern world demands and most faculty members support. There is an increased use of educational technology, especially for distance education, but all too often this emulates traditional didactic teaching and testing instead of promoting student curiosity and autonomy. In other words, there is too often a poor alignment, to use a term coined by Biggs (1999), between what is taught and the competencies students will need in their later lives and work settings.

Curriculum Planning and Review

These are problems that affect both instructional methods (how we teach) and curriculum planning (what we teach). Until recently, educational developers have focussed on the former, and matters of program planning, assessment, and reform have been left to the disciplines. But there is increasing recognition that effective and relevant learning requires attention to both teaching methods and curriculum-planning processes. Designing a curriculum has traditionally been seen as largely a matter of assembling courses that reflect the conventional wisdom in the field, with the goal that students will master the basic concepts of the discipline. In the words of Hubball and Gold (2007): "Traditional approaches to undergraduate programming in higher education ... are often characterised by well-intentioned, select committees making ad hoc decisions about adding, modifying, or "tinkering" with individual course offerings [and] rely on students' efforts to make sense of the whole (if at all) from a broad set of often fragmented and unconnected individual course learning experiences" (8).

Professional faculties tend to emphasize students' acquisition of certain key skills relevant to professional practice. But in traditional programs (as opposed to, say, inquiry or problem-based approaches), the teaching of these skills often takes place quite late and only after a foundation of basic knowledge has been accumulated. Often more generic or "soft skills" (e.g., team work, written and oral communication, self-evaluation, and reflection) are not taught at all, even though they are widely believed to be important by employers and professional associations. This is especially problematic in a context where the nature of professional work changes rapidly, and many—perhaps most—students, even in the professions, will never practise their "discipline" directly in their later careers.

Although few professionals work in isolation (e.g., engineers must frequently deal with social, aesthetic, and environmental issues as well as the purely technical), students are rarely required to engage meaningfully with other disciplinary perspectives. While many departments require students to take courses outside the major, there is generally no attempt at integration of ideas and values from different areas, except for the few students who are enrolled in interdisciplinary programs outside the traditional departmental structure. Such programs often struggle to find a place in the modern university, and the rewards are often sparse for the faculty who teach in them.

Most universities have complex (and often cumbersome) processes for the approval of individual courses, but the scrutiny of entire programs is much rarer. And reviews tend to focus primarily on content coverage and research qualifications of teachers, rather than stressing learning outcomes and the student-learning experiences that might help to achieve them. Rarely do course or program reviews examine evidence of change in student knowledge, skills, and values that can be linked to program goals and attributed to the teaching that has taken place.

Hubball et al. (2007) have provided a valuable wholistic framework for curriculum evaluation that transcends the usual indicators (such as student grades or graduate career success), and instead focuses on real change and impacts on learning and development related to program goals. The authors are realistic enough to identify the many barriers to adopting such an approach to curriculum review. In fact, we found in the Oxford study described above that the strategies recommended by Hubball et al. are much more likely to be adopted when a program or discipline is facing a major crisis—for example, a lack of demand for its graduates or widespread dissatisfaction on the part of employers.

How We Might Do Better

To summarise, a major challenge for universities, especially at a time of resource constraints, is to organise teaching so as to maximize learning effectiveness. As I have argued earlier, a major obstacle to change is the fact that most faculty members are not trained for their teaching role and are largely ignorant of the research literature on effective pedagogy. Yet the need for change is urgent, and a number of commentators have offered suggestions of what types of changes should be adopted (e.g., Biggs 1999; Kember 1997; Prosser and Trigwell 1999; Weimer 2002).
   Ideas include:

- Teaching methods that stress student activity and task performance rather than just acquisition of facts;
- Opportunities for meaningful personal interaction between students and teachers;
- Opportunities for collaborative team learning;
- More authentic methods of assessment that stress task performance in naturalistic situations, preferably including elements of peer and self-assessment;
- Making learning processes more explicit, and encouraging students to reflect on the way they learn;
- Learning tasks that encourage integration of information and skills from different fields;
- Curriculum planning that focuses on realistic student-learning outcomes rather than disciplinary traditions and faculty prefer- ences. By realistic, I mean outcomes that will equip students with knowledge and skills, both generic and discipline-based, that can be transferred to the world beyond the university throughout their lives and careers.

   For example, both problem-based and inquiry methods encourage active learning, meaningful interaction with a teacher, team learning, reflection, authentic assessment, and integration of knowledge from different fields. And even traditional research tasks, such as the under- graduate thesis, have the great advantage of encouraging students to take ownership of their own learning, with the teacher as facilitator, guide, and subject-matter expert. The universities that have under- taken such initiatives can take credit for encouraging teaching based on evidence of good practice—even if in some cases they perhaps did so inadvertently!

Conclusion

Despite some achievements in making teaching more scholarly and more effective, clearly there is much more to do if teaching is to be practised in a way that is as professional and systematic as our approach to research. This certainly involves efforts by individual teachers, but it also requires structural changes that can only be brought about by academic leaders (presidents and deans)—including hiring practices and reward structures that recognise the importance of teaching expertise, quality-assurance approaches that measure learning processes and outcomes in a much more sophisticated way than has been customary, support for research in university teaching and learning, and changes in the way we accredit universities and prepare new entrants to the profession. Moreover, as the Gibbs, Knapper, and Piccinin study (2008) has shown, change in teaching also requires effective leadership at the departmental level; leadership that is knowledgeable about pedagogical issues, articulates a convincing rationale for change, supports colleagues and students who can help transform teaching and learning practice, gathers evidence for the effectiveness of the new approaches, and ensures that teaching achievements are recognised across the institution and beyond.

Note

[1] The official title of the project is *Departmental Leadership for Quality Teaching: An International Comparative Study Of Effective Practice*, and it was funded by the Leadership Foundation for Higher Education (UK) and the (British) Higher Education Academy.

References

Astin, A.W. 1993. *What Matters in College? Four Critical Years Revisited*. San Francisco: Jossey-Bass.

Barr, R.B. and J. Tagg. 1995. From Teaching to Learning: A New Paradigm for Undergraduate Education. *Change* 27(6):13-25.

Bertrand, D. and C.K. Knapper. 1991. Contextual Influences on Students' Approaches to Learning in Three Academic Departments. Unpublished honours thesis, University of Waterloo.

Biggs, J. 1999. *Teaching for Quality Learning at University: What the Student Does*. Buckingham, UK: Society for Research into Higher Education and Open University Press.

Boyer, E.L. 1990. *Scholarship Reconsidered: Priorities of the Professoriate*. Princeton, NJ: Princeton University Press and the Carnegie Foundation for the Advancement of Teaching.

Entwistle, N.J. and P. Ramsden. 1983. *Understanding Student Learning*. London: Croom Helm.

Gibbs, G., C. Knapper, and S. Piccinin. 2008. Disciplinary and Contextually Appropriate Approaches to Leadership of Teaching in Research-Intensive Academic Departments in Higher Education. *Higher Education Quarterly* 62:416-36.

Hubball, H. and N. Gold. 2007. The Scholarship of Curriculum Practice and Undergraduate Program Reform: Integrating Theory into Practice. In *Curriculum Development in Higher Education: Faculty-Driven Processes and Practices*, ed. P. Wolf and J. Christensen Hughes. San Francisco: Jossey-Bass.

Hubball, H., N. Gold, J. Mighty, and J. Britnell. 2007. Supporting the Implementation of Externally Generated Learning Outcomes and Learning-Centered Curriculum Development: An Integrated Framework. In *Curriculum Development in Higher Education: Faculty-Driven Processes and Practices*, ed. P. Wolf and J. Christensen Hughes. San Francisco: Jossey-Bass.

Kember, D. 1997. A Reconceptualisation of the Research into University Academics' Conceptions of Teaching. *Learning and Instruction* 7:255-75.

Kember, D. and L. Gow. 1994. Orientations to Teaching and their Effect on the Quality of Student Learning. *Journal of Higher Education* 65:58-74.

Knapper, C.K. 1995. Understanding Student Learning: Implications for Instructional Practice. In *Successful Faculty Development: Strategies to Improve University Teaching*, ed. W.A. Wright. Bolton, MA: Anker.

Knapper, C.K. 2004. *Research on College Teaching and Learning: Applying What We Know*. Background discussion paper prepared for the Teaching Professor Conference, May, Philadelphia.

Knapper, C.K. and A.J. Cropley. 2000. *Lifelong Learning in Higher Education*, 3rd edition. London: Kogan Page.

Marton, F. and R. Saljo. 1976a. On Qualitative Differences in Learning: I – Outcome and Process. *British Journal of Educational Psychology* 46:4-11.

Marton, F. and R. Saljo. 1976b. On Qualitative Differences in Learning: II – Outcome as a Function of the Learner's Conception of the Task. *British Journal of Educational Psychology* 46:115-27.

Pascarella, E.T. and P.T. Terenzini. 1991. *How College Affects Students: Findings and Insights from Twenty Years of Research*. San Francisco: Jossey-Bass.

Prosser, M. and K. Trigwell. 1999. *Understanding Learning and Teaching: The Experience in Higher Education*. Buckingham, UK: Society for Research into Higher Education and Open University Press.

Ramsden, P. and N.J. Entwistle. 1981. Effects of Academic Departments on Students' Approaches to Studying. *British Journal of Educational Psychology* 51:368-83.

Watkins, D.A. and J. Hattie. 1981. The Learning Processes of Australian University Students: Investigations of Contextual and Personological Factors. *British Journal of Educational Psychology* 51:384-93.

Weimer, M. 2002. *Learner-Centered Teaching: Five Key Changes to Practice*. San Francisco: Jossey-Bass.

The advent of the Internet, the need for employability skills, pressure for greater accessibility, declining resources, changing student demographics, and challenges in K-12 all suggest that universities must embrace change or risk obsolescence.

14

Pressures for Change and the Future of University Education

Alastair J.S. Summerlee and Julia Christensen Hughes

Introduction

Universities worldwide are facing a number of apparently contradictory and competing pressures ranging from underfunding and increased demand, to questions concerning the very nature of universities, their roles in society and—as has been amply demonstrated throughout this book—concerns about their effectiveness in fulfilling their educational mandate. Combined, these factors call into question the very future of one of our most venerable institutions. For all of these reasons we need to change. If we do not, society will likely find different ways to deliver on the promise of higher education and we may become obsolete.

The Promise of Universities and Contemporary Global Challenges

First established in Europe during medieval times, universities have long served as bastions of ideas, repositories of knowledge, and training grounds for intellectuals and the professions—theology, law, and medicine (Altbach 1999; Rait 1912). Accordingly, they have long stood as beacons for philosophical thought, ethical debate, and social reform and service.

In the 19th century, this mandate was challenged as Germany positioned the university as a mechanism for "nation building" and for conducting research in support of "national development and industrialization," establishing graduate education and the doctoral degree in support of such aims (Altbach 1999, 17). Other countries soon followed, which irrevocably changed the nature of universities around the globe (Altbach, Reisberg, and Rumbley 2009).

Criticizing the Germanic educational model, noted educational philosopher Dewey (1916) observed that with its focus on "military, industrial, and political defense and expansion" (94), the stated aim of education had become to "form the citizen, not the 'man,'" and that the educational process had become "one of disciplinary training rather than of personal development" (94). In contrast, Dewey argued that education should serve as "the fundamental method of social progress and reform" (1897, NP), and that "through the full development of private personality" (1916, 96), humanity would be enhanced. According to Dewey, education was the key underpinning of democratic society, preparing people with the ability to articulate and understand disparate points of view and to resolve complex issues of social importance collaboratively.

In the mid-1900s, the mandate of the university was challenged once again, this time in North America. With the advent of the Servicemen's Readjustment Act of 1944 and the Veteran's Readjustment Assistance Act of 1952 (referred to as the GI Bills), access to higher education in the US became unprecedented (Cuban 1999). Described as "the first country to achieve mass higher education," by 1960 the US had achieved a 40-percent participation rate (Altbach et al. 2009, vi). Hence, the dual mandate of conducting complex scientific research while preparing large numbers of undergraduates for rewarding careers became an established expectation at universities across North America, creating tension in our sense of purpose that has been with us ever since.

Despite the enormity of these challenges, in a recent report prepared for the UNESCO 2009 World Conference on Higher Education, Altbach et al. (2009) argued that those challenges we have encountered within higher education over the past decade have been even more profound "due to their global nature and the number of institutions and people they affect" (iii). Some of the challenges they identified in making this point include:

- Increased competition by students (for admission) and by universities (for status, ranking, and funding), alongside significant growth in private higher education, i.e., "30 percent of global higher education" is now private (xiv).

- Globalization, including the establishment of English as "the dominant language of scientific communication" (iv) and new forms of collaboration, e.g., the Bologna Process and Libson Strategy.
- Massification: there are currently "150.6 million tertiary students globally, roughly a 53-percent increase over 2000" (vi).
- Concentration: there are 24 "mega-universities" in the world today, "a number of which boast over one million students" (xviii).
- Growing concern with access inequality and economic barriers to participation.
- Increasing student mobility: by 2020, over seven million students will be studying abroad, up from 2.5 million currently (viii).
- Growing pressure for innovative pedagogy due to an increasingly diverse student body.
- The increasing prioritization of quality assurance and accountability frameworks.
- Information and communications technology: with the Internet revolutionizing how information is communicated.
- Changes in the "social contract," with higher education being increasingly "seen as a private good, largely benefiting individuals" (xii).
- The current economic crisis.

With respect to this last point, over the past year the New York Times has published numerous articles attesting to the dire financial situation being faced by universities in the US. According to Davidoff (2009), for example, growing endowments and tuition increases in the early part of the 21st century resulted in overbuilding and a "faculty and program expansion spree" (NP). With the economic crisis of 2009, and declining endowments, many universities today are facing dire financial consequences. At Harvard, for example, endowments are down by as much as 30 percent, threatening as much as one-third of Harvard's operating budget.

As a result of these economic pressures, combined with changes in the social contract, academic institutions and their students are being expected to pay larger portions of the actual cost of education, there is growing pressure to conduct research with the potential for commercial application, class sizes and teaching loads are increasing, part-time faculty are replacing full-time academic staff, and universities are being redirected away from their "traditional social role and service function" (Altbach et al. 2009, xii-xiii).

In summarizing their report, Altbach et al. (2009) state:

> We are convinced of the centrality of the higher education enterprise globally and the need for strong, vibrant post-secondary institutions to support the knowledge economy as well as to provide the knowledge necessary for

the social mobility and economic progress essential to societies across the globe. The role of higher education as a public good continues to be fundamentally important and must be supported…. The multiple and diverse responsibilities of higher education are ultimately key to the well-being of society, but this expanded role adds considerable complexity and many new challenges. (xxi)

Within Canada, there is no question that Post-Secondary Education (PSE) has for some time been associated with job creation and the economy. A report by the Council of Ministers of Education (CMEC 1999) stated that, in addition to high-quality, affordable, and accessible education, the purpose of PSE in Canada is to:

> … prepare graduates for good jobs … contribute to, and draw from the international network of research that supports prosperity and well-being … [and] serve as pillars of regional economic growth and global competitiveness. (1)

Yet, as Altbach et al. (2009) suggest, we are faced with numerous challenges that may affect our ability to deliver on these expectations. In the section that follows, select challenges and their implications are explored, including the information explosion, concerns with the employability skills of our graduates, accessibility and funding issues, demographic changes within the student body, and challenges within the K-12 system.

The Ubiquity of Information

Pressures of the information explosion, the democratization of information through open access, and the advent of knowledge-based economies have changed the educational landscape. Information, often taken as a surrogate for knowledge, is now ubiquitously available through the Internet. Free and ready access to information, without an appreciation of the limits of such information, undermines and obviates the ability to think critically and to explore, in detail, issues that should lie at the heart of the important questions facing every society. While universities have been the bastions of information, the quality of our work has come from taking that information and fashioning knowledge and helping students learn to do the same. But as so aptly suggested by Kunstler (2006) in a special issue of the futurist journal *On the Horizon*, we are facing "a media / cyber-culture in which synchronistic, instantly gratified responses and visual cues substitute for the rhythms and structures of multi-layered meaning that is the greatest virtue of the substantive written text" (63).

We must find ways to effectively teach our students information-literacy skills (Lorenzo and Dziuban 2006) so they are able to piece together the fragments of information they glean from the Internet and create a critically evaluated sense of knowledge, fostering as Marton and Säljö (1976) suggested, deep learning. According to Breivik (2005), "it has become one of education's greatest challenges to teach students the skills needed to test the reliability, currency, and relevance of the information they find" (22). This will require new partnerships between faculty and librarians and the broad-scale adoption of active learning pedagogies (particularly inquiry-based and problem-based) as assessed by Prince (2004) and advocated by Noel Entwistle, Maryellen Weimer, and Jillian Kinzie in this volume.

Employability Skills

Another pressure for change concerns the employability skills of our graduates. Whatever the academy wishes, the "product" of our undergraduate educational process is predominantly comprised of individuals who will enter the workforce. For some time, employers (industry, commerce, and the professions) have been expressing dissatisfaction with that "output." They need employees who can think creatively, communicate effectively, work collaboratively, solve complex problems, understand issues from multiple and global perspectives, manage themselves along with tasks and others, and provide leadership for innovation and change (Evers, Rush, and Berdrow 1998). The Conference Board of Canada (referenced earlier in this volume by Alenoush Saroyan) has organized these skills into three broad areas: fundamental skills, personal management skills, and teamwork skills. Learning process, more than content, will be vital for producing these outcomes.

And how have universities responded to this repeated message? In general, we have not responded well. We have continued to uphold a traditional concept of an undergraduate degree where the teaching is designed around content, taught in silos, and does not focus on process or skill development. In fact, our efforts have remained very much in keeping with the behaviourist tradition advocated by Skinner (1954) who argued that "the whole process of becoming competent in any field must be divided into a very large number of very small steps, and reinforcement must be contingent upon the accomplishment of each step" (94). Skinner's work in the early 1950s reinforced the conception of learning as mastering atomistic bits of knowledge in sequential and hierarchial order that has dominated much of university teaching, particularly in the sciences, to this day.

Accessibility

We are also being pressured to make higher education more accessible, increasing our enrollments year after year, and this, paradoxically, is also negatively affecting the quality of education. In many jurisdictions around the world, the imperative of accessibility combined with changes to the social contract has translated into "doing more with less;" universities are expected to teach more and more students with either less money or less money per student. In Canada, for example, full-time equivalent student enrollments increased by 56 percent between 1987 and 2006, while the numbers of faculty increased by only 18 percent during this same period (AUCC 2008, 4).

Universities have not responded to such pressures by changing the ways students are taught. Instead, as Altbach et al. (2009) suggest, we have simply moved to an expedient solution—larger and larger classes and heavier teaching loads. And, as the research presented in this volume by Maryellen Weimer shows, we tend to rely on the old warhorse of the traditional lecture when it clearly is not effective as the underpinning of a quality undergraduate experience.

Student Demographics

Students are changing too and these differences have implications for student learning. Consistent with the data in most developed countries (Altbach et al. 2009), women now form the majority of the entering student cohort at the University of Guelph (The First Year Experience at the University of Guelph 2007, 8). And, our incoming students report some interesting gender-based differences. For example, based upon their last year in high school, female students reported being more likely than their male counterparts to frequently "feel overwhelmed by all they had to do, study with other students, tutor another student, do volunteer work, use a library" (Incoming Students Survey Results 2008, 2). Males, on the other hand were "much more likely than females to frequently drink beer, use computer software packages, and do computer installations (hardware and software)" (Incoming Students Survey Results 2008, 2).

There are also increasing numbers of students with recognized challenges in learning who we have a duty to accommodate. At Guelph, for example, approximately 9 percent of incoming students now report having a disability (Incoming Students Survey Results 2008, 2).

Another important factor pertains to commitments outside of school. For example, a recent study found that 87 percent of first-year University of Guelph students occasionally or frequently participated in volunteer work in the year prior to their arrival (The First Year Experience at the University of Guelph 2007, 8), and 30 percent "indicated that they would be working part-time either on or off campus while at school" (Incoming Students Survey Results 2008, 2).

Finally, many of today's students are Millennials or Generation N (i.e., born during or after 1982). Having "come of age in the Internet bubble of the 1990s and Web boom of the 2000s" (Feiertag and Berge 2008, 457), many university students inhabit a world that is vastly different from the experience of most faculty and administrators (for an elaboration of these differences, see Tapscot 2009). Reportedly, the learning preferences of this group of students include "teamwork, experiential activities, structure, [and] the use of technology" and their strengths include "multitasking, goal orientation, positive attitudes, and a collaborative style" (Oblinger 2003, 38).

As with any work that attempts to identify characteristics common to a particular group of people, however, generalized claims about Generation N have not been without challenge. For example, Feiertag and Berge (2008) caution that such descriptions do not apply equally to every student. Further, Lorenzo and Dziuban (2006) and Breivik (2005) challenge the depth to which Millennials are tech-savvy and suggest that when it comes to technology, few have actually mastered more than the use of email and word processing. Consistent with this last point, incoming Guelph students rate their abilities lowest on computer skills, along with "artistic ability, problem solving skills and mathematical ability" (Incoming Students Survey Results 2008, 2). In contrast, they rate themselves highest on "drive to achieve, maturity, and competitiveness" (Incoming Students Survey Results 2008, 2).

Research has also challenged the notion that Millennials exhibit particularly positive attitudes. In fact, the results of one recent study of US undergraduates suggest that many may possess a strong sense of entitlement (Greenberger et al. 2008). Greenberger et al. (2008) found that 66 percent of respondents agreed with the statement: "If I have explained to my professor that I'm trying hard, I think he/she should give me some consideration with respect to my course grade" (1196). Further, many thought they should get a "B" grade if they completed most of the reading (41.1 percent) or attended most classes (34.1 percent). Over 10 percent (11.2) agreed that "a professor should be willing to meet with me at a time that works best for me, even if inconvenient for the professor" and just less than 10 percent (9.5 percent) agreed "a professor should let me arrange to turn in an assignment late if the due date interferes with my vacation plans" (1196).

Greenberger et al. (2008) also found support for several hypothesized relationships (1197). For example, academic entitlement was found to be positively associated with a number of personality measures (e.g., narcissism), parenting practices (e.g., giving rewards for high grades), and academic dishonesty; academic entitlement was negatively associated with work orientation (e.g., work ethic), social commitment (e.g., disposition to work for social good), and self-esteem.

While there are exceptions, universities by and large do not appear to have spent much time considering how to adapt educational processes given all of these differences, or how to meet or challenge the expectations, abilities, and habits of today's student. We should be paying much more attention to these differences and reflecting on their implications for helping students adapt to and succeed at university.

Challenges and Changes in the K-12 System

Finally, concern is increasingly being expressed with challenges and changes occurring in the K-12 system, including issues of retention and grade inflation, that are affecting the expectations, work habits, knowledge, skills and abilities that students are bringing with them to post-secondary education. According to Abeles (2006):

> In the US, there is pressure to accept students from secondary institutions into post-secondary studies even though many are thinly qualified. Today, many of those who are admitted are receiving their college degrees and are still deficient in basic skills, not just reading, writing and arithmetic, but also critical thinking and other capabilities often considered hallmarks of the "liberal college education." (38)

Within Canada, concern has been voiced with respect to similar issues (Côté and Allahar 2007). Most recently, practices of social promotion (i.e., no-fail policies) that have reportedly become widespread in Canadian schools have met with criticism. Zwaagstra and Clifton (2009) argue against such practices, suggesting that "post-secondary institutions and employers must be confident that students who receive diplomas have the necessary skills and knowledge to function in post-secondary institutions and as productive citizens in society" (6).

In focusing on issues of literacy in Canada, O'Sullivan et al. (2009) similarly state that "many of the students who reach secondary school have problems in comprehension, inadequate vocabulary, insufficient background knowledge, poor reading fluency, and little or no motivation to read" (8). Further, they report that one-third of Canadian youth aged 16 to 25 read below a level "determined to be essential for living and working in modern society" (15) and suggest that such an outcome is "unacceptable" for youth who have attended school for ten years or more (15).

Further fueling the question of the preparedness of high-school students for university are the high rates of cheating that some Canadian high-school students report. In a study by Christensen Hughes and McCabe (2006), first-year university students were presented with a list of 24 questionable behaviors and asked whether they had demonstrated such behavior during high school. Almost all of the listed behaviours (21/24) were reported by 10 percent or more of the student respondents. Sample behaviours and the percentage of students indicating they had engaged in each included: getting questions and answers from someone who had already taken a test (73 percent); fabricating or falsifying lab data (50 percent); receiving unpermitted help on an assignment (45 percent); helping someone else cheat on a test (41 percent); fabricating or falsifying a bibliography (30 percent); using unpermitted crib notes during a test

(30 percent); turning in work done by someone else (22 percent); copying material almost word for word from a written source and turning it in as your own work (20 percent); writing or providing a paper for another student (15 percent); altering a graded test to try to get additional credit (10 percent); and turning in a paper obtained in large part from a paper "mill" or website (9 percent) (Christensen Hughes and McCabe 2006, 13).

Suggesting the existence of some high-school environments or cultures in which there is little perceived risk for engaging in these behaviours: "only 12 percent [of the students] agreed or strongly agreed that students who cheated during high school would be embarrassed to tell their friends they had done so; only 13 percent thought it likely or very likely that a student would report an incident of cheating; only 14 percent agreed that students who cheated were likely to be caught; and less than half (43 percent) agreed that students who were caught cheating would be given significant penalties for having done so" (8).

In summary, universities around the world are experiencing an unprecedented number of challenges and pressures for change. Those that may be particularly seminal in Canada include the advent of the Internet, the expectation that we will become more effective at helping our students develop employability skills, the need to provide access to increasing numbers of students despite declining resources, the changing demographics and characteristics of our students, and changes in the K-12 system affecting the preparedness of students for university-level expectations. And all of this is happening at a time when the world is facing unprecedented challenges of its own—challenges that could benefit from the rigours of intellectual debate and processes of inquiry that universities are uniquely well-suited to provide. Our overarching challenge is to ensure our central place in society as the forum for intellectual debate while educating increasing numbers of students with declining resources, and in ways that are relevant to their future places of work, and the ways that they think about and process information. These factors, combined with the research presented in the earlier chapters of this book, suggest that we are faced with an imperative for change.

How Should We Respond?

Much has already been written in this volume with regard to the ways in which our teaching practice needs to change. To this discussion we add the need to instill in students the belief that they have the ability and indeed the responsibility to participate in processes of inquiry and debate, and contribute to helping resolve the complex issues facing the world today. To this end, they must become independent learners who can be critical of the information available, work with others, and make informed judgments on subjects where they have to find and evaluate the information available. The challenge is doing this in an environment where students have largely been trained to accept passively and un-critically that which they have been told. The literature on self-efficacy (Bandura 1977, 1986) and empowerment (see, e.g., Conger and Kanungo 1988) may be particularly instructive in this regard.

Writing from within the management domain and considering how employees—having experienced hierarchical and authoritarian control, feeling a sense of powerlessness, and lacking in self-efficacy belief—might come to assume more responsibility, Conger and Kanungo (1988) made a number of suggestions. In particular, they argued that desired behaviours such as initiation and persistence are best supported by the identification and removal of conditions that foster a sense of powerlessness, along with the use of empowerment-inducing strategies (e.g., participation, collaborative goal setting, effective feedback, interesting work, and the provision of meaningful rewards).

Conger and Kanungo (1988) further suggested that, in order to be ef-fective, these strategies must include self-efficacy confirming information, involving four possible sources: "enactive attainment," e.g., the experi-ence of mastering a task; "vicarious experience," e.g., the experience of observing peers successfully mastering a task; "verbal persuasion," e.g., positive verbal encouragement and feedback; and a positive "emotional arousal state," e.g., a supportive and positive environment (479).

These concepts arguably have much relevance to the higher-education domain, where initiation and persistence are exactly the kind of behav-iours that will help lead to deep learning. As suggested by Maryellen Weimer in this volume, Pintrich's work on student motivation affirms the importance of self-efficacy. Explicitly linking these concepts, he wrote: "It has been a major finding from the earliest models of achieve-ment motivation and behavior that when people expect to do well, they tend to try hard, persist, and perform better" (Pintrich and Schunk 2002, 671). These concepts may be particularly useful in understanding the educational experience of students from traditionally under-represented groups. Writing on race, Wlodkowski and Ginsberg (1995) suggested that:

> ... how students feel about the setting they are in, the respect they feel from the people around them, and their ability to trust their own thinking and experience powerfully influence their concentration, their imagination, their effort, and their ability to continue. People who feel unsafe, unconnected and disrespected are unlikely to be motivated to learn. (2)

Other motivational constructs highlighted by Pintrich (2003) include: beliefs about control—"students who believe they have more personal control of their own learning and behavior are more likely to do well and achieve at higher levels than student who do not" (673); intrinsic motivation—"research on both personal and situational interest has shown that higher levels of both are associated with more cognitive engagement, more learning, and higher levels of achievement" (674); value—"whether students care about or think the task is important in some way" (675); and goals—"goals serve to motivate and direct behavior in classroom contexts" (675).

Accordingly, Pintrich (2003, 672) identifies a number of design principles that should enhance student motivation, including providing students with:

- clear and accurate feedback regarding competence and self-efficacy ... [and] focusing on the development of competence, expertise, and skill;
- tasks that offer opportunities to be successful, but also challenge;
- feedback that stresses process nature of learning, including importance of effort, strategies, and potential self-control of learning;
- opportunities to exercise some choice and control;
- stimulating and interesting tasks ... that are personally meaningful and interesting;
- activities that are relevant and useful;
- co-operative and collaborative groups;
- task, reward, and evaluation structures that promote mastery. (672)

In addition to incorporating more of these design principles in our teaching, we must also recognize that work *outside* the classroom can be a vital component of a quality learning experience (see, e.g., work cited by Jillian Kinzie and Christopher Knapper in this volume, such as Astin 1993; Kuh 2001; and Pascarella and Terenzini 2005). In fact, there is considerable evidence that the amount of time and energy that students devote to external activities that are linked to an overall educational purpose is directly related to their ultimate success and performance. The implications are clear; universities that engage their students more fully in the life of the university and its community will be able to claim to be of a higher quality than those that do not.

All of this suggests that university education should be about process, not content; it should be about teaching people how to learn rather than memorizing facts; it should be centred on problems, not disciplines, so as to create a context in which to learn more; it should marry theoretical and applied knowledge to help the learner understand why it is necessary to understand the material; it should be involved in, and not isolated from, the communities where students and faculty live and work; it should be about working together in teams and real-life situations; and it should be relevant to international issues, not limited to the local or national context.

Making this vision a reality for the majority of our students will not be easy. In fact, it will require us to reflect deeply on our purpose, recommit to teaching and learning, and challenge some deeply held myths and assumptions, particularly those associated with the faculty role and institutional resources. For example, we need to ensure that teaching is fully valued at our institutions; that it is not seen as being of secondary importance but at the core of what society expects from us and needs us to do. We also need to challenge conceptions of what teaching and learning "look" like. In our mind's eye: Do we conjure neat rows of students quietly taking notes while a teacher speaks from the front of the room, or do we see something quite different? Relatedly, we will need to invest time and energy in supporting the development of faculty as facilitators of efficacious learning (and celebrate and reward them for doing so), as well as creatively address the issue of class size, providing increased opportunity for small group learning. And this will require a fundamental rethinking of how we direct institutional resources.

Reporting on a large-scale project funded by the Pew Charitable Trusts, Ewell (2008) observed that "one of the most pervasive and unassailable myths about higher education has to do with the relationship between outcomes and money" (10). Ewell (2008) suggested that "variations in spending have little to no effect on institutional or state higher education performance" (10) and concluded that "it is not *how much* is invested in a given collegiate experience that is important; it is instead *how intentionally* these resources are directed" (11). Yet studies showing how learning can be enhanced through the redirection of resources are often dismissed. Underscoring this point, Ewell cited a study by Twigg, carried out through the National Center for Academic Transformation (NCAT), involving the redesign of large first-year courses at several US institutions. In most cases, the redesigns involved replacing some faculty contact time with a combination of technology, peer learning, and applied learning. Twigg found that the redesigns led to better learning, increased retention, and reduced costs. Ewell underscored the resistance that such change efforts can derive (2008):

> Because these results run against the grain of conventional wisdom, they have frequently met with skepticism or downright disbelief. Even many faculty and administrators who were directly involved in these redesign efforts at first insisted on seeing the project only as a thinly disguised way to save money at the expense of learning. The article of faith that cutting costs invariably yields diminished quality was too firmly entrenched to be overturned, even when the evidence was in. (11)

In summary, suggestions for change have been made along several dimensions, including: fostering student self-efficacy and motivation; providing enriching learning activities outside of the formal curriculum; recommitting to our teaching mandate; and challenging myths and assumptions associated with traditional faculty roles and the allocation of scarce resources. While examples of these suggestions can be found on most Canadian university campuses, the challenge we face is having them become the norm.

Should (or Will) Universities Continue to Exist?

Given the pressures for change previously outlined and the inherent challenge in implementing the foregoing suggestions on a broad scale, it is perhaps important to ask a fundamental question: Should (or will) universities continue to exist? Some futurists such as Abeles (2006) suggest that the future is bleak. Given the opportunities presented by the Internet along with forces of global consolidation and the commodification of education, Abeles argues that "the probability of institutional closings, whether public or private and regardless of size, is high" (40). The prognosis by Altbach et al. (2009) is not so dire. They argue that "the demise of the traditional university will ... not take place any time soon" (xvii), although with respect to the current economic situation, they do suggest that "higher education is entering a period of crisis, unprecedented since World War II, and the full impact is as yet unclear" (xx).

Whether one believes we are facing imminent obsolescence or not, there is no question that we must adapt. As institutions, we have withstood the test of centuries—as well as the past ten years!—but historical longevity alone is not sufficient reason for our continuation. There must be palpable and important reasons for remaining at the centre of our society, even if some of the functions that were once the purview of tertiary education are hived off to other venues. For example, in some jurisdictions research has been peeled off into private and publicly funded research institutes, and job training has been centred in vocational colleges and polytechnics. The principal argument for universities' continued existence should be the centrality of our commitment to the well-being of society and to the pursuit of that old academic "chestnut," truth—truth in the context of solving the multi-dimensional interdisciplinary problems that face the world, alongside our students, not apart from them. As Hinchcliff (2006) suggested, there is an absolute need for us to create a place "where educated and responsible advocates openly prepare themselves to change the world" (83). Universities will continue to exist as long as we are sincerely committed to—and have a demonstrated track record at—developing students' abilities to lead meaningful lives and to contribute to the quality of society as a whole.

The Way Forward

Many academic institutions have begun to take steps in an effort to address the challenges identified. We offer here as one example an overview of some of the initiatives being taken at our own institution, the University of Guelph. In 1995 we adopted a strategic plan (Making Change 1995) which embraced research intensiveness and learner-centredness as our two primary strategic directions (1), along with a commitment to active and experiential learning, the integration of research with teaching (e.g., inquiry-based learning), student-skill development, and the promotion of self-reliant learning (8).

More recently, the provost released a "white paper" (The Lighting of a Fire 2005) which promoted many of the active-learning concepts mentioned throughout this volume and provided the impetus for further discussions across campus. Stemming from the white paper, a 21st Century Curriculum Committee was formed which resulted in 14 specific recommendations (21C Final Report 2007). These recommendations dealt with a range of issues, including: the need to provide more variety in course-credit weightings, ultimately reducing the number of courses students might take at any one time; creating more opportunities for students to engage in inquiry-based learning and research; the provision of a greater number of international learning opportunities; extending opportunities for hybrid learning (blending face-to-face with on-line learning); the creation of curricular maps with skill-based, program-level learning outcomes for all programs; and enhancing both the first and fourth years through integrative and applied introductory and "capstone" experiences.

Following the presentation of this report, a retreat was held, attended by all of the university's vice-presidents and deans, at which we focused on identifying innovative strategies for reforming the undergraduate learning experience. As a result, each of our core undergraduate programs is currently undergoing review, many significant changes have been proposed, and several have already been implemented. We are also looking at all of our systems and practices that may either be catalyzing or constraining further innovation and doing what we can to align them in support of student learning. Perhaps most significantly, we have implemented a new approach to integrated planning and are in the midst of introducing new systems of goal setting, accountability, resource allocation, and merit-based pay for our deans and associate deans with the purpose of further aligning all of our key administrators in support of our stated goals.

At the same time that Guelph has been placing increased emphasis on pedagogical innovation and the quality of student learning, so too has the government of Ontario, the province in which Guelph is located. In 2005, The Honourable Bob Rae was appointed by the government to provide leadership for a commission looking into higher education in the province. Specifically, he produced a report which called on Ontario to establish itself as "A Leader in Learning" (Rae 2005), placing greater focus on accessibility and quality, providing additional resources, and improving accountability and collaboration throughout the educational system.

Associated with this report, in 2005 the Ontario government released *Reaching Higher: The McGuinty Government Plan for Postsecondary Education*

(Sorbara 2005, 10-22) and, more recently, made funding conditional on the creation of customized "multi-year agreements" and "multi-year action plans" complete with institutional-specific strategies, indicators, and results (see Multi-Year Action Plan 2006). With respect to such indicators, we believe the principal measure of quality should be the willingness of institutions to experiment and change, collect data on the impact of such changes, and in the spirit of continuous improvement, change again.

Rae also recommended the establishment of the Higher Educational Quality Council of Ontario (HEQCO) which has been tasked with the development of a quality framework for the province. Of note, the government is particularly interested in student access, engagement, satisfaction, and success, and has mandated that all institutions participate in the National Survey on Student Engagement (NSSE), discussed in an earlier chapter by Jillian Kinzie, as well as other quality-related research. Guelph is firmly entrenched in these processes, is using data from our NSSE surveys to further inform our efforts, and is participating in HEQCO-sponsored research.

CONCLUSION

Universities worldwide have encountered many pressures for change over time, but in particular during the past ten years. What is now needed is a period of reflection, reformation, and renaissance. Amidst the frenzy of our day-to-day experiences, we need to reestablish the university as a place of contemplation and reasoning while demonstrating a willingness, even a passion, to participate in civil and civic engagement and debate. At the same time, we need to regenerate our understanding of, and approach to, teaching and learning. It is these goals which will drive the pressing need to reform the undergraduate experience in universities worldwide. More specifically, teaching and learning need to become focused on the *process* of learning, and helping the learner understand exactly how learning occurs. To drive learning, students should be motivated and empowered, and that means both building self-efficacy and setting the learning in the context of problems that are relevant, or have an intrigue or immediacy that makes investigating them and understanding them an absolute challenge.

Inherent in these suggestions are a number of principles about university education that challenge our current approaches and systems. For example, these opportunities should be available regardless of gender, creed, race, age, or economic status. Universities should not be places for the elite but rather places for an "eliteness" of thinking that is accessible to all. They should present problems and issues as complex and integrated, not reduced to readily digestible units (often referred to as disciplinary courses). Finally, they should concentrate on innovation, relevance, and applicability and should develop skills related to employability and an ability to function within global policies, economies, and cultures.

This is a call to action, a plea to think seriously about what we are doing, to value pedagogical research, and to ensure our instituional policies and practices are well aligned with the very important work that needs to be done. Our future depends on it.

REFERENCES

21C Final Report. 2007. Accessed 9 May 2009 at http://www.21c.uoguelph.ca/
Abeles, T.P. 2006. Do We Know the Future of the University? *On the Horizon* 14(2):35-42.
Altbach, P.G. 1999. Patterns in Higher Education Development. In *American Higher Education in the 21st Century: Social, Political and Economic Challenges,* ed. P.G. Altbach, R.O. Berdhal, and P.J. Gumport. Baltimore, ML: John Hopkins University Press.
Altbach, P.G., L. Reisberg, and L.E. Rumbley. 2009. *Trends in Global Higher Education: Tracking an Academic Revolution.* A Report Prepared for the UNESCO 2009 World Conference on Higher Education. Accessed 13 September 2009 at http://www.unesco.org/tools/fileretrieve/2844977e.pdf
Association of Universities and Colleges of Canada (AUCC). 2008. *Trends in Higher Education – Volume 3: Finance.* Ottawa: Association of Universities and Colleges of Canada. Available at http://www.aucc.ca/publications/auccpubs/research/trends/trends_e.html
Astin, A.W. 1993. *What Matters in College? Four Critical Years Revisited,* 1st edition. San Francisco: Jossey-Bass.
Bandura, A. 1977. Self-Efficacy: Toward a Unifying Theory of Behavioral Change. *Psychological Review* 84:191-215.
Bandura, A. 1986. *Social Foundations of Thought and Action: A Social-Cognitive View.* Englewood Cliffs, NJ: Prentice Hall.
Breivik, P.S. 2005. 21st Century Learning and Information Literacy. *Change* March/April:20-7.
Christensen Hughes, J. and D. McCabe. 2006. Academic Misconduct Within Higher Education in Canada. *Canadian Journal of Higher Education* 36(2):1-21.
Conger, J.A. and R.N. Kanungo. 1988. The Empowerment Process: Integrating Theory and Practice. *Academy of Management Review* 13(3):471-82.
Côté, J.E. and A.L. Allahar. 2007. *Ivory Tower Blues: A University System in Crisis.* Toronto: Toronto University Press.
Council of Ministers of Education (CMEC). 1999. *A Report on Public Expectations of Postsecondary Education in Canada.* Toronto: Council of Ministers of Education. Available at http://www.cmec.ca/Publications/Lists/Publications/Attachments/22/expectations.en.pdf
Cuban, L. 1999. *How Scholars Trumped Teachers: Constancy and Change in University Curriculum, Teaching and Research, 1890–1990.* New York, NY: Teachers College Press.
Davidoff, S.M. 2009. Harvard, Private Equity and the Education Bubble. New York Times, the Deal Professor, 3 March. Accessed 15 Nov-

ember 2009 at http://dealbook.blogs.nytimes.com/2009/03/03/harvard-private-equity-and-the-education-bubble

Dewey, J. 1897. My Pedagogic Creed. *The School Journal* 54(3):77-80. Accessed 13 September 209 at http://dewey.pragmatism.org/creed.htm

Dewey, J. 1916. *Democracy and Education*. New York: The Free Press.

Evers, F., J.C. Rush, and I. Berdrow. 1998. *The Bases of Competence: Skills for Lifelong Learning and Employability*. San Francisco: Jossey-Bass.

Ewell, P. 2008. No Correlation: Musings on Some Myths About Quality. *Change* 40(6):8-13.

Feiertag, J. and Z.L. Berge. 2008. Training Generation N: How Educators Should Approach the Net Generation. *Education and Training* 50(6):457-64.

Greenberger, E., J. Lessard, D. Chen, and S. Farruggia. 2008. Self-Entitled College Students: Contributions of Personality, Parenting, and Motivational Factors. *Journal of Youth and Adolescence* 37:1193-1204.

Hinchcliff, J. 2006. The Future of the University: Some Ethico-Epistemological Explorations. *On the Horizon* 14(2):77-83.

Incoming Student Survey Results. 2008. Incoming Students: Trends in Population from 2000 to 2008. Accessed 7 May 2009 at http://www.uoguelph.ca/analysis_planning/studentresults/

Kuh, G.D. 2001. Assessing What Really Matters to Student Learning: Inside the National Survey of Student Engagement. *Change* 33(3):10-7, 66.

Kunstler, B. 2006. The Milliennial University, Then and Now: From Late Medieval Origins to Radical Transformation. *On the Horizon* 14(2):62-9.

Lorenzo, G. and D. Dziuban. 2006. *Ensuring the Net Generation Is Net Savvy*. Educause Learning Initiative. Accessed 12 September 2009 at http://net.educause.edu/ir/library/pdf/ELI3006.pdf

Making Change. 1995. *The Strategic Plan for the University of Guelph*. Accessed 7 May 2009 at http://www.uoguelph.ca/secretariat/download/strategicplan.pdf

Marton, F. and R. Säljö. 1976. On Qualitative Difference in Learning. I-Outcomes and Processes. *British Journal of Educational Psychology* 46:4-11.

Multi-Year Action Plan. 2006. Accessed 13 September 2009 at http://www.uoguelph.ca/analysis_planning/images/pdfs/UniversityofGuelph

Oblinger, D. 2003. Boomers, Gen-Xers & Millennials: Understanding the New Students. *Educause* (July/August):37-47.

O'Sullivan, J., P. Canning P., L. Siegel, L., and M.E. Oliveri. 2009. Key Factors to Support Literacy Success in School-Aged Populations: A Literature Review. *Canadian Education Statistics Council*. Accessed 8 September 2009 at http://www.cmec.ca/Publications/Lists/Publications/Attachments/201/key-factors-literacy-school-aged.pdf

Pascarella, E.T. and P.T. Terenzini. 2005. *How College Affects Students: A Third Decade of Research*. San Francisco: Jossey-Bass.

Pintrich, P.R. 2003. A Motivational Perspective on the Role of Student Motivation in Learning and Teaching Contexts. *Journal of Educational Psychology* 95(4):667-86.

Pintrich, P.R. and D.H. Schunk. 2002. *Motivation in Education: Theory, Research, and Applications*, 2nd edition. Upper Saddle River, NJ: Prentice Hall.

Prince, M. 2004. Does Active Learning Work? A Review of the Research. *Journal of Engineering Education* (July):1-9.

Rae, B. 2005. Ontario: A Leader in Learning. Accessed 8 May 2009 at http://www.edu.gov.on.ca/eng/document/reports/postsec.pdf

Rait, R.S. 1912. *Life in the Medieval University*. Cambridge: Cambridge University Press.

Skinner, B.F. 1954. The Science of Learning and the Art of Teaching. *Harvard Educational Review* 24:86-97.

Sorbara, G. 2005. Paper A: Investing in People—Managing Ontario's Finances, the Plan for 2005. *2005 Ontario Budget: Investing in People, Strengthening our Economy*. Toronto: Queen's Printer for Ontario. Accessed 8 January 2010 at http://www.fin.gov.on.ca/en/budget/ontariobudgets/2005/pdf/papera.pdf

Tapscot, D. 2009. *Grown Up Digital: How the Net Generation is Changing Your World*. New York: McGraw-Hill.

The First Year Experience at the University of Guelph. 2007. Report of the Student Affairs First Year Experience Committee. Accessed 3 May 2009 at http://www.uoguelph.ca/studentaffairs/home/documents/thefirstyearexperiencefinal-report.doc

The Lighting of a Fire. 2005. Reimagining the Undergraduate Experience. Accessed 9 May 2009 at http://www.21c.uoguelph.ca/whitepaper.html

Wlodkowski, R.J. and M.B. Ginsberg. 1995. Diversity and Motivation: Culturally Responsive Teaching. San Francisco: Jossey-Bass.

Zwaagstra, M. and R.A. Clifton. 2009. An "F" for Social Promotion. Frontier Centre for Public Policy. 79 (August). Accessed 7 September 2009 at http://www.troymedia.com/Reports/FCPP/An-F-For-Social-Promotion.pdf

> *An urgent call for effective leadership to bring about much needed pedagogical and curricular change that will align all components of the PSE system in support of evidence-based practice.*

15

A CALL TO ACTION: BARRIERS TO PEDAGOGICAL INNOVATION AND HOW TO OVERCOME THEM

Julia Christensen Hughes and Joy Mighty

INTRODUCTION

The intent of this book has been to "take stock" of the evidence on teaching and learning in higher education. Clearly, much is known, and in fact has been known for some time, which suggests that our most common teaching method—the traditional didactic lecture—is not all that conducive to student learning. The question that confronts those of us that now know this is: What will we do with this knowledge?

This final chapter begins with a brief synopsis of the key findings that have been consistently and repeatedly supported throughout this volume. Next, we review calls for change in higher education from a historical perspective. The point is made that these calls have been made since at least the late 1800s; what we are advocating is not new. Possible barriers that have prevented change from occurring are then presented. Finally, we move to the current day and provide an overview of what changes are needed if we are to adopt broad-based, evidence-based approaches in our teaching practice. The chapter concludes with a call to

Taking Stock: Research on Teaching and Learning in Higher Education, ed. J. Christensen Hughes and J. Mighty. Montreal and Kingston: McGill-Queen's University Press, Queen's Policy Studies Series. © 2010 The School of Policy Studies, Queen's University at Kingston. All rights reserved.

the academy—faculty, administrators, educational developers, and other academic staff—along with its most important stakeholders (students, employers, government, and the community as a whole) to embrace such change. We suggest that nothing short of a renaissance in education is required, driven by determined and commited leadership. Who will lead this change? Who will follow? And who will continue to resist, impairing the educational potential of our institutions, our students, and ourselves?

Taking Stock

Based on the evidence, the chapters in this book have clearly and consistently presented three key findings. The first is that *students vary in their approaches to learning*, which have been broadly classified as deep or surface (Marton and Säljö 1976).

The second is that *variation in student learning is in part determined by the learning context*. This was largely the focus of Sari Lindblom-Ylänne's and Keith Trigwell's contributions, with others providing further support. For example, in his chapter, Christopher Knapper cited the work of Ramsden and Entwistle (1981) who found an association between deep learning and various aspects of "good teaching." Carl Weiman similarly found that student approaches to learning were all affected by the learning context, with students becoming more novice-like in their learning approaches as a result of experiencing a traditionally taught first-year class. Works cited by Dr. Knapper further reinforced this point. For example, Watkins and Hattie (1981) found that student learning orientations became progressively more surface-oriented, ostensibly as a result of an examination system which emphasized rote learning. Presenting a more positive view, in a large-scale US study, Astin (1993) found that quality student-faculty interaction led to enhanced intellectual and personal student growth.

Recognizing that there is a relationship between faculty approaches to teaching and student approaches to learning is critical. Simply put, what faculty and administrators do matters. As the chapter by Maryellen Weimer suggested, we control much of the learning context. Therefore, we control much of the approach that students take to their learning. When faculty wonder about the negative behaviours of their students—their lack of attention, their lack of preparedness—one place they should look for answers is in their own pedagogical mirrors. This is not to say that students do not present their own diverse abilities and dispositions with respect to learning, as reinforced in the chapters by Noel Entwistle, and Alastair J.S. Summerlee and Julia Christensen Hughes, including attitudes of entitlement (Greenberger et al. 2008), or that faculty concerns about increasing class size and teaching load are unwarranted. But it is to suggest that there is much we can and should be doing differently.

The third finding identifies why surface learning and the conditions that foster it are problematic; *variation in student approaches to learning leads to variation in learning outcomes.* These outcomes pertain to both the extent to which knowledge is acquired and retained, as well as the extent to which learning and other crucial skills are developed. For example, Carl Wieman's chapter indicated that the extent to which information is retained, the degree of understanding basic concepts as well as the discipline and knowledge in general, skill development, and persistence and retention—are all affected. Jillian Kinzie's chapter further identified "moral reasoning, leadership, well-being, critical thinking, intercultural effectiveness" as being outcomes of a more engaged, deeper approach to learning. Simply put, surface-learning approaches lead to less robust learning outcomes than deep-learning approaches.

Finally, given the complex problems faced by society today and the concomitent need for graduates with the skills and abilities to address them, coupled with the significant investment that both students and society make in higher education, these types of learning deficits are clearly problematic. With this knowledge in hand, it is imperative that we find the means to create the conditions that are conducive to deep learning. Or, as stated by Jan H.F. Meyer in this volume:

> … it seems self-evident that we can, *and should*, use this knowledge to improve the learning and teaching experiences of students … if the knowledge and the efficient means exist to do this then it is unethical to deny students these opportunities.

One area that holds promise for helping bring about such change is related to a fourth observation made in several of the preceding chapters. That is the finding that *how faculty perceive their disciplines may influence their approach to teaching practice.* For example, Michael Prosser's chapter presented evidence that the ways in which faculty "experience their research is related logically and empirically to the way they experience their teaching and their subject matter." Building on Dr. Prosser's earlier work with Martin and Trigwell (Prosser, Martin, and Trigwell 2007), Noel Entwistle in his chapter also drew attention to this finding, expressing particular concern regarding its implications for the sciences:

> Knowledge in the sciences is more firmly established and more impersonal, while it remains more contested and people-centred in the social sciences. What does that imply for perceptions of pedagogy? Does the teaching of science really have to remain impersonal? It may be … that the ways science faculty tend to think about teaching remains both too impersonal and too atomistic to make it easy for many students to develop an integrated personal understanding.

Finally, building on Ramsden's (1992) "theories of teaching"—along with Saroyan (2000), Saroyan, Dagenais, and Zhou (2008), and Gow and

Kember (1993)—Alenoush Saroyan suggested in this volume that epistemic beliefs strongly influence teaching methods, the selection of learning tasks and assessments, and workload. Underscoring the significance of this finding, Dr. Saroyan observed that "knowing about the influence of personal beliefs on approaches to teaching is ... the first step if a change is to be made in one's teaching approach."

Recognition of the relationship between disciplinary paradigms and approaches to teaching further suggests that in order to improve student learning, we need to help faculty identify the underlying assumptions of their disciplines and understand the limits of these assumptions with respect to teaching and learning. Or, we need to find ways to work within these limits more effectively. For example, the suggestion by Noel Entwistle that much can be gained in the lecture by introducing pauses for students at 15-minute intervals, to clarify their notes with a peer, would be an example of working within an existing paradigm. Similarly, Dr. Wieman's call for a scientific approach to science education is an argument that is consistent with the values base of his discipline.

The Call for Change: A Historical Perspective

The call for change resulting from these four insights is certainly not new. In fact, individuals have been challenging the higher-education system for decades. In his noteworthy book, *How Scholars Trumped Teachers*, Cuban (1999) documented efforts to transform the university system dating back to the late 1800s. According to Cuban, at the crux of the problem is the dual mandate of universities (previously described by Alastair J.S. Summerlee and Julia Christensen Hughes in this volume). North American universities having combined both British and Germanic traditions, have traditionally emphasized both the development of student knowledge, values, and character on the one hand, and scientific research and faculty autonomy on the other. Reflecting this dualism, Cuban cites the late David Jordan, president of Stanford University, as having said in an 1891 address: "Some day our universities will recognize that their most important professors may be men who teach no classes, devoting their time and strength wholly to advanced research" (18-19). Then again, in 1899, President Jordan spoke in support of teaching: "The great teacher never fails to leave a ... mark on every young man and young woman with whom he comes in contact." Tensions associated with this dual mandate have been with us ever since.

Cuban further suggests that during the late 1800s, despite having much smaller class sizes than we do today, the dominant pedagogy included lectures, recitations, weekly quizzes, major exams, and laboratories. In an 1895 article written in the *Daily Palo Alto*, Stanford's student newspaper, the negative consequences of this approach were highlighted:

In some of the larger classes where the students are not called upon daily to recite, there springs up a strange hesitancy to speak.... The professor, although he prefers to spend most of his time in lecturing, finds it discouraging, when he does ask something to be met with an appalling silence savoring of stupidity.... The students ... often know perfectly the answer, but are not used to speaking in a lecture class. (as cited in Cuban 1999, 18)

It was also at about this time that Dewey was advancing his own ideas about teaching and learning. In a 1929 newsreel address (Hickman 2001) Dewey suggested that learning and the acquisition of a college credential were not necessarily one and the same:

I am not here to knock going to college. If a young person has the opportunity to do so and has the character and intelligence to take advantage of it, it is a good thing. But going to college is not the same thing as getting an education, although the two are often confused. A boy or a girl can go to college and get a degree and not much more. (2)

Dewey argued that effective teachers appreciate the individuality of each student and facilitate transformative learning experiences through actively engaging their students in solving problems that have clear relevance to their lives and society. Arguing the benefits of this approach, Dewey suggested that "if he cannot devise his own solution (not, of course, in isolation but in correspondence with the teacher and other pupils) and find his own way out he will not learn, not even if he can recite some correct answer with one hundred percent accuracy" (Dewey 1916, 160).

Given that these suggestions have been made for over a hundred years, why hasn't change been more forthcoming? In answer to this question, Cuban (1999) cited a 1957 Stanford review which concluded that teaching was not sufficiently rewarded:

We would like to see good teaching rewarded as a prime value in the life of the university. We do not wish to imply that good teaching should be rewarded to the neglect of scholarly and scientific research. We are, however, perturbed by a fairly general impression, and particularly among younger faculty members, that advancement is achieved almost exclusively through research and publication. (30)

Further, citing a 1979 Stanford faculty study, Cuban (1999, 41) reported that while approximately 50 percent reported most admiring a colleague who had demonstrated competence as a scholar; only 9 percent most admired a colleague who had demonstrated competence as a teacher; and only 28 percent viewed teaching effectiveness as important in tenure and promotion decisions. Finally, citing a general US-based study involving

35,000 faculty and 400 institutions, Cuban (1999, 48) reported that 80 percent of faculty felt research was the highest priority and, while 98 percent believed being an exemplary teacher was an important goal, only 10 percent believed their institutions rewarded good teaching.

Suggesting that these same biases have been present in Canada, a Commission of Inquiry on Canadian University Education by Stuart Smith (1991) concluded that "teaching is seriously undervalued at Canadian universities and nothing less than a total recommitment to it is required" (63). A few years later, Ernest Boyer, then president of the Carnegie Foundation for the Advancement of Teaching, headed a National Commission on Educating Undergraduates in the Research University (1995) in the US. Echoing the words of Dewey, almost a hundred years later, the Commission's report suggested:

> Many students graduate having accumulated whatever number of courses is required, but still lacking a coherent body of knowledge ... without knowing how to think logically, write clearly, or speak coherently.... The university has given them too little that will be of real value beyond a credential that will help them get their first jobs. (6)

Common within many of these quotes is the sense that for some, teaching and learning in higher education may simply involve practices of convenience; whereby students and faculty alike go through the motions, engaging in surface teaching and learning approaches, in order to meet an administrative requirement or receive a credential, without a deep or transformative experience having occured.

In contrast, without question, we can all point to wonderful and committed faculty, educational developers, and administrators, and innovative and engaging courses and curricular-reform projects. The Society for Teaching and Learning in Higher Education (STLHE) celebrates such people and their accomplishments every year through, *inter alia*, its 3M National Teaching Fellowship, Alan Blizzard Award, and Christopher Knapper Lifetime Achievement Award programs. However, given that calls for change have been heralded for years and continue to this day, it is important to reflect on why these accomplishments have not become more widespread. Rather than being the norm on our campuses, they often exist as "special" projects and in this way are vulnerable to changes in funding, faculty, and leadership.

The *lack of prestige* associated with teaching competence identified by Cuban is surely one potential explanation. The *lack of expectation for professional competence and demonstrated continuous improvement* identified by Christopher Knapper earlier in this volume is another. Both tend to be reinforced by *human-resource practices* (selection, tenure, and promotion) that incorporate too little emphasis on, and less than rigorous approaches for, assessing teaching effectiveness and outcomes. This is not a question of valuing teaching at the expense of research, but rather establishing high expectations for both and achieving a more appropriate balance given the dual mandates of our institutions.

The fact that *few faculty are formally prepared* for their teaching roles is another area that warrants attention. With some countries now requiring new faculty to participate in educational development activities, we wonder what messages might be sent, what new competencies would be developed, and what outcomes would result if new faculty in Canada were routinely required to, or given release from other responsibilities in order to, participate in such a program.

Lastly, *growing enrollments alongside declining resources*, coupled with *myths concerning the lack of benefit of the reallocation of resources* (see Alastair J.S. Summerlee and Julia Christensen Hughes, this volume) arguably only further support the status quo.

Underlying these impediments to change is another host of issues to do with the *conceptual and pedagogical capability of the faculty*, along with *cultural and political dimensions of the educational context*. Alenoush Saroyan's chapter provided a framework for understanding these impediments, in the form of four dilemmas, first suggested by Windschitl (2002). While Windschitl's contribution is centred around the successful implementation of constructivism within the K-12 system, his work arguably holds important insights for pedagogical transformation, in general, within PSE. Windschitl suggests that teachers find the implementation of non-traditional constructivist pedagogies "far more difficult than the reform community acknowledges" (131). He offers that:

> ... the most profound challenges for teachers are not associated merely with acquiring new skills but with making personal sense of constructivism as a basis for instruction, reorienting the cultures of classrooms to be consonant with the constructivist philosophy, and dealing with the pervasive educational conservatism that works against efforts to teach for understanding. (131)

Windschitl's first set of dilemmas are described as conceptual, whereby the teacher "attempts to understand the philosophical, psychological, epistemological underpinnings of constructivism" (132). The second set is pedagogical, which relates specifically to efforts to design curricula and "learning experiences that constructivism demands" (132). According to Windschitl (2002): "one of the most powerful determinants of whether constructivist approaches flourish or flounder in classrooms is the *degree to which individual teachers understand the concept* [original emphasis]" (138). With only a superficial or naive understanding, teachers tend to focus on the provision of constructivist learning activities (e.g., encouraging student participation) for its own sake, paying little attention to the "intellectual implications" underlying the activity. This in turn can lead to the impression of educational reform, while "preserving fundamental ideas about the subject matter, teaching and learning" (139). This observation is similar to one made by Noel Entwistle in this volume, who, drawing on Shulman's (1987) idea of pedagogical content knowledge and the work of Entwistle and Walker (2002), emphasized that effective teachers draw "from three overlapping knowledge bases—about the subject, about the range of teaching methods available to them, and about how students learn their subject."

Windschitl's third set of dilemmas is cultural, which can occur between teachers and students when classroom roles and expectations are radically transformed. The fourth and final set is political. Both of these types of dilemmas involve stakeholder expectations. Stakeholders that may resist constructivist pedagogies within higher education include parents, students, prospective students, accrediting bodies, and graduate schools as well as other faculty and administrators who may want to be assured that a certain amount of content has been "properly covered," that students are assessed through traditional exams and, as one recent study by Oakes et al. (2000) found, expect a classroom to be "quiet and orderly, with students seated and not talking to each other" (as cited in Windschitl 2002, 150). Windschitl (2002) concludes that "the most effective forms of constructivist teaching depend on nothing less than the reculturing of the classroom, meaning that familiar relationships, norms, and values have to be made public and be critically reevaluated" (164).

In summary, lack of prestige and reward, lack of expectation or requirement for professional competence or the continuous improvement of one's skills as a teacher, lack of requirement and opportunity for knowledge acquisition and skill development, growing enrollments coupled with declining resources, challenges associated with understanding and implementing non-traditional pedagogies, and issues of classroom culture and stakeholder politics all serve as significant barriers to pedagogical reform.

Where to from Here?

The preceding chapters contain many suggestions for ways in which teaching might change in support of student learning. Several also contain suggestions for how these changes might best be brought about. Clearly, institutional vision, leadership, culture, systems, resources, and policies and practices are all important considerations, along with the establishment of appropriate measures of success. Arguably, the extent to which all of these attributes are brought into alignment with and prioritize pedagogical and curricular innovation, the more likely it is that successful change will occur.

In keeping with this perspective, Barr and Tagg (1995) argue that the entire higher-education system needs to change, beginning with a *reexamination of our mission or purpose*. They suggest that we need to ask ourselves if our mission is to offer courses and confer degrees and other

credentials (as is implied by our practice), or is it to foster transformational learning and develop productive and effective citizens? In support
of the latter, they suggest that we challenge the criteria we currently use
to measure our success (e.g., entering student grades, number of faculty
with Ph.D.s), our teaching and learning structures (e.g., the 50-minute
lecture in tiered classrooms with fixed seating), and the nature of faculty
roles (e.g., a predominant focus on covering content, combined with the
assumption that anyone with a Ph.D. can teach). Instead, we should focus
on measuring improvements in student learning, reduce the number of
courses students take at any one time, develop flexible "learning spaces,"
and recognize that faculty—along with other academic staff such as educational developers and librarians—need support in becoming effective
facilitators of learning.

Further reinforcing this point, Jillian Kinzie in this volume suggested
that student engagement or "the extent to which students take part in
educationally effective practice" results from two components. The first is
the "time and effort students put into their studies and other educationally
purposeful activities." The second pertains to the institutional context, in
particular, "how the institution deploys its resources and organizes the
curriculum, other learning opportunities, and support services to induce
students to participate in activities that lead to ... persistence, satisfaction,
learning, and graduation."

While senior *institutional leadership* is clearly needed to help bring this
type of complex change about, understanding the role of more local or
distributed leadership—the dean, departmental chair, program co-ordinator,
curriculum committee chair, or faculty advisor—may be equally if not
more important, as it is at this level that the institution's mission, priorities,
and practices are interpreted and judged, and accepted or dismissed. In
fact, one of the most significant barriers to academic change may be this
very culture; where decentralized decision-making structures, along with
concepts of collegiality and academic freedom, can foster the impression
that faculty are more or less independent contractors who can largely do
as they choose as long as they fulfill basic role expectations. Of course, to
the extent that senior administrators have discretion over the allocation
of resources, and use that discretion wisely, they can exert some degree
of influence. As Noel Entwistle earlier suggested in this volume:

> Attempts to introduce innovations in either teaching or assessment can
> be encouraged or constrained by the resources provided and the types of
> teaching rooms available, while institution-wide curriculum changes can
> sometimes be bitterly opposed within departments. The teaching and learn-
> ing policies and strategies evolved within institutions and policies clearly
> frame what is possible for faculty to achieve within their teaching activities,
> but how lecturers feel about them affects how these are implemented, and
> whether they will be successful.

In studying the attributes of "local leaders" who have been effective at bringing faculty on board with curricular change, Gibbs, Knapper, and Piccinin (2008) identified pedagogical knowledge, the ability to articulate a convincing argument for change, the provision of support for those who are committed to helping bring about change, the ability to gather evidence of the effectiveness of the innovation, and adeptness at bringing about recognition for the achievements made as being particularly important.

Departmental leaders can also affect change through their day-to-day activities and their impact on local cultures, such as the extent to which they: reinforce high pedagogical expectations; include discussions of pedagogy in departmental meetings and integrating, as Thomas Carey earlier suggested, "craft knowledge, professional knowledge, and scientific knowledge;" and are clearly associated with and supportive of the institution's teaching centre. In addition, their approach to faculty-teaching assignments and teaching resource-allocation decisions (e.g., is teaching a first-year course seen as a scourge or an honour?), the care with which teaching assistants are selected and trained, and the extent to which they are seen to value teaching and learning as part of selection, promotion, and tenure decisions—all send a message. In fact, W. Alan Wright's study of educational developers presented earlier in this volume found that "demonstrated leadership on teaching matters by deans and academic department heads and recognition and emphasis on teaching in employment policies and practices" were perceived to have the most potential to improve teaching practice.

These latter observations suggest that *educational developers or teaching centres* may have a particularly essential role to play—both directly and indirectly through their support of faculty champions—in helping bring about pedagogical innovation. New-faculty orientation programs, learning groups, courses, workshops, conferences, private consultations, curricular mapping and design exercises, and support for the scholarship of teaching and learning are all important services. However, to the extent that such activities remain voluntary or outside mainstream expectations, which is almost always the case in the North American context, they tend to attract those who already have an interest in and aptitude for teaching as opposed to those who might benefit the most. Potentially, as previously suggested, one of the most effective ways of transforming the system might be to provide all new faculty with work release for participating in an *educational development program* in which they gain exposure to the pedagogical literature and conduct a study pertaining to the effectiveness of their own teaching practice. Such a program would ideally be designed in keeping with the four prerequisites for large-scale pedagogical reform advocated by Centra (1993), and cited by Alenoush Saroyan in this volume, including the perception that (a) the pedagogical knowledge is important and valid, (b) it is from a credible source, (c) the faculty member has the ability to change, and (d) the faculty member is motivated to change.

Jan H.F. Meyer, in this volume, further suggested that such programs be taught in a *discipline-specific* as opposed to a generic manner and include the identification of *threshold concepts* particular to that discipline. Consistent with this view, Davies and Mangan (2007) suggest that threshold concepts "focus our attention on the relationship between big shifts in thinking in the subject and transformative changes that learners have to experience in their thinking" (721). Noel Entwistle similarly argued in this volume that "discussion of threshold concepts can transform lecturers' ways of thinking about the nature of knowledge in their subject areas and in so doing, also affect their ideas about teaching and learning." This is also in keeping with the advice of Prosser et al. (2005): "If we want to change and develop the ways in which teachers approach their teaching and help their students to learn, we need to help them to think carefully about what they are teaching and how it relates to and coheres with the field as a whole" (153).

In addition to orientation and developmental support, other human-resource practices may also be particularly useful. For example, in *selection decisions*, the importance of teaching and learning should be emphasized and pedagogical and curricular competence assessed. Peer review, the use of teaching dossiers, and having students participate in the process could all be beneficial.

The same should apply to our reward systems, particularly *promotion and tenure decisions*. To this end, the adoption of Boyer's conception of scholarship may be highly appropriate. In *Scholarship Reconsidered: Priorities of the Professoriate* (1990, 15), Boyer advocated the adoption of four types of scholarship: the scholarship of discovery (advancement of knowledge, original research); the scholarship of integration (integration of knowledge, synthesis, interdisciplinarity); the scholarship of application (application of knowledge, professional service); and the scholarship of teaching (transformation and dissemination of knowledge, pedagogical research). Such an undertaking would not only legitimize the activity of—and encourage—faculty who are interested in studying the impact of their own teaching practice, but it would also provide the department with disciplinary-based evidence on which to base future pedagogical and curricular decisions. This was the point made by Carl Wieman earlier in this volume when he called for the use of "objective data rather than … anecdote or tradition."

Of course, in order for such an approach to be successful, it would be helpful if *grants in support of the scholarship of teaching and learning* were more widely available. While many universities already provide some degree of funding in this regard, more could be done. This is something that both the provincial and federal governments could champion, perhaps by extending the chairs in higher education through the Canada Research Chairs (CRC) program, so as to include "*teaching chairs*" in a variety of disciplines. Such a program could provide experts who can mentor faculty in carrying out educational research in their disciplines, either within or across institutions. Finally, those who get involved in such activity will ideally be mindful of Maryellen Weimer's plea in this volume, to disseminate one's results in an accessible manner. Pointing to Prince and Felder's (2006) article as an example of how to do it well, Dr. Weimer argued that functional, integrative, and accessible scholarship remains in short supply.

Other possible suggestions pertain to the provision of *effective learning spaces* (both physical and virtual). Institutions could do a much better job of providing classrooms that are conducive to collaborative learning (e.g., with tables and chairs on castors), as well as space outside of class that promotes student interaction. In support of this outcome, many of our libraries are going through a renaissance of sorts and establishing collaborative-learning spaces alongside learning and research-support services (e.g., learning commons). Another area for consideration is the extent to which we provide support for the effective use of technology, the development of online resources, or the creation of hybrid courses, and ensure that we are not simply replicating the worst of didactic teaching methods in online or technology-enhanced environments, but using technology to foster deep learning. In keeping with this view, Noel Entwistle earlier offered:

> There is a lack of research that brings together technological advances with the findings about teaching and learning in a coherent way. They seem at times to be marching to different drums: the one creating excitement about the latest way of presenting information or administering courses and the other focusing more on students' conceptual development and change.

There is also the need to place increased focus on the *assessment and development of curricula along with the specification of program-level learning outcomes*, including skills and attitudes as well as more traditional knowledge domains (Wolf and Christensen Hughes 2007). Program-level outcomes help guide curriculum development and provide criteria for assessing the achievement of educational objectives. Often, they are also a response to expressions of concern about the quality of higher education and calls for accountability from governments and employers. Explicitly articulated program-level outcomes or graduate attributes also facilitate credit transfers, admission to graduate programs, and accreditation of professional programs.

In this regard, the recent system-wide adoption of degree-level expectations in the province of Ontario may be instructive (Hubball et al. 2007). In 2005, the Council of Ontario Universities (COU), the organization of executive heads of Ontario's publicly assisted universities, proactively established a task force made up of members of one of its subgroups, the Ontario Council of Academic Vice-Presidents (OCAV), to develop "Guidelines for University Undergraduate Degree Level Expectations" (UDLEs) to serve as a framework for describing expectations of attributes and minimum levels of performance by graduates of universities in Ontario. Effective June 2008, it was expected that all existing undergraduate programs in Ontario would have integrated into their curriculum the OCAV UDLEs, which consist of the following six generic categories of intellectual and creative development of graduates: depth of knowledge; knowledge of methodologies; application of knowledge; communication skills; awareness of limits of knowledge; and autonomy and professional capacity. As individuals and departments try to make sense of program-level outcomes and apply them to their disciplines, threshold concepts may once again play a particularly useful role. In implementing such processes, educational staff such as those situated within teaching support units can be particularly helpful.

Some efforts have also been made to rethink graduate education. As suggested by Alenoush Sarayon in this volume, a recent US study has identified weaknesses employers perceive in Ph.D. holders, such as fear of risk taking, not seeing the big picture, poor "people skills," and poor project management. Similarly, within Canada, there has been growing concern that many graduate students often lack an array of generic skills that are essential if they are to use their technical, discipline-specific research skills effectively in professional practice.

In 2007, the co-editors of this volume were invited to co-ordinate and co-facilitate a think tank of approximately 50 individuals representing a wide range of stakeholders in graduate education, including graduate students, researchers, educational developers, deans of graduate schools, and representatives from industry and government. The event was sponsored by the three major federal granting agencies—the Natural Sciences and Engineering Research Council (NSERC), the Social Sciences and Humanities Research Council (SSHRC), and the Canadian Institute of Health Research (CIHR)—and the Canadian Association for Graduate Studies (CAGS) in collaboration with the STLHE. Its purpose was to identify the most important professional skills as learning outcomes for graduate programs in Canada. Not surprisingly, one of the skills identified was "teaching competence."

This collaboration has had several implications for the development of graduate curricula and has been a significant step toward enhancing the quality of graduate education in universities across Canada. For example, to ensure that graduate students have the capacity to communicate their ideas effectively and support the learning of others, some graduate programs now explicitly require students to participate in courses on pedagogy. In addition, in 2008, one of the granting agencies, NSERC, established a new grant aptly named the Collaborative Research and Training Experience (CREATE) Program to encourage collaborative training approaches, and facilitate the transition of graduate students and post-doctoral fellows to the Canadian workforce. It also encourages the acquisition and development of important professional skills, students' mobility nationally and internationally, and interdisciplinary research.

Conclusion

In summary, what is being advocated here is significant change within higher education—a change that will require effective leadership at all levels with an unwavering commitment to embracing evidence-based pedagogical practice. If we are to walk this path, then a multi-dimensional process of change is required, beginning with the re-articulation of what we are trying to achieve within our institutions, and including our commitment to deep and transformational learning and the implementation of meaningful measures through which we can chart our progress. We need to clarify the place these activities hold amongst our other priorities and align our systems, including the allocation of scarce resources, against their achievement. Key additional levers for change have been identified as including:

- Effective pedagogical leadership at all levels;
- Departmental cultures in which teaching and learning are valued, and in which an ethos of pedagogical creativity and experimentation is encouraged;
- Professional-development opportunities that are offered in collaboration with educational developers and local teaching centres and that encourage faculty to engage with discipline-specific pedagogical literature, to identify threshold concepts, and to participate in research projects with respect to their own pedagogical practice;
- Support for the scholarship of teaching and learning, including the provision of grants and the establishment of teaching chairs;
- Faculty recruitment, selection, promotion, and tenure processes where teaching and learning competence and scholarship are adequately assessed and valued;
- Pedagogically sound physical and virtual learning spaces;
- A focus on curriculum assessment and development and the achievement of generic program-level learning outcomes.

In closing, we have taken stock of the research on teaching and learning in higher education and have concluded that at least four key observations can be made:

- Students vary in their approaches to learning;
- Variation in student learning is in part determined by the learning context;
- Variation in student approaches to learning leads to different learning outcomes;
- Faculty perceptions of their disciplines and their research influence their approaches to teaching and the learning contexts they create.

Most importantly, when faculty adopt active-learning pedagogies, students are more likely to engage in deep-learning approaches, leading to improved mastery and retention of knowledge and skills, and more sophisticated learning approaches. When faculty adopt traditional transmission-oriented pedagogies, students are more likely to engage in surface-learning approaches, leading to learning and skill-based deficits and more novice-like understandings of their disciplines, to the detriment of themselves and society.

The question, as stated at the outset, is: What will we now do with this knowledge? What system-wide changes need to occur in order for us to broadly and effectively make use of this evidence in our practice? Key levers for change have been suggested. Our hope is that we—faculty, educational developers, administrators, policy makers—will use this information as a call to action, as a catalyst to revisit the purpose of our educational institutions and our roles, to challenge practices of convenience, to commit to providing learning environments that encourage deep learning and transform our students and societies in the process, and to align our systems and cultures in support of such a worthy goal.

REFERENCES

Astin, A.W. 1993. *What Matters in College? Four Critical Years Revisited*, 1st edition. San Francisco: Jossey-Bass.

Barr, R.B. and J. Tagg. 1995. From Teaching to Learning: A New Paradigm for Undergraduate Education. *Change* 27(6):12-25.

Boyer, E.L. 1990. *Scholarship Reconsidered: Priorities of the Professoriate*. Lawrenceville, NJ: Princeton University Press.

Centra, J.A. 1993. *Reflective Faculty Evaluation: Enhancing Teaching and Determining Faculty Effectiveness*. San Francisco: Jossey-Bass.

Cuban, L. 1999. *How Scholars Trumped Teachers: Change Without Reform in University Curriculum, Teaching, and Research, 1890–1990*. New York, NY: Teachers College Press.

Daily Palo Alto. 1895. 14 November, p. 2 (cited in Cuban 1999, 18).

Davies, P. and J. Mangan. 2007. Threshold Concepts and the Integration of Understanding in Economics. *Studies in Higher Education* 32: 711-26.

Dewey, J. 1916. *Democracy and Education*. New York: Macmillan. Accessed 13 September 2009 at http://www.ilt.columbia.edu/Publications/dewey.html

Entwistle, N.J. and P. Walker. 2002. Strategic Alertness and Expanded Alertness Within Sophisticated Conceptions of Teaching. In *Teacher Thinking, Beliefs and Knowledge in Higher Education*, ed. N. Nativa and P. Goodyear, 15-40. Dordrecht: Kluwer Academic Publishers.

Gibbs, G., C. Knapper, and S. Piccinin. 2008. Disciplinary and Contextually Appropriate Approaches to Leadership of Teaching in Research-Intensive Academic Departments in Higher Education. *Higher Education Quarterly* 62:416-36.

Gow, L. and D. Kember. 1993. Conceptions of Teaching and Their Relationship to Student Learning. *British Journal of Educational Psychology* 63:20-33.

Greenberger, E., J. Lessard, D. Chen, and S. Farruggia. 2008. Self-Entitled College Students: Contributions of Personality, Parenting, and Motivational Factors. *Journal of Youth and Adolescence* 37:1193-1204.

Hickman, L. 2001. Additional Comments, *John Dewey: An Introduction to His Life and Work*. Accessed 8 May 2009 at www.davidsonfilmsstore.com/2007_LG_WORD/Dewey_Additional_Comments.doc

Hubball, H., N. Gold, J. Mighty, and J. Britnell. 2007. Supporting the Implementation of Externally Generated Learning Outcomes and Learning Centred Curriculum Development: An Integrated Framework. In *Curriculum Development in Higher Education: Faculty-Driven Processes and Practices*, ed. P. Wolf and J. Christensen Hughes. *New Directions for Teaching and Learning* 112: 93-105. San Francisco: Jossey-Bass.

Marton, F. and R. Säljö. 1976. On Qualitative Differences in Learning. II – Outcome as a Function of the Learner's Conception of the Task. *British Journal of Educational Psychology* 46(2):115-27.

National Commission on Educating Undergraduates in the Research University. 1995. Reinventing Undergraduate Education: A Blueprint for American's Research Universities. Accessed 15 November 2009 at http://naples.cc.sunysb.edu/pres/boyer.nsf/673918d46fbf653e852565ec0056ff3e/d955b61ffddd590a852565ec005717ae/$FILE/boyer.pdf

Oakes, J., K. Hunter-Quartz, S. Ryan, and M. Lipton. 2000. *Becoming Good American Schools: The Struggle for Civic Virtue in Educational Reform*. San Francisco: Jossey-Bass.

Prince, M. and R. Felder. 2006. Inductive Teaching and Learning Methods: Definitions, Comparisons, and Research Bases. *Journal of Engineering Education* 95(2):123-38.

Prosser, M., E. Martin, K. Trigswell, P. Ramsden, and G. Lueckenhausen. 2005. Academics' Experiences of Understanding of their Subject Matters and the Relationship to their Experiences of Teaching and Learning. *Instructional Science* 33:137-57.

Prosser, M., E. Martin, and K. Trigwell. 2007. Academics' Experiences of their Teaching and of their Subject Matter. In *British Journal of Educational Psychology Monograph Series II, Number 4* – Student learning and university teaching, ed. N.J. Entwistle and P.D. Tomlinson, 49-60. Leicester: British Psychological Society.

Ramsden, P. 1992. *Learning to Teach in Higher Education*. London: Routledge.

Ramsden, P. and N.J. Entwistle. 1981. Effects of Academic Departments on Students' Approaches to Studying. *British Journal of Educational Psychology* 51:368-83.

Saroyan, A. 2000. Addressing the Needs of Large Groups: The Lecturer: Working with Large Groups. In *Teaching Alone/Teaching Together: Transforming the Structure of Teams for Teaching*, ed. J. Bess, 87-107. San Francisco: Jossey-Bass.

Saroyan, A., J. Dagenais, and Y. Zhou. 2008. Graduate Students' Conceptions of University Teaching and Learning: Formation for Change. *Instructional Science* DOI 10.1007/s11251-008-9071-8.

Shulman, L.S. 1987. Knowledge and Teaching: Foundations of the New Reform. *Educational Researcher* 152:1-22.

Smith, S. 1991. *Commission of Inquiry on Canadian University Education*. Ottawa: Association of Universities and Colleges of Canada.

Watkins, D.A. and J. Hattie. 1981. The Learning Processes of Australian University Students: Investigations of Contextual and Personological Factors. *British Journal of Educational Psychology* 51:384-93.

Windschitl, M. 2002. Framing Constructivism as the Negotiation of Dilemmas: An Analysis of the Conceptual, Pedagogical, Cultural, and Political Challenges Facing Teachers. *Review of Educational Research* 72(2):131-75.

Wolf P. and J. Christensen Hughes, eds. 2007. *Curriculum Development in Higher Education: Faculty-Driven Processes and Practices. New Directions for Teaching and Learning* 112. San Francisco: Jossey-Bass.

Queen's Policy Studies
Recent Publications

The Queen's Policy Studies Series is dedicated to the exploration of major public policy issues that confront governments and society in Canada and other nations.

Manuscript submission. We are pleased to consider new book proposals and manuscripts. Preliminary enquiries are welcome. A subvention is normally required for the publication of an academic book. Please direct questions or proposals to the Publications Unit by email at spspress@queensu.ca, or visit our website at: www.queensu.ca/sps/books, or contact us by phone at (613) 533 - 2192.

Our books are available from good bookstores everywhere, including the Queen's University bookstore (http://www.campusbookstore.com/). McGill-Queen's University Press is the exclusive world representative and distributor of books in the series. A full catalogue and ordering information may be found on their web site (http://mqup.mcgill.ca/).

School of Policy Studies

Architects and Innovators: Building the Department of Foreign Affairs and International Trade, 1909–2009/Architectes et innovateurs : le développement du ministère des Affaires étrangères et du Commerce international,de 1909 à 2009, Greg Donaghy and Kim Richard Nossal (eds.), 2009, Paper 978-1-55339-269-9 Cloth 978-1-55339-270-5

Academic Transformation: The Forces Reshaping Higher Education in Ontario, Ian D. Clark, Greg Moran, Michael L. Skolnik, and David Trick, 2009, Paper 978-1-55339-238-5 Cloth 978-1-55339-265-1

The New Federal Policy Agenda and the Voluntary Sector: On the Cutting Edge, Rachel Laforest (ed.), 2009. Paper 978-1-55339-132-6

The Afghanistan Challenge: Hard Realities and Strategic Choices, Hans-Georg Ehrhart and Charles Pentland (eds.), 2009. Paper 978-1-55339-241-5

Measuring What Matters in Peace Operations and Crisis Management, Sarah Jane Meharg, 2009. Paper 978-1-55339-228-6 Cloth ISBN 978-1-55339-229-3

International Migration and the Governance of Religious Diversity, Paul Bramadat and Matthias Koenig (eds.), 2009. Paper 978-1-55339-266-8 Cloth ISBN 978-1-55339-267-5

Who Goes? Who Stays? What Matters? Accessing and Persisting in Post-Secondary Education in Canada, Ross Finnie, Richard E. Mueller, Arthur Sweetman, and Alex Usher (eds.), 2008. Paper 978-1-55339-221-7 Cloth ISBN 978-1-55339-222-4

Economic Transitions with Chinese Characteristics: Thirty Years of Reform and Opening Up, Arthur Sweetman and Jun Zhang (eds.), 2009. Paper 978-1-55339-225-5 Cloth ISBN 978-1-55339-226-2

Economic Transitions with Chinese Characteristics: Social Change During Thirty Years of Reform, Arthur Sweetman and Jun Zhang (eds.), 2009. Paper 978-1-55339-234-7 Cloth ISBN 978-1-55339-235-4

Dear Gladys: Letters from Over There, Gladys Osmond (Gilbert Penney ed.), 2009. Paper ISBN 978-1-55339-223-1

Immigration and Integration in Canada in the Twenty-first Century, John Biles, Meyer Burstein, and James Frideres (eds.), 2008. Paper ISBN 978-1-55339-216-3 Cloth ISBN 978-1-55339-217-0

Robert Stanfield's Canada, Richard Clippingdale, 2008. ISBN 978-1-55339-218-7

Exploring Social Insurance: Can a Dose of Europe Cure Canadian Health Care Finance?
Colleen Flood, Mark Stabile, and Carolyn Tuohy (eds.), 2008.
Paper ISBN 978-1-55339-136-4 Cloth ISBN 978-1-55339-213-2

Canada in NORAD, 1957–2007: A History, Joseph T. Jockel, 2007.
Paper ISBN 978-1-55339-134-0 Cloth ISBN 978-1-55339-135-7

Canadian Public-Sector Financial Management, Andrew Graham, 2007.
Paper ISBN 978-1-55339-120-3 Cloth ISBN 978-1-55339-121-0

Emerging Approaches to Chronic Disease Management in Primary Health Care,
John Dorland and Mary Ann McColl (eds.), 2007. Paper ISBN 978-1-55339-130-2
Cloth ISBN 978-1-55339-131-9

Fulfilling Potential, Creating Success: Perspectives on Human Capital Development,
Garnett Picot, Ron Saunders and Arthur Sweetman (eds.), 2007.
Paper ISBN 978-1-55339-127-2 Cloth ISBN 978-1-55339-128-9

Reinventing Canadian Defence Procurement: A View from the Inside, Alan S. Williams, 2006.
Paper ISBN 0-9781693-0-1 (Published in association with Breakout Educational Network)

SARS in Context: Memory, History, Policy, Jacalyn Duffin and Arthur Sweetman (eds.),
2006. Paper ISBN 978-0-7735-3194-9 Cloth ISBN 978-0-7735-3193-2
(Published in association with McGill-Queen's University Press)

Dreamland: How Canada's Pretend Foreign Policy has Undermined Sovereignty,
Roy Rempel, 2006. Páper ISBN 1-55339-118-7 Cloth ISBN 1-55339-119-5
(Published in association with Breakout Educational Network)

Canadian and Mexican Security in the New North America: Challenges and Prospects,
Jordi Díez (ed.), 2006. Paper ISBN 978-1-55339-123-4 Cloth ISBN 978-1-55339-122-7

*Global Networks and Local Linkages: The Paradox of Cluster Development in an Open
Economy,* David A. Wolfe and Matthew Lucas (eds.), 2005. Paper ISBN 1-55339-047-4
Cloth ISBN 1-55339-048-2

Choice of Force: Special Operations for Canada, David Last and Bernd Horn (eds.), 2005.
Paper ISBN 1-55339-044-X Cloth ISBN 1-55339-045-8

Force of Choice: Perspectives on Special Operations, Bernd Horn, J. Paul de B. Taillon, and
David Last (eds.), 2004. Paper ISBN 1-55339-042-3 Cloth 1-55339-043-1

New Missions, Old Problems, Douglas L. Bland, David Last, Franklin Pinch, and
Alan Okros (eds.), 2004. Paper ISBN 1-55339-034-2 Cloth 1-55339-035-0

*The North American Democratic Peace: Absence of War and Security Institution-Building in
Canada-US Relations,* 1867-1958, Stéphane Roussel, 2004.
Paper ISBN 0-88911-937-6 Cloth 0-88911-932-2

Implementing Primary Care Reform: Barriers and Facilitators, Ruth Wilson, S.E.D. Shortt,
and John Dorland (eds.), 2004. Paper ISBN 1-55339-040-7 Cloth 1-55339-041-5

Social and Cultural Change, David Last, Franklin Pinch, Douglas L. Bland, and
Alan Okros (eds.), 2004. Paper ISBN 1-55339-032-6 Cloth 1-55339-033-4

Clusters in a Cold Climate: Innovation Dynamics in a Diverse Economy, David A. Wolfe and
Matthew Lucas (eds.), 2004. Paper ISBN 1-55339-038-5 Cloth 1-55339-039-3

Canada Without Armed Forces? Douglas L. Bland (ed.), 2004.
Paper ISBN 1-55339-036-9 Cloth 1-55339-037-7

Campaigns for International Security: Canada's Defence Policy at the Turn of the Century,
Douglas L. Bland and Sean M. Maloney, 2004. Paper ISBN 0-88911-962-7
Cloth 0-88911-964-3

Understanding Innovation in Canadian Industry, Fred Gault (ed.), 2003.
Paper ISBN 1-55339-030-X Cloth 1-55339-031-8

Delicate Dances: Public Policy and the Nonprofit Sector, Kathy L. Brock (ed.), 2003.
Paper ISBN 0-88911-953-8 Cloth 0-88911-955-4

Beyond the National Divide: Regional Dimensions of Industrial Relations, Mark Thompson, Joseph B. Rose, and Anthony E. Smith (eds.), 2003. Paper ISBN 0-88911-963-5
Cloth 0-88911-965-1

The Nonprofit Sector in Interesting Times: Case Studies in a Changing Sector, Kathy L. Brock and Keith G. Banting (eds.), 2003. Paper ISBN 0-88911-941-4 Cloth 0-88911-943-0

Clusters Old and New: The Transition to a Knowledge Economy in Canada's Regions, David A. Wolfe (ed.), 2003. Paper ISBN 0-88911-959-7 Cloth 0-88911-961-9

The e-Connected World: Risks and Opportunities, Stephen Coleman (ed.), 2003.
Paper ISBN 0-88911-945-7 Cloth 0-88911-947-3

Centre for the Study of Democracy

The Authentic Voice of Canada: R.B. Bennell's Speeches in the House of Lords, 1941-1947, Christopher McCreery and Arthur Milnes (eds.), 2009. Paper 978-1-55339-275-0
Cloth ISBN 978-1-55339-276-7

Age of the Offered Hand: The Cross-Border Partnership Between President George H.W. Bush and Prime-Minister Brian Mulroney, A Documentary History, James McGrath and Arthur Milnes (eds.), 2009. Paper ISBN 978-1-55339-232-3
Cloth ISBN 978-1-55339-233-0

In Roosevelt's Bright Shadow: Presidential Addresses About Canada from Taft to Obama in Honour of FDR's 1938 Speech at Queen's University, Christopher McCreery and Arthur Milnes (eds.), 2009. Paper ISBN 978-1-55339-230-9 Cloth ISBN 978 1 55339-231-6

Politics of Purpose, 40th Anniversary Edition, The Right Honourable John N. Turner 17th Prime Minister of Canada, Elizabeth McIninch and Arthur Milnes (eds.), 2009.
Paper ISBN 978-1-55339-227-9 Cloth ISBN 978-1-55339-224-8

Bridging the Divide: Religious Dialogue and Universal Ethics, Papers for The InterAction Council, Thomas S. Axworthy (ed.), 2008. Paper ISBN 978-1-55339 219-4
Cloth ISBN 978-1-55339-220-0

Institute of Intergovernmental Relations

The Democratic Dilemma: Reforming the Canadian Senate, Jennifer Smith (ed.), 2009.
Paper 978-1-55339-190-6

Canada: The State of the Federation 2006/07, vol. 20, *Transitions – Fiscal and Political Federalism in an Era of Change*, John R. Allan, Thomas J. Courchene, and Christian Leuprecht (eds.), 2009. Paper ISBN 978-1-55339-189-0 Cloth ISBN 978-1-55339-191-3

Comparing Federal Systems, Third Edition, Ronald L. Watts, 2008.
Paper ISBN 978-1-55339-188-3

Canada: The State of the Federation 2005, vol. 19, *Quebec and Canada in the New Century – New Dynamics, New Opportunities*, Michael Murphy (ed.), 2007.
Paper ISBN 978-1-55339-018-3 Cloth ISBN 978-1-55339-017-6

Spheres of Governance: Comparative Studies of Cities in Multilevel Governance Systems, Harvey Lazar and Christian Leuprecht (eds.), 2007. Paper ISBN 978-1-55339-019-0
Cloth ISBN 978-1-55339-129-6

Canada: The State of the Federation 2004, vol. 18, *Municipal-Federal-Provincial Relations in Canada*, Robert Young and Christian Leuprecht (eds.), 2006.
Paper ISBN 1-55339-015-6 Cloth ISBN 1-55339-016-4

Canadian Fiscal Arrangements: What Works, What Might Work Better, Harvey Lazar (ed.), 2005. Paper ISBN 1-55339-012-1 Cloth ISBN 1-55339-013-X

Canada: The State of the Federation 2003, vol. 17, *Reconfiguring Aboriginal-State Relations,* Michael Murphy (ed.), 2005. Paper ISBN 1-55339-010-5 Cloth ISBN 1-55339-011-3

Canada: The State of the Federation 2002, vol. 16, *Reconsidering the Institutions of Canadian Federalism,* J. Peter Meekison, Hamish Telford, and Harvey Lazar (eds.), 2004. Paper ISBN 1-55339-009-1 Cloth ISBN 1-55339-008-3

Federalism and Labour Market Policy: Comparing Different Governance and Employment Strategies, Alain Noël (ed.), 2004. Paper ISBN 1-55339-006-7 Cloth ISBN 1-55339-007-5

The Impact of Global and Regional Integration on Federal Systems: A Comparative Analysis, Harvey Lazar, Hamish Telford, and Ronald L. Watts (eds.), 2003. Paper ISBN 1-55339-002-4 Cloth ISBN 1-55339-003-2

John Deutsch Institute for the Study of Economic Policy

Retirement Policy Issues in Canada, Michael G. Abbott, Charles M. Beach, Robin W. Boadway, and James G. MacKinnon (eds.), 2009. Paper ISBN 978-1-55339-161-6 Cloth ISBN 978-1-55339-162-3

The 2006 Federal Budget: Rethinking Fiscal Priorities, Charles M. Beach, Michael Smart, and Thomas A. Wilson (eds.), 2007. Paper ISBN 978-1-55339-125-8 Cloth ISBN 978-1-55339-126-6

Health Services Restructuring in Canada: New Evidence and New Directions, Charles M. Beach, Richard P. Chaykowksi, Sam Shortt, France St-Hilaire, and Arthur Sweetman (eds.), 2006. Paper ISBN 978-1-55339-076-3 Cloth ISBN 978-1-55339-075-6

A Challenge for Higher Education in Ontario, Charles M. Beach (ed.), 2005. Paper ISBN 1-55339-074-1 Cloth ISBN 1-55339-073-3

Current Directions in Financial Regulation, Frank Milne and Edwin H. Neave (eds.), Policy Forum Series no. 40, 2005. Paper ISBN 1-55339-072-5 Cloth ISBN 1-55339-071-7

Higher Education in Canada, Charles M. Beach, Robin W. Boadway, and R. Marvin McInnis (eds.), 2005. Paper ISBN 1-55339-070-9 Cloth ISBN 1-55339-069-5

Financial Services and Public Policy, Christopher Waddell (ed.), 2004. Paper ISBN 1-55339-068-7 Cloth ISBN 1-55339-067-9

The 2003 Federal Budget: Conflicting Tensions, Charles M. Beach and Thomas A. Wilson (eds.), Policy Forum Series no. 39, 2004. Paper ISBN 0-88911-958-9 Cloth ISBN 0-88911-956-2

Canadian Immigration Policy for the 21st Century, Charles M. Beach, Alan G. Green, and Jeffrey G. Reitz (eds.), 2003. Paper ISBN 0-88911-954-6 Cloth ISBN 0-88911-952-X

Framing Financial Structure in an Information Environment, Thomas J. Courchene and Edwin H. Neave (eds.), Policy Forum Series no. 38, 2003. Paper ISBN 0-88911-950-3 Cloth ISBN 0-88911-948-1

Our publications may be purchased at leading bookstores, including the Queen's University Bookstore (http://www.campusbookstore.com/) or can be ordered online from: McGill-Queen's University Press, at **http://mqup.mcgill.ca/ordering.php**

For more information about new and backlist titles from Queen's Policy Studies, visit http://www.queensu.ca/sps/books or visit the McGill-Queen's University Press web site at: **http://mqup.mcgill.ca/**